Delivering Results

Lawrence P. Carr · Alfred J. Nanni, Jr.

Delivering Results

Managing What Matters

 Springer

Lawrence P. Carr
Babson College
Accounting & Law Div.
231 Forest Street
Babson Park MA 02457
USA
carr@babson.edu

Alfred J. Nanni, Jr.
Babson College
Accounting & Law Div.
231 Forest Street
Babson Park MA 02457
USA
nanni@babson.edu

ISBN 978-1-4419-0620-5   e-ISBN 978-1-4419-0621-2
DOI 10.1007/978-1-4419-0621-2
Springer Dordrecht Heidelberg London New York

Library of Congress Control Number: 2009927131

Printed on acid-free paper

Springer is part of Springer Science+Business Media (www.springer.com)

To our students and clients who taught us so much

Preface

There is no shortage of techniques and models available to a manager trying to effectively execute a strategy. This book doesn't try to add to that list. Instead, *Delivering Results: Managing What Matters* takes a holistic, systems approach to strategy implementation. Our objective is to bring together and integrate the variety of factors a manager must consider when executing a strategy.

This book provides managers with insight into how to balance various management techniques and models in order to influence their subordinates' joint and individual behavior toward pursuit of strategic goals. Our *Management System for Delivering Results* (MSDR) demonstrates how various popular management techniques can be employed in concert under specific firm circumstances. We show how to choose an effective blend of management approaches under specific strategies, industry dynamics, organizational structure and culture, management style, and possible incentive systems.

This book is aimed at managers at any level who need guidance on how to pull all the pieces together and implement the strategy effectively and efficiently. The principles and guidelines in the book will work equally well for first-time managers concerned with running a single department to senior managers tired of "big ideas" with no guidance on follow-through. The book is concise and illustrative (and designed to be read and digested during a long flight and revisited as needed). The book is realistic in nature, designed for a practicing manager. The reader will be able to use the outlined techniques immediately. There are many examples of both effective and ineffective implementations from a wide variety of companies. These provide the reader with a context for understanding the design of an effective strategy delivery system. We provide a hierarchy of things to consider that helps the manager think in a systems manner and set priorities among competing demands.

Delivering Results makes a good sourcebook for advanced executive training sessions and is very useful for MBA students looking for a single source to help them integrate thoughts from a wide range of contemporary management disciplines: strategy, operations, organizational behavior, and management accounting/control.

The genesis of this book came from the demand of our many undergraduate, graduate, and executive students who wanted a straight forward model for decision-making, something they could use right away. Inundated with many theories and the latest management fads, they struggled to link both the big picture and the day-to-day operational decision-making demands. The students challenged us to develop material they could use on the job that is clearly understood by all levels in the organization, applicable in all types of industries, and relevant for not-for profit organizations. We moved from using textbooks and cases to a set of class notes, readings and relevant cases. This was the start of *Delivering Results*. We were encouraged by the many e-mails and feedback from our graduates who were using and benefiting from the course frameworks. We were regularly asked to put the material in a form they could share with their managers and colleagues.

We extend heartfelt thanks to the many people who have shared their experiences with us, both flattering and embarrassing. Their willingness to participate in the professional learning process has benefited many future leaders. A special thanks to Bob Badelt of Nortel, Ernesto Bertarelli of Serono, Robert Bohn and Mike Ouest of Oshkosh Truck, David Carberry of Johnson & Johnson, Jeff Carney of Putnam, Mike Crosby of Override, Bill Fonvielle of Performance Measurement Associates, Harry Hadiaris of Irving Oil, Ted Lapres of Nypro, Ken Luttio of LTI- Philips, Mike Ruettgers of EMC, and Jeff Vander Wolk of The Waterway Café and The Inn of the Governors. Additional thanks to the many others who confided in us. The practice of management is best understood in the rich contextual background provided by their freely told stories.

There are many hands that touched the production of this work. Our editor, Nick Philipson, saw the value and pushed us to be clear and consistent. Sara Gaum, our research assistant, did an excellent job finding supporting data and taking a critical view of our messages. Our proof reader, Janice Reynolds and administrative assistant, Randee Lucia, were invaluable in managing the details and making many of the technical corrections. Joe Boudreau and a number of our current students made very helpful comments on the working draft.

We are grateful to Babson College for giving us the time to do the work, valuing a desire to excel in the classroom, and encouraging the pursuit of practical management knowledge.

Wellesley, MA   Larry Carr
                                                                     Fred Nanni

Contents

Chapter 1
Introduction

Today's senior managers grapple with a common problem: their organization is straying from its strategic intent. All too often, senior managers realize that their organizations' departments are not synchronized, and in the worst cases, these out-of-synch departments actually conflict with each other. Siemens, a $52 billion multinational corporation, struggled to establish their US market position in the medical equipment business. The US Siemens team was working hard to build their market. They knew 50% of the world's demand for medical equipment was in the United States and their less than 10% market share was unacceptable. Corporate made the US market a strategic priority. Most of the medical equipment was manufactured in Germany. Manufacturing processed the US market demand the same as requests from Germany and operations from the rest of the world. Orders from Argentina, Nigeria, Portugal, and other countries were treated with the same priority. Further, Siemens had a tendency to delay the products for the United States due to some regulatory and special product requirements. The results were that products were delivered late and did not respond to the US demand. Manufacturing did not share the importance and urgency of the US market. Executives were frustrated with the lack of progress. They did not have strategic alignment.

Frustrated by their company's inefficiency, managers frequently ask us to define the correct set of measures or to provide the best incentive system to motivate their people. In short, they want to know the secret of consistently delivering results. This book contains that secret!

Okay, anyone whose gut response is to argue, "There is no secret," is absolutely right and already knows the first lesson of this book. The past is littered with clever management innovations, maze-like operational frameworks, and faddish methodologies. If any of them had been the "secret," we wouldn't have had to write this book, and no one would need to read it.

Yet smart managers understand that effective management often means adhering to the old adage, "You get what you measure." Consequently, many managers seek a universal approach to implementing strategy; but in doing so they labor under the very common misconception that such a thing exists. Searching for the secret—the "holy grail" of management strategy—is both fruitless and misguided.

There is no "one size fits all" management system. Every firm needs to employ a custom management system that motivates employees to behave in ways that

L.P. Carr, A.J. Nanni, Jr., *Delivering Results*, DOI 10.1007/978-1-4419-0621-2_1,
© Springer Science+Business Media, LLC 2009

advance specific goals. Different strategies call for different approaches to managing and measuring performance. For example, a firm pursuing a low-cost strategy in a mass market, like Wal-Mart, has different priorities than a firm selling high-end products to a niche market, like Nordstrom's. Highly desirable behavior in the niche market such as wide aisles and appealing displays may be considered wasteful in the Wal-Mart low-cost firm. Conversely, cost-reduction methods that are viewed as top priorities in the mass market may be strategically destructive in the niche market. Wal-Mart has one set of cashier queues and store personnel are focused on filling shelves while Nordstrom has department cashiers and store personnel are knowledgeable and focus on customer service.

But suppose two companies do pursue the same strategy—should they therefore measure performance the same way? No, because a customized performance and measurement system works not only because it fits a particular business strategy but also because it responds to the company's culture and context. A strategy must be able to adapt to the particulars of a company; thus any single strategy, when followed by two different firms, will require very different kinds of work. Consider the variables that affect strategy in two given firms: Do both firms face the same kind of competition? Are the prices and availabilities of required resources the same for both firms? Are the organizational capabilities the same? Do the firms face equivalent regulatory and compliance restrictions? Is the strategy a natural fit to the way people think in the organization or does it represent a break from past behavior? The answers to these questions will determine what matters in implementing the strategy and, therefore, which performance measures the company should choose.

General Electric (GE) and Philips compete in the Lighting Industry. Philips has very cutting-edge technology and is in need of more US market penetration. GE has a dominant market share and strong distribution with an excellent sales and marketing team. GE needs to find better ways to commercialize technology and introduce more innovative products. Philips must build its customer relationship, distribution, and marketing. The factors of success in the same served market are different for each company.

But even once a company has thoroughly examined itself and its context to find "what matters," it cannot preserve the results in a static set of procedures and performance measures. A good management system, like any other part of the organization's infrastructure, needs constant attention, maintenance, and upgrading. Organizations are constantly changing—responding to the needs of the served market and the competitive environment. An effective set of measures is only good for a limited time. Excellent management systems are dynamic and responsive.

Thus, concerned managers must learn to ask the right questions and to ask them often: not questions about finding a good performance measurement system *product* but about identifying a good *process* for measuring what matters. Designing and using custom performance measurement systems to implement organizational strategy requires careful thought and significant effort, and there are no shortcuts.

But the rewards can be great. In our academic, consulting, and professional careers, we have crafted, implemented, utilized, analyzed, critiqued, and repaired hundreds of management systems. Collectively, we have been working at this for over 50 years. We have found that, although there are no "silver bullets," there are productive ways of thinking about delivering strategic results. Thinking clearly about delivering results means looking for compatible organizational structures, linked performance measures, and reliable processes. This book comprises a set of guidelines to help managers assess what kinds of strategic measurements they need as well as advice about how to design those measures, to implement them, and to use them to motivate strategic behavior. We want to show you how to bring your strategy to life.

Our Philosophy of Management Systems

To achieve strategic results, a management system must align the effort of all the members of the organization. Effective execution requires that everyone in the organization pull in the right direction at the right time.

We take a holistic systems approach to delivering results. A management system for delivering results must be in harmony with the strategy, the environment, and the organization. When we say "holistic" and "harmony," we are not talking about New Age mysticism; instead, we are talking about a hard-headed and rational approach to strategy execution, one in which all the parts fit together and work toward a common goal with little wasted effort or energy. The primary active mechanism in the performance measurement part of the management system is feedback. Using feedback, a manager may measure the magnitudes of strategically important performance improvements, assess causes and effects, learn how to make effective improvements, and motivate people to take actions that lead to those improvements. But only when all the parts of the management system line up can feedback be harnessed to encourage behavior that delivers strategic results. Harmonious design of the management system must take into account the nature of the business, the type of products or services it offers, and its strategic priorities. The organizational architecture must be compatible with the strategy. Furthermore, the organization's culture, as well as its operational capabilities and strategic strengths and weaknesses, must be reflected in the system design.

Ultimately, promoting strategic behavior is the objective of system design. First and foremost, delivering results depends upon influencing employees' behavior. The term "management system"—something that measures results and directs activities—sounds mechanistic, but nothing could be farther from the truth. Delivering results, from the organization's perspective, is not merely measuring and reporting; instead, it is the amalgamation of all the decisions made and all the actions taken by the organization's people. Thus a management system is more about human judgment than quantitative analysis. In assessing these judgments, a good manager must examine them from many angles: Are the employees' decisions and actions in the best interest of the firm? Are they aligned with the strategy? Do they open new options for the organization? Do they represent best efforts? Do they expose the organization to undesirable risks? Do they develop strategic resources?

Yet even when the behavior stays the same, the responses to these questions may differ depending upon the situation.

Our message of delivering results is very applicable to not-for-profit organizations. They, more than for-profit firms, are challenged with aligning the efforts of the parts of their organization with the shared strategy. The common financial goals (ROI, profit, EVA, etc.) are not applicable as overall measures. They need a system that coordinates roles and motivates people to implement the strategy as designed.

How to Use the Book

The challenge of designing and implementing a management system for delivering results can be daunting for several reasons:

- Different strategies call for different competencies.
- Specific competitive environments may reorder the priorities of these competencies.
- The professional model may determine how an organization operates.
- Leadership styles influence behavior.
- Variations in organizational structures can lead to dissimilar strategic opportunities or limits within an organization.
- Information technology can enhance or limit the flow of necessary data.
- Skills and knowledge change over time.
- No two people are exactly the same.

Managers who can navigate these variables and chart a route for their own organization's strategy will reach their goals faster and more efficiently than their competitors. Knowing how to create and direct management systems that deliver results is, in itself, a strategic resource.

Developing this strategic resource is the purpose of this book. Managers can use the guidelines in this book to develop their own philosophy of strategic management and performance measurement and then to enact this philosophy in their organizations. Students can use this book, along with a forthcoming companion casebook, to study the process of designing and employing performance management systems. Business professors who teach courses on control from a tools' perspective can use this book as an additional resource to provide a complementary "big picture" view of strategic control.

The inspiration for this book comes from the managers we have worked with, from our own experiences as practicing controllers and senior managers, and, most importantly, from our students at Babson College. At Babson, we offer two popular courses entitled "Managing and Achieving Strategic Results," one for MBA students and one for advanced undergraduates, in which we use competitive strategy as a foundation to teach a behavioral approach to formulating solutions. These project-based classes, which function as "capstone" courses just prior to graduation, have received very positive feedback. Working MBA students, who can immediately apply the course's tools and techniques to their jobs, applaud the results they produce. Graduates of the course have also encouraged us to put our system into writing so that they can share it with their colleagues and superiors.

Outline of Content and Application

As a response to such requests, our purpose in this book is pragmatic rather than theoretical. Although we do acknowledge and make reference to current research on strategy and management, our intent is to provide a practical guide for the working manager. Thus, the book's organization parallels the process of diagnosing and solving performance management problems.

The first part of the book focuses on the broad issue of strategy and execution. Chapter 2 provides an extended example that illustrates our idea of a "holistic and harmonious management system" and explains why the system's traits are critical to strategic execution. In Chapter 3, we outline the major components of a management system for delivering results (an MSDR), along with cautionary examples that show how a poor fit of any single component can cause strategic failure.

The second part of the book focuses on the context within which the organization's management system operates. In order to be effective, the management system must fit both the strategy and the context; therefore, a management system must match the competitive environment, connect with the organization's capabilities, and harmonize with the organization's culture. Chapter 4 provides a synopsis of the strategic context in which management systems operate. In this chapter, we show that the success of strategy implementation depends upon markets and competition: herein we find the opportunities, barriers, and threats to strategic success. We also show managers how to analyze these contextual factors to determine which behaviors the management system should explicitly encourage, which behaviors it can ignore, and which behaviors it should actively discourage.

The next two chapters offer ways to understand the relationships between a strategy's key success factors and the organization's internal environment. Chapter 5 explains how the organization has to be attuned to both the strategy and the realities of the market in which it is being executed. Internal culture and leadership can either help or hinder a company's execution of its strategy. When managers can tap into its strengths, organizational culture may be the most potent source for delivering results. Chapter 6 examines the influence of management upon the contextual factors that affect the delivery of strategic results. We start with a look into the governance structure as a way of determining the strength of the organizational foundation.

The final chapters teach managers to use our process for determining and implementing measurement systems and also for using incentives to propel good results. Chapter 7 provides an overview of how management systems work, outlining the complementary roles of measures and controls in a management system. The managerial structure of an organization determines, to a great extent, whether an individual manager will be able to build and deploy critical competences. The ability to deliver results is also predicated upon how the organization is populated and how the people's skills and capabilities contribute to the organization. We discuss how to diagnose and adjust these factors. The chapter also contrasts balance with *alignment*, two measurement features that are necessary for strategic success. Chapter 8 investigates balance in more detail, examining balanced scorecard and other frameworks. Chapter 9 extends the discussion, emphasizing the alignment between the management system and the strategy, while also describing the processes through which managers can select meaningful and effective measures, diagnose the currency of the measures, and renew or replace them over time.

Chapter 10 delves more deeply into the realm of designing measurement systems, describing several approaches to creating and maintaining alignment among strategy, actions, and measures. Chapter 11 adds the final ingredient: attaching rewards and incentives to measures. Rewards can range from recognition (like formal celebrations and informal "ataboys"), to promotions and pay increases, to significant financial bonuses. The kinds of incentives and the conditions under which they are used can make a big difference to both short-term and long-term strategic outcomes. Chapter 11 provides a perspective for the manager wrestling with the inherent trade-offs. The book's conclusion pulls together the lessons of the previous chapters. In Chapter 12, we examine life cycles of strategies and delivering results. We discuss the inextricable relationship between strategy implementation control and management; we show how to make strategic management systems dynamic while maintaining a harmony with the contextual environment; and we reveal how the process of creating and using measurement systems can become the primary weapon in the manager's arsenal for both strategy execution and strategy renewal.

Part I
Delivering Results—Strategy and Execution

Chapter 2
Management as a System

A Tale of Two Companies—Success and Failure of Strategic Execution

The year was 1997. A new CEO at AT&T Corporation, C. Michael Armstrong, initiated a bold strategy. Realizing that his company's core business, long distance, was rapidly becoming obsolete, Armstrong embarked on a $100 billion acquisition spree to launch AT&T into the up-and-coming cable market. The move won rave reviews and Wall Street embraced the idea, especially viewed against the background of AT&T's market slide prior to Armstrong's hiring.[1]

Armstrong knew the cable market. During his previous stint as CEO of Hughes Electronics, he had built the largest satellite-TV service in the United States competing directly against cable. Furthermore, he could foresee a key advantage of cable: It would offer direct lines into customers' homes, a benefit AT&T had lost years ago. With such easy access to customers, AT&T would be poised to offer television, Internet, and phone services, separately or bundled. Armstrong also intended to catapult the company into first-mover position in offering voice-over-Internet phone (VOIP) service. Ten-plus years later, after we have witnessed the emergence of successful VOIP companies like Vonage and Skype, and seen subscriptions to bundled cable packages in 15 million American homes, we can appreciate the prescience of Armstrong's strategy.[2]

Rewind to 1996, about a year before Armstrong made his move toward cable, another new CEO, Robert G. Bohn, began a more modest strategic shift at Oshkosh Truck Corporation. Oshkosh manufactured heavy trucks, primarily for the U.S. armed services, which accounted for over 60% of its sales in fiscal year 1996. But in the late 1990s the U.S. military cut spending on heavy trucks in favor of a rapid-deployment military, hurting Oshkosh. Bohn responded by crafting a new strategy at Oshkosh: First, he introduced lean manufacturing techniques to reduce production costs in the company's core business; next, he intended to stimulate growth through forward-integration into non-military heavy truck markets. Like Armstrong's strategy execution, Bohn's would involve healthy doses of acquisition.

Bohn knew lean manufacturing, but Oshkosh didn't—nor did any of the company's acquisition targets—so change would require effort. By reworking the

L.P. Carr, A.J. Nanni, Jr., *Delivering Results*, DOI 10.1007/978-1-4419-0621-2_2,
© Springer Science+Business Media, LLC 2009

manufacturing process in Oshkosh's established and newly acquired businesses, Bohn hoped to extract greater profits from them. The business and corporate strategies were smart, but barely noteworthy. In fact, the only reaction in the analyst community at the time was that Oshkosh paid too much for its first acquisition. The change was not particularly innovative; in fact, Raytheon and several other military contractors were already pursuing variations on the same theme. With its emphasis on hard work and sound business sense, Bohn's strategy lacked the glamour of Armstrong's visionary sweep at AT&T.

We all know how Armstrong's story ends. Price competition undercut AT&T's long-distance revenue, and a $65 billion debt crippled the company's strides into the cable and wireless markets. Unable to secure adequate funds in the financial markets, AT&T was forced to break up in 2001. The stock price lost half its value between the date Armstrong was hired (October 1997) and the date he announced the planned split (October 2000), falling from $45.19 to $23.38.[3] For people under the age of 25, AT&T is now known as the company that offers service for the iPhone. Of course, that's just the name AT&T. Under the brand, it's Cingular Wireless!

On the other hand, few people know how Bohn's story at Oshkosh Truck Corporation unfolded over the same span of time. Under Bohn's leadership Oshkosh transformed its production operations in its original business, decreasing costs and increasing productivity, and then successfully deployed the same changes into each of Oshkosh's acquisitions. Corporate revenues grew from $413 million in 1996 to $1.324 billion in 2000. Net income improved from minus $3 million (−$0.23 per share) to $49.7 million ($3.03 per share) during the same period ($75.6 million in 2003). The company's stock traded at $1.75 per share (adjusted) at the beginning of 1997 and $11.00 per share (adjusted) at the end of 2000.[4]

Bohn and Armstrong were both smart, ambitious CEOs with enough experience to understand the potential impact of the strategic changes they proposed for their companies. Why did one fail so spectacularly while the other quietly succeeded? Armstrong cites fraudulent financial activity and reporting by his competitors at WorldCom and Quest Communications as major contributors to AT&T's failure. He claims their falsified reported results made AT&T look bad by comparison. Judged on a more level-playing field, Armstrong maintains that AT&T would have been perceived more favorably by Wall Street, allowing more time and money for his strategy to produce the desired results. However, in their book, *Execution*, Larry Bossidy and Ram Charan describe Armstrong's AT&T as a company that simply could not follow through on its strategy.[5] We are inclined to agree. Unethical business practices by competitors notwithstanding, AT&T simply did not have a management system that could deliver results.

Bohn, on the other hand, was able to deliver results at Oshkosh Truck. Granted, Bohn's situation was less difficult than Armstrong's. For a Fortune 1000 company, Oshkosh Truck suffered far less scrutiny and competitive price pressure than AT&T. Perhaps good luck played a role. Nevertheless, Bohn was able to produce significant changes in his core business and, subsequently, in his acquisitions. It is important to note that, while the business strategy at Oshkosh Truck was far from unique, very few companies have actually been able to pull it off. Everybody knows about lean manufacturing principles and the related benefits, but only a handful of companies—Toyota, FedEx, Southwest Airlines—have applied these principles successfully. On a similar note, the corporate strategy of extracting value from acquisitions through synergy and the exploitation of special knowledge and skills is quite common. Yet, again, over 50% of business combinations based on these premises fail where Bohn has succeeded.

We believe that the central reason for the vastly different outcomes at AT&T and Oshkosh Truck is that Oshkosh had a management system for delivering results and AT&T didn't.

Management Systems

Ultimately, managers at every level are judged by their ability to deliver desired results. Shareholders normally measure results using a financial barometer (EPS, ROI, and EBITDA are a few examples), and they expect senior managers to deliver them. Senior managers meet the shareholders' financial targets by setting expectations for each of the divisions, departments, and units of their organizations. Within each division, subordinate managers, in turn, must motivate their people to meet goals. And so it goes down the organizational hierarchy.

To consistently make money or meet expectations, an organization needs managers who can define and execute a solid organizational strategy. Regrettably, we are bombarded with news of high-profile deviations like Enron, Lucent-Alcatel, or Lehman Bros., which claim to meet shareholder expectations and protect shareholder value, but which paper-over poor execution (or execute a bad strategy all too well). Nonetheless, most managers would agree that the best way of systematically creating value as measured by financial returns is the old-fashioned way: They gain a sustainable advantage over their competition—or simply put, they develop a strategy. Choosing and implementing the strategy is the role of the management system.

A system is simply a collection of inter-related parts that work together toward a common purpose. In a plumbing system, these parts are pipes and valves. In an organization's management system, these parts are attitudes, habits, policies, rules, and measures. The combination of these organizational components is critical. Only when these components fit together appropriately and are focused on the common strategic goal will the system deliver the desired results. If any of the critical parts is missing, or if any of the types of parts is overlooked, the results can be haphazard.

While this principle may sound pretty obvious, a surprising number of organizations fail to grasp it. Often an organization's design actually impedes execution of strategy, and senior managers are consistently disappointed in their company's lackluster performance. In other cases, the performance measures for one business function simply generate unnecessary work for other business functions, disrupting harmony among the divisions. Still other companies violate this principle when the dominant culture of its organization undercuts its own strategic priorities. Time and again, we are amazed at the degree to which business organizations ignore the delicate balance among the parts of their organizations and treat strategy, competitive analysis, culture, organizational design, capability development, and performance measurement as separate and independent problem spaces.

To achieve our purpose in this book—creating and using a system to execute a strategy that delivers results—we must unite all of these "problem spaces" in one broad view. Though our focus is performance management through measurement and feedback, we cannot speak sensibly about performance measurement unless we acknowledge and analyze the effects of other parts of the management system on delivering strategic results. The desirability of any set of performance measures is meaningless when they are considered out of context.

Strategy is valuable only when it is executed well. Thus, a unique but poorly executed strategy like Armstrong's is far inferior to a mundane, me-too strategy that is carried out skillfully. Delivering results does not start with crafting a strategy. It starts by laying the groundwork for strategic success: Members of the organization must first establish the right priorities, then find the critical problems blocking the achievement of those priorities, and finally take the right actions at the right times to remove the barriers to success.

When all the members of an organization prepare this way, the company can be secure in the knowledge that what the strategy says is desirable is actually the right thing to do. Thus, a management system for delivering results (an MSDR) must communicate the firm's strategy, along with its implications for action, to every member of the organization. The management system's designers, therefore, need not only an explicit understanding of the firm's strategy but also the knowledge of how the strategy maps onto the organization's capabilities and attributes and how to systematically encourage desirable individual actions.

The Management System at AT&T

Let's turn again to C. Michael Armstrong's leadership at AT&T. Under Armstrong, AT&T floundered not in the strategy, but in the execution. The CEO recognized that the long-distance business was doomed, and he created a strategy to redirect the company. He saw the enormous capacity in a fixed-cost business. Since variations in the sound quality of phone calls were undetectable to the vast majority of consumers, Armstrong focused on volume rather than on quality as a path to financial success. But since the local operating companies, the descendents of the Baby Bells, owned the physical connections to the customers, Armstrong had to find a way to forge direct connections to customers through cable broadband. Out of context, it still sounds like a good idea. So what went wrong?

Competitive Environment

The cash that AT&T spent to make acquisitions in support of its strategy came from its long-distance business. While Armstrong's complaint that some of AT&T's competitors were reporting false results turns out to be valid, the low price for long-distance communication in the late 1990s was the real factor in AT&T's decline. In 1998, there were over 500 long-distance companies in the United States and prices had fallen 60% since AT&T's 1984 breakup. Consequently, AT&T's market share had fallen from 90% to 50%. In 1999, prices were still falling. Meanwhile, competition was driving an increase in costs, particularly in sales and advertising. To further complicate the picture, the regulatory framework had changed to allow the Baby Bells to enter the long-distance market.[6]

Spurred largely by AT&T's acquisition spree, the cable industry consolidated, and many providers began upgrading themselves in order to offer "next generation" services. Qwest, for example, had already announced Internet-based long distance by the end of 1997. Cable prices were rising, but not fast enough to cover the investments AT&T was making in its system. Even as AT&T's broadband revenues rose, its net cash flows continued to fall.

AT&T misread the competitive environment, failing to predict that their long-distance competitors would most likely continue to reduce prices in the future. At this crucial moment, Armstrong should have paused to ask some serious questions: If long-distance prices were to fall further, should the company still leverage itself so highly in order to acquire the cable assets? What would be the likelihood of AT&T finding a "sweet spot" in long-distance service? Is it possible that the bundled, cable-based services would produce a positive cash flow quickly—or at least quickly enough to sustain the company's acquisitions?

Suppose Armstrong had considered all of these questions. From our perspective, the only successful resolution of this scenario would hinge on AT&T's ability to redirect its phone service to heavy users—a hotly contested segment—and to integrate its cable acquisitions quickly, taking advantage of its scale of operations. The resulting cost reductions would preserve the cash needed to service the company's debt without compromising strategic targets. The management system should have been tightly focused on increased sales to heavy long-distance users and on quick digestion of newly acquired cable providers.

In fact, the company did acknowledge these requirements in its plans for 2000. Despite the urgent need to deliver results quickly, it is unclear from published reports whether AT&T changed its management system to aggressively pursue its goals. It is clear, however, that the goals were not obtained. Under intense pressure of time and competition, Armstrong should have rapidly organized the company to isolate redundancies and motivate his most strategically capable employees. Let's look at how Armstrong and AT&T responded at this crucial moment.

Organizational Culture

Any significant change in strategy requires unity of purpose throughout the levels of personnel, and the strategy Armstrong was proposing demanded an especially flexible and nimble workforce. Yet AT&T still had a highly bureaucratic, hierarchical culture, even more than 10 years after its initial breakup. The dominant culture in the core AT&T organization emphasized the traditional notions of internal service quality (e.g., uninterrupted service or, in the industry parlance, maintaining the "dial tone"). The old guard was staff-centric; they adhered to a rigid chain of command and followed the rules that led to lifetime employment. Several attempts to shake up the staunch culture failed, and it endured intact into the late 1990s.[7]Any infusion of new blood—like the entrepreneurs brought into AT&T through its acquisitions—tended to leave quickly rather than boost the company's faltering vitality. Twelve of them left senior executive positions between 1996 and 1999, and many observers blamed clashes of culture for their departures. The problem of retaining talented people did not only afflict the senior levels of the organization, but extended deeply into the organization. AT&T regularly reported reductions in personnel during the period from 1997 to 2000. The company even created an internal "temps" agency in the late 1990s to fill empty positions. Soon thereafter, 10,000 jobs were cut in 2002. With so much employee upheaval, Armstrong could have seized the opportunity to "unfreeze" the old culture, but instead the company failed to communicate any sense of purpose to its remaining workforce. External reports show that Armstrong and others at the top of the organization ignored the need to rebuild the culture. As Jim Collins, author of "Built to Last", said, "Instead of re-finding a sense of purpose, AT&T tried to substitute charismatic leadership."[8]Communications to employees throughout the period, memos that merely papered-over the emotional turmoil, reinforce this observation. Inspirational leadership counts, as we discuss later, but inspiration involves action and processes for getting things done.

Armstrong was left with a company whose internal reality was inconsistent with its strategic desires. AT&T's strategy required that its acquisitions be quickly absorbed into the parent company and that the newly absorbed personnel supply fresh skills and an entrepreneurial perspective. Yet the parent company was not culturally prepared to learn from its feisty new children.

Organizational Design

AT&T's hierarchical and bureaucratic culture was mirrored by its hierarchical and functional organization. Within the multiple layers of management, direct-report headcount was a marker of organizational clout. Into this complicated hierarchy, AT&T had to integrate their new acquisitions and operations, create a streamlined infrastructure, and thereby extract the many potential synergies. This would give the organization a much-needed scale advantage over its competition. The competitive advantage that never materialized was stalled by an organization ill-suited for efficiency.

Instead of reorganizing to integrate its acquisitions, AT&T maintained its functional orientation creating a loose association of free-floating entities rather than a tightly woven organization. Once again, the strategic mindset conflicted with the organizational reality. For example, even though cable's "direct access" to customers' homes was supposed to be the salvation of the phone business, broadband and phone were managed separately. The new digital-cable phone company was likewise managed apart from the original phone company—and the emerging voice-over-Internet phone business would be separate also. The relationship to the consumer was made more complicated rather than simpler. There was no synergy.

Lack of synergy extended to operations. Four years after Armstrong's arrival, AT&T still could not pull all of its services (cable, wireless, and long-distance), onto a single customer bill. This is a particularly telling detail because it reveals a miss on efficiency of operation, a miss on strategic priorities, and a miss on customer service.

Armstrong's strategy was to offer a new bundled product to each consumer household, and he realized his strategy meant anticipating and satisfying a range of customer needs. But since AT&T's organization was fragmented into separate companies, it did not present a single face to its customers. Simply operating under a single brand was not enough. The individual service organizations continued to operate as disaggregate entities. At its heart, the organization was focused not on the customer, but on the old corporate manuals.

Motivating Strategic Capabilities

AT&T had a problem. Any system of policies and performance measures that might have delivered results in one division of the company probably would have been tripped up by the management system in other divisions. At the very least, policies and performance measures might have clearly communicated the strategy or impelled strategic behavior. Yet no system, no matter how smart, could have unleashed enough ingenuity for employees to leap over the roadblocks—competitive, cultural, and organizational—that AT&T had set up for itself.

In our view, Armstrong's strategy failed at the first test of "executability." The company was fundamentally unprepared for its new strategy. Not only did it lack reliable cash flow to manage its debt plus expanded operations, but it was also stuck in a culture that was ignorant of operational innovation and inattentive to customer needs. It had neither the structure nor the infrastructure to allow rapid absorption of its cable acquisitions. Despite having the deal-making savvy to acquire strategically important businesses, the company could not retain people with the skills and experience to realize the potential scale or increased access to customers that the acquisitions brought. In short, AT&T did not have a management system capable of delivering results consistent with the company's new strategy.

Any bold strategy introduces risks, but it is especially foolhardy for an organization to pursue a course of action when nearly everything about the company—from its market conditions to its corporate culture—conflicts with the strategic intent. Certainly, there is little a company can do to create favorable market conditions (although that doesn't stop some companies from trying). In fact, it is typically the mismatch between the old ways of doing things and market conditions that creates the need for a bold new strategy. This means that an organization's main requirement under a new strategy is crafting the management system, an area where it does have direct influence. Strategy is worthless without execution, and execution requires both opportunity and preparedness.

The Management System at Oshkosh Truck

Competitive Environment

When Robert G. Bohn arrived as a new CEO in 1996, Oshkosh Truck's competitive environment bore a striking resemblance to AT&T's, only on a much smaller scale. Like AT&T's, Oshkosh Truck's core business was in danger. The demand for military vehicles had dropped significantly, but Oshkosh's outlook was less stark than AT&T's because the basic economics of profitability in the heavy truck industry was unchanged. While innovations in technology may have impacted military aircraft production and sales in the 1990s, military trucks remained essentially the same for years. Oshkosh Truck's core competence had always been turning out long lines of nearly identical, robust, heavy-duty truck platforms. Scale and volume production drove profits, and this had been the case for decades.

Because the heavy-truck industry had chugged forward reliably for so many years, Oshkosh Truck and its competitors still resembled the automobile industry of the 1950s at the height of mass production. Unlike most modern consumer vehicle producers, Oshkosh still practiced quality control through inspection and rework, and the military market had always tolerated the requisite long lead times. However, during the Reagan years, military spending was refocused from maintaining large standing military forces to planning for a smaller "Rapid Deployment Force." By the early 1990s, that planning was beginning to show up as reduced military spending. The drop in military demand exacerbated the existing problem of excess capacity throughout the industry. Oshkosh and its competitors would be hard-pressed to adapt to the new multi-segment, customer-driven, high-variety world of commercial markets. Incremental changes would be insufficient to allow Oshkosh Truck to cope in such an environment—drastic measures would have to be taken for the company's survival.

Bohn rose to the challenge. He decided to rebuild the strategic capabilities of the company and fashion Oshkosh Truck into a world-class lean manufacturer. The plan called for a costly internal investment to launch a new operation that would eventually lower production costs and improve responsiveness. The reinvigorated manufacturing muscle would provide the platform from which the company could integrate vertically into commercial markets. However, this second phase of the plan would require another round of heavy investment in the company.

To generate enough cash to cover its investments, Oshkosh Truck, like AT&T, could not abandon its core business. Military trucks would have to be the prime internal source of funds for the company's rebirth. But Oshkosh Truck would have to compete with other desperate manufacturers to win the increasingly rare contract bids for fewer numbers of trucks. It was clear that price competition would be the hallmark of the new era for military truck makers. Bohn would have to teach his company to operate more efficiently—and in short order.

Two CEOs faced a crucial moment in their companies, but both were armed with the background knowledge to do the job: Bohn came to Oshkosh Truck with experience in lean manufacturing, just as Armstrong had arrived at AT&T with experience competing with cable. Also, like AT&T, Oshkosh Truck's management system would have to achieve near-term results and employ the tactics to deliver them. Otherwise, the strategy would fail—and this is where the two CEOs differ. Let's look at how Bohn avoided the pitfalls that thwarted Armstrong.

Organizational Culture

Bohn's strategy may have been simple, but implementing it would be complicated. The changes at Oshkosh Truck would have to be huge. To shift to lean manufacturing, the company would have to redefine and expand job responsibilities on the shop floor; but the structure of the company would not make it easy. First of all, the constraints on unionized workers' job designs and levels of seniority would be hard to overcome. Second, the many rigid layers of supervision and control that categorized jobs in production management would prevent the quick, nimble transitions that Bohn sought. In short, Oshkosh Truck, like AT&T, began with a hierarchical, by-the-book organizational culture.

But unlike AT&T's leadership, Bohn was acutely aware that he would have to convince his workforce to fully embrace change. He led a direct and sustained effort to break up the old ways of thinking and replace them with the new vision. He made the company's dire situation quite clear and stark. Rather than trying to hide the likelihood of pain and potential job loss in the transition, he communicated his strategy as the only alternative to continual downsizing.

The culture change was aggressive. Bohn energized his management team to find opportunities for improvement. To publicly validate his claims that success depended on the labor force, he initiated a program for employee empowerment and management–labor cooperation. Training programs flourished. Improvements were documented and celebrated. All the while, Bohn and his direct reports maintained a high profile. By striving to persuade all of the organization's heads to internalize its strategic priorities, Oshkosh Trucks nurtured a culture of change.

Organizational Design

Having changed the thinking of his people, Bohn still had to change its organization. He streamlined Oshkosh Truck's design toward lean manufacturing principles. He also had to eliminate layers of middle management to align the organizational structure with the new cultural emphasis on worker involvement. In fact, the great majority of headcount reduction came from the management ranks. Labor was then reorganized into self-managed teams, and production systems were reconfigured along lean manufacturing principles. All vehicles were now produced on the same assembly line, with military trucks and commercial vehicles intermingled as they passed down the line. The manufacture of new products and their associated production methods were pioneered in a separate, specialized development facility. Workers cycled through the development area and the main production line in order to move knowledge and people fluidly between the two.

Oshkosh Truck Corporation also had to redesign its relationships with suppliers. The company worked with fewer suppliers but exchanged more information with them. By outsourcing some subunit manufacture, Bohn reduced the variety of work on the assembly line while increasing output variety. To further promote efficiency, the company developed and implemented integrated information systems.

To vertically integrate into commercial markets, Bohn's next step was to acquire firms that manufactured fire and emergency vehicles, concrete mixer/delivery vehicles, and municipal service vehicles. With each acquisition, the synergies were immediately exploited. At its original base truck manufacturer, changes in vehicle design allowed new downstream businesses to meet customer needs more efficiently. Bohn also cross-fertilized company management, bringing new managers from the acquisitions into the corporate headquarters and sending corporate managers into the new businesses.

Rather than force the acquired businesses to follow the procedures, rules, and organizational structures of the core truck business, Bohn let the new businesses reorganize themselves. The unifying element that was exported to all acquisitions was Oshkosh's organizational process for problem finding and problem solving. This process-focused approach to integrating acquisitions has proven quite effective at Oshkosh. Although each business in the organization kept its own customer-oriented strategy, all of the businesses shared the same basic strategic vision and set of operational priorities.

Motivating Strategic Capabilities

In contrast to AT&T's, Oshkosh Truck Corporation's strategy was both competitive and feasible. Robert Bohn, an experienced CEO who had led his prior company into lean manufacturing, was only one cause of the company's success. Another factor in the company's favor was its financial wherewithal to purchase acquisitions in the short run. The company's financial projections for the lean manufacturing business strategy were predicated on earning fatter returns under current market prices or, if prices fell, on maintaining current margins at lower prices. Finally, the company operated in ways that exploited potential synergies as it implemented its strategy. By forming a management system that complemented and reinforced the strategy, Bohn aligned organization with strategy. The company dedicated itself to implementing the strategy, not just having the strategy.

Oshkosh Truck's ability to execute was finally nailed down by its collection of policies and performance measures. With the culture and structure oriented toward the new strategy, the performance management system could more efficiently direct attention and motivate improvement. To do this, Oshkosh Truck rebuilt its entire set of performance measures.

Each of Oshkosh Truck's business units was evaluated against financial performance measures, but the desired outcomes were also logically decomposed into short-term operational goals and measures. On the whole, the performance measures were balanced across internal and external measures, short- and long-term perspectives, and financial and operational measures. All of the measures were driven by and aligned with the business unit strategies.

Conclusion

Strategic success depends on the complete management system. Shortcomings in any area could derail that success. Business strategy addresses the market within which a company operates, but executing strategy addresses all of the company's parts—norms and values, design and structure, people and policies, rules and measures, and rewards and incentives. All parts of the management system should complement each other. If any one part is out of alignment with the strategy, execution will suffer. If several are out of alignment, as we saw in AT&T circa 2000, the strategy will fail.

A management system that delivers results must be consciously crafted. It will not arise spontaneously. We've seen how Robert Bohn at Oshkosh Truck planned specifically for the company's competitive operating environment, along with all its constraints and contingencies, and how both the organization's structure and its culture were modified to promote strategic priorities. Having met these conditions, Bohn created the policies and performance measures needed to impel the whole system into motion. In subsequent chapters, we will peel the complicated management system apart to examine each of its components before reassembling them into a management system that delivers results.

Notes

1. Hofmeister, Sallie. "ATT Cable Executive Hindery to Leave Firm," *Los Angeles Times*, (October 7, 1999).
2. ATT Corp—Company History from fundinguniverse.com http://www.fundinguniverse.com/company-histories/ATamp;T-Corporation-Company-History.html
3. For a brief history of AT&T, company milestones and stock prices, visit the corporate web site at www.corp.att.com/history
4. Annual reports and stock price information from 1994 to present can be obtained on the Oshkosh corporate web site, www.oshkoshcorporation.com, by clicking on the Investor link.
5. Bossidy, L and Charan, R., *Execution*, (New York, Random House, 2002).
6. Kastre, Michael. "The Demise of AT&T," www.adti.net/telecom/whitepaper_demiseattmkastre122000.html
7. Maney, Kevin. "Former Execs "Walk All Over" AT&T," *USA Today*, (September 24, 1998).
8. Maney, Kevin. "Failure to Define Purpose Leads to AT&T Split," *USA Today* (2000).

Chapter 3
The Key to Delivering Results

Nothing succeeds like dumb luck. Unmerited and unanticipated, fortunate events can sometimes elevate a company's prosperity almost immeasurably. Take the case of Microsoft Corporation. Today, one of the world's largest corporations, the Redmond giant owes its dominance to just such an initial stroke of fantastic luck. Yet luck had little to do with its eventual rise.

The story is the stuff of legend: Roughly a quarter-century ago, the world's dominant computer company, International Business Machines, established a project "skunk works" in Boca Raton, FL, far from its bureaucratic Armonk, NY, corporate headquarters. The goal for this "independent business unit" was both radical and urgent. Instead of making huge computers for centralized data processing, it would quickly design an easy-to-use microcomputer that could run on a desktop—a personal computer that would become the IBM PC. For speed, the business unit broke from IBM's policy of using proprietary components and software. Instead, it chose to assemble the PC from "off-the-shelf" industry parts and software.

Back then, not many companies produced software for microcomputers. Nor did IBM think the PC was going to be anything more than a niche product for a growing hobbyist market that it quickly needed to fill. So it approached the pip-squeak Microsoft to supply the PC's operating system. True to its name, Microsoft had only one small offering, a version of BASIC. Nonetheless, the little shop agreed to supply the operating system. Bill Gates and his then-obscure cohorts took their own shortcut, buying the rights to another microcomputer operating system; they then set about to develop and extend its best features. Thus was born MS-DOS (PC-DOS, as sold by IBM).

For Microsoft, this was a complete bolt out of the "Blue," guaranteeing sizable profits. Moreover, IBM's visibility and brand turned the microcomputer into a real business tool, not just a toy for nerds. Any company riding IBM's coattails would thus become a serious business. But it could not necessarily stay one by simply remaining a supplier. Presciently, Gates convinced IBM to let Microsoft retain the rights to market its operating system for PCs other than IBMs. Not only would Microsoft have IBM sales but they would also provide the platform for all PC clones—and be able to run the most popular application software, such as Lotus 1-2-3 and WordPerfect.[1]

L.P. Carr, A.J. Nanni, Jr., *Delivering Results*, DOI 10.1007/978-1-4419-0621-2_3,
© Springer Science+Business Media, LLC 2009

Luck had played its part. But it's a testament to Bill Gates, Paul Allen, and their associates that Microsoft was able to extend that advantage into an enduring, dominant presence. Crucial to their eventual success, they didn't mistake their windfall for good management. Rather, they learned from their experience and developed a repetitive strategy of co-opting open-system software products and concepts, improving them, and then integrating them with their operating systems. In other words, luck opened the door; but a thoughtful strategy and its careful execution sealed success.

Too many companies fail to understand their active role in managing luck, whether good or bad. When their results are poor, they ascribe it to bad luck or unfair competition. Alternately, they conclude that good luck was the inevitable result of their clever innovations, their outstanding management skills, or their unassailably superior products and services. Luck is what you make of it. But the key to delivering results is not just having a good strategy but implementing it well. More often than not, being in the right place and the right time with the right capabilities is the result of careful preparation rather than dumb luck.

By definition, a management system that delivers results (MSDR) makes allowances for luck. It starts by assisting in the shaping of an executable strategy and then supports and assures complete follow-through on that strategy. Strategy creation, we believe, is far easier than actually delivering against strategic objectives.

Thus, the majority of this chapter analyzes management control—the execution part of the system. It entails a never-ending process of integrating strategic objectives into the firm's infrastructure and measurement system. Indeed, an MSDR must be woven into the fabric of an organization so that it influences every decision. MSDR's primary integrating mechanism relates to measuring the performance of manager's activities. However, in some important areas, determining how well the strategy is being pursued involves other mechanisms, as we discuss below.

Strategy

Let's start first with what we mean by "strategy" and how we test it. We can characterize business unit strategy as a hypothesis about how a company can create value and capture some of it.[2] But for management to be able to genuinely assess the true merit of the hypothesis, an organization must first execute its strategy effectively and efficiently. That requires an MSDR, which is designed to deliver flawless execution of the strategy.

Strategy can take on many guises. At one end of the spectrum, strategy is a theme or an attitude about how work will be done in an organization (e.g., "We're about quality!"). At the other end, some people speak of strategy as the organization's long-term plans (e.g., rolling out and expanding a new product line). It is true that you cannot have and execute a strategy without a thematic core and an implementation plan, but having an idea of what is important does not mean you have a strategy. Neither does having a plan.

What we consider to be strategy connects those two things: strategy is competitive positioning. At the business unit level, strategy means choosing markets. It also means defining what the organization will provide for those markets, the interface to the markets, and specifying why customers in those markets will want to buy what is offered (the customer value proposition). Strategy at the corporate level is about building business units that exploit strengths the corporation already has. It's also about creating the additional skills and resources needed to be able to take advantage of competitive opportunities. In other words, corporate strategy depends on the collective MSDRs of all of the business units.

No one knows, at the outset, whether a strategy will be effective. In a sense, the strategy is an informed hunch that a particular value proposition, aimed at a particular market and executed well, will create wealth for the company and its owners. Neither can the organization know with certainty what plans the competition has nor can it foresee changing customer preferences, economic conditions, or emergent substitutes. Nonetheless, a manager can influence his or her "luck" by building critical organizational strengths and purposefully eradicating weaknesses. Moreover, he can understand his role in the team that is executing the strategy.

Because market conditions change (customers, competitors, technology), MSDRs need to be course correcting. The various elements of the strategic execution system must be able to respond to shifts. Moreover, performance and results gauges must be constantly calibrated to the various pressures of the environment. We'll detail the primary mechanisms for delivering results below, but first we'll discuss some concepts about staying in balance amid constant change.

Management Control

Effective management means making hard decisions and taking actions based on good feedback about what is strategically important. That is not simple. Not only are managers reliant on the quality of the feedback they get, they often must balance progress toward apparently competing goals. In order to thrive tomorrow, the organization must survive today. Good managers are both tactical and strategic. They balance the short-run results with the long-term targets. They consider the demands of the stockholders for financial results as well as the responsibility to the employees for an enriching environment. They encourage entrepreneurial thinking and risk taking, but at the same time demand predictable results that meet expectations. They balance the drive for market share and the desire for profits.

Finally, amid all this duality, good managers deliver the pledged results; they execute the strategy.

The practice of management may be a balancing act—and it may differ by product, industry, culture, or style—but in all cases it involves using measurements to manage and control the organization.

A company's internal rules, standard procedures, and performance measures are often referred to as its management control system. Sometimes that nomenclature can be problematical. The word control is derived from the Latin *contra-rotulus*, literally "counter-roll." At its root, it means staying in balance. But in many situations, the term takes on a negative connotation, as in the removal of freedom. However, we view strategic control as corrective feedback, not as a limiting factor. The primary objective of strategic control is to make corrections for deviations from the strategy, as illustrated in Fig. 3.1.

The thermostat in your home is a classic, and benign, control mechanism. You set the temperature highs and lows to regulate the heating and cooling. The thermostat then monitors the atmosphere and, if the temperature varies from the settings, it switches on the furnace or the air conditioning system. Measurement and feedback about deviations from a desired state are central to control, mechanical or human. But strategic control is more like manipulating a host of gauges that must be reset constantly.

Performance measures, rules, and standard procedures must be actively coordinated with the strategy, along with the competitive environment and the organization's characteristics. Moreover, good feedback frequently requires more than just tuning. Often, delivering results requires managers to make wholesale adjustments to the strategy or to the organization's characteristics. This whole set of dynamic relationships encompasses the management system for delivering results. And central to its gyroscopic mission is getting the human element of management right.

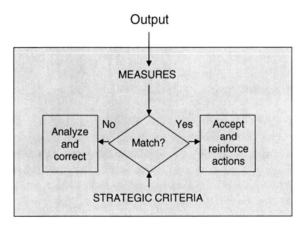

Fig. 3.1 Feedback control loop

Our model of managing for results also heavily weights the human behavior and motivation for course-correcting actions and decisions. And that is because managing for results focuses on the behavior necessary to achieve results. An MSDR is therefore a critical determinant of effective leadership.

Indeed, what the members of the organization do determines whether the organization is "on target." Put another way, an organization's real strategy is in its actions, not its words. In practice, this inherent strategy does not always turn out to be the intended one. Affected by leadership, the organization's actions are determined by what the organization's members believe is important and how they approach the priorities established by those beliefs. They also tend to coincide with what is measured, not desired.[3] In *Delivering What You Promise*, Jeff Weinstein discusses how food service organizations carry out service guarantees.[4] An example is Rally's "Get it right or get it free" campaign. During the five-week management training course, managers role-play customer interactions in order to understand how to correctly understand complaints and how to correct the problem. Managers are then expected to teach and enforce this training to their hourly employees. To monitor their staff's customer interactions, managers give employees coupons at the beginning of their shift to be issued when a problem arises. Coupons can be for anything from a free soda to an entirely free meal and are issued at the discretion of the employee, not the manager. The manager collects unused coupons at the end of the day and discusses the reasons behind the used coupons with the employee. "If a crew member does something wrong, it gives them a learning opportunity," says Rally's VP of Training, Larry Smith. "But we teach our people to go beyond guest expectations. If that is the worst thing that happens, we are happy. If employees don't go far enough, that is a disappointment." Rally's commitment to service extends from its corporate office down through its organization due to its established training program, coupon system, and constant reinforcement of both programs.

The most common example of not "walking the talk" is the division manager who manages by budget compliance but talks about strategy and business growth. The actions speak louder than the words, and the people understand that budget observance is the main focus of the leadership.

To understand the difference between professed and inherent strategies, consider the experience one of us had assisting a major health products company with its performance measurement systems. This is a major player. If you walked into a Walgreen's or a CVS today, you would find this company's products throughout the store. Yet we encountered one of these implicit strategy management systems in one of the company's major divisions.

Questioning the division's leaders and their subordinates on what the current performance measures emphasized, we found they did not align with what was deemed important at the strategic level. Many of these managers were well aware of the lack of fit, but, not unexpectedly, they had managed to the measures. Further, the implicit strategy defined by their beliefs was not really a strategy at all. Their de facto strategy was "Make and sell what we made and sold yesterday for our existing customers, only cheaper and better." The board reluctantly agreed that this statement reflected what the division was really doing. However, the real intended strategy was "Innovate: develop new products to emerging market needs and design lean processes to produce and distribute them quickly."

Based on our experience, such a disconnect is far from uncommon. Strategic results are only delivered when the things decision makers believe and do align with the intended strategy. This means that an MSDR is not a carefully elaborated strategy statement, a list of measures, or even the result of having all those things. Rather, an MSDR is the entire guidance system for the organization, one that establishes harmony between the intended strategic direction and current actions—and is pressure tested and revised to achieve actual good results.

Strategic management requires aligning the group objective with the individual objectives. This is one of the major roles of performance measures, which direct attention, establish priorities, and provide feedback on strategic execution. However, performance measures alone are not well suited to creating an understanding of the strategy or at preventing unintended consequences.

That is the job of a management system, which is a *process* for influencing behavior. Unfortunately, most managers immediately think of this process in terms of performance measures and the associated system of outcomes to which those measures are attached. Performance measures do generate attention, and we will show how they can be used to create strategic alignment within an organization. However, they are not the first step in the entire MSDR process. Before you explore performance measures there needs to be a clear strategic direction and an articulated set of key success factors.

Step back and think about how our behavior is influenced outside of the business environment. Our behavior is constrained or motivated, for example, by our attitudes and beliefs, by the norms of our society, by peer groups and family, and by legal and ethical boundaries. Each of us can find examples in our lives of making a decision or taking an action because we wanted to be like other people. Conversely, we have also attempted to stand out at other times. Motivations run the gamut from wanting to be recognized, to gaining financial rewards, to minimizing undesirable risks, to avoiding punishment, and to proving something to ourselves. These same influences come into play in the development of a management system for delivering results.

The Key to Delivering Results

Once everyone is on board, control feedback can be achieved in a variety of ways. Sometimes a formal reporting system creates a feedback loop. Sometimes a casual conversation over coffee can be an equally effective feedback. Small entrepreneurial firms will likely use different techniques than, say, GE. And a data-driven manager will have different information requirements from a concept-oriented manager.

Not only will the manner of feedback change but also its substance and style. For instance, those companies competing on price will employ different measures than those dominating a market segment based on some unique features or customer benefits. And the values and culture of the organization will place different emphasis on certain aspects of management systems. These variations in management systems will accurately reflect the organization's strategy, values, people, and current competitive situation.

Indeed, the mix of measures in the portfolio will be unique to each enterprise and should snugly fit the specific needs of the firm. Often, the root cause of recurring business problems can be traced directly to an ill-fitting MSDR. We often measure the wrong things that are not well connected to the actions needed for success.

A good way to illustrate how an MSDR is tailor-made is to look at the system from the "inside-out," starting with the performance measures first. Performance measures count things—dollars of income, customer complaints, points of market share, or average number of rings before the phone is answered.

Performance measures fall into three major types: those that focus on *results*, those that focus on *actions*, and those that focus on *resources*. Results measures are primarily motivators—they help direct people's attention and provide some impetus for achieving desired strategic results. Results measures are the organization's strategic "gas pedal." Action measures tend to be focused on uniformity of behavior in "best practices." They are intended to improve safety, mitigate risk, and standardize the implementation of management decisions. They are the organizations' strategic "brakes." Resource measures establish another kind of limitation, work capacity. They define the horsepower available to each strategic initiative.

In the sections below, we describe these measures and discuss the risks and benefits of using each.

Results Measures

Results measures focus on the outcomes of decisions and actions. They are most common to situations where there are clear metrics for individual unit performance. Companies employ an array of operational and financial performance measures to guide the training, development, and performance of the people in their organization. Typical measures codify sales level, return on investment (ROI), profit, number of defects, or number of on-time deliveries. These standards are well known and referenced during performance reviews. They are also easily defined and typically established on a regular basis.

Yet it is not sufficient to simply measure results. The results measured must be strategically important. They have to be complete, including the effects of competition and the business environment. They have to be believed and accepted by managers. They also have to be balanced across time, organizational skill sets, and organizational subunits. Even the accuracy of assumptions used in strategic planning is critical to the usefulness of results measures.

Results measures should thus provide managers with clear indications that things are (or are not) strategically on track. These metrics are also important in judging a manager's performance. Yet they are not all inclusive. A maximum score in one area does not necessarily indicate the best performance. For example, a division attaining its annual ROI goal may have a declining market share that is not captured in this results measure. Therefore, a single overall measure, or even a set of measures, may not effectively lead to reaching strategic goals.

Results measures can't tabulate everything achieved. Financial results are important to know to keep score. But measures must motivate managers to excel at *all* the important dimensions of strategic performance. After all, regular feedback guides corrective action only when managers are able to address deviations of which they are aware. For the same reason, some must be outwardly focused to assure timely course corrections in the face of quickly changing customer requirements and markets. When the environment changes, proven strategies of the past may become ineffective.[5] Remember results measures drive behavior. People want to score well and will do what is necessary to achieve high scores. Consider the behavior implications of your results measures more than the assessment of performance.

Action Measures

Action measures enforce organizational standards and local best practices, reflecting organizational policies and procedures. Such rules define how decisions should be made, who has the authority to make decisions, and what actions are prohibited. Thus, some action measures are simply on/off or yes/no rules. They ask the question, "Was the policy followed?"

Decision-making authority is typically established through delegation rules. For example, a policy might specify the job title and level of authorization required to sign checks or contracts. Increased organizational complexity usually requires greater distribution of authority so that units can function and react to changing conditions. On the flip side, dispersed authority also requires increased specificity in defining the scope and scale of each manager's authority.

Other action measures count the number of times or the degree to which actual behavior meets or exceeds desired levels. These kinds of measures are frequently used when it is difficult to get a measure of a specific desired outcome. For example, we may not be able to determine how satisfied our customers are, but we can count how long they have to wait in the phone queue. Similarly, we may not be able to determine how motivated our employees are; but we can count the requests for transfers.

Standard operating procedures (SOPs) guide daily business processes. They might specify the documentation required prior to approval of a project or the nature of the decision-making process itself. These kinds of action controls help assure that all decisions are made with proper care and in a consistent way. We've all been exposed to poorly run organizations that suffered from too many or too few action measures. And where SOPs are not supported by management action, ethical dilemmas often crop up.

Finally, some action controls specifically exclude certain decisions or actions. An MSDR in this category might prohibit pursuit of opportunities that run counter to strategic direction. For example, there may be a profitable business opportunity predicated on establishing a special low price. However, if the business strategy were based on maintaining an upscale market brand image, such an option would be blocked. These strategic action controls are also frequently established to safeguard prime organizational ethical standards.

Task controls are a subset of action measures. These SOPs exist at the day-to-day operations level. They ensure that organizational functions are carried out effectively and efficiently. For example, has a certain piece of equipment been properly maintained as scheduled? Or has the server storage backup been run today?

Leaders do not normally get directly involved in task control, but they rely heavily on the assumption that this function is being carried out. These protocols serve as a basis for operational management. Many of the internal inspections conducted by a corporation are simply an audit of the use of task protocols. In order to make task controls effective, the leader must support the system. They cannot be considered trivial. The accounting, control, and reporting systems developed as a result of the Sarbanes–Oxley Law can be considered an essential task protocol within the action management system.

Resource Measures

Resource measures are a critical but often forgotten component of the MSDR. Their implications are often overlooked or misunderstood.

Resource controls define the horsepower available to do strategic work. When set too tight, the organization is starved for the fuel to reach major milestones. When too loose, the organization expends too much and becomes a "gas guzzler."

Resource controls can take many forms. Probably the most obvious is the functional or departmental budget. While the organization-wide budget is primarily a planning tool used to project and test future financial results, departmental or work-group budgets are often used as target spending limits. They inherently constrain managers' options for action. Middle-level managers tend to spend to their budget limits. In fact, it is typically in a manager's best interest to slightly overspend the budget—enough to establish the need for more resources in the future, but not so much as to be identified as an overspending trouble spot.[6]

A related kind of resource control is associated with allocating time among projects. Time budgets can be explicit, or they can be buried within the distribution of work. In many businesses, the word "resources" is synonymous with the term "available personnel." How a manager distributes work among subordinates is the final determinant of how much horsepower is available for various strategic tasks. A manager with six improvement projects will obviously have less time and energy to devote to each project than if there were only two projects. And a new product development team of four full-time engineers has more horsepower than a team of four engineers assigned to the project on a part-time basis.

Another guise for resource controls is physical resource allocation. The organization's capital budget process is a variation of this kind of resource control. Other bureaucratic policies and procedures can also constrain the number and type of productivity-enhancing assets assigned to various work initiatives.

It is helpful to think of resource controls from the perspective of production bottlenecks. To gain the most results from our management system, we need to open the bottlenecks. Resource controls should be focused on allocating sufficient work capacity to strategic bottlenecks. Resource controls should also be focused on limiting the amount of capacity created in non-bottleneck areas. This means that management's typical reaction to poor financial performance across the board budget cuts—may be the worst strategic reaction possible. How often do you see management cutting the marketing spend when sales are behind budget? They want to deliver the intended profit and cutting marketing expenses does not generally involve cutting people. They deliver the short-term results frequently at the expense of the future.

Delivering Results as a System

Delivering results is the direct outcome of the organization's decision makers acting in concert with the strategy.

So how do we get from our list of performance measurements to an effective management control system? This is the focus of the rest of this book. An MSDR needs to be custom-built for each organization. The system must fit so well that good results can be, if not assured, at least likely. So let's pause to consider the essentials in your MSDR's portfolio of results, action, and resource controls.

Figure 3.2 depicts a conceptual model of the MSDR system. Figure 3.2A focuses on the external view. Choosing appropriate components with which to build your system requires an understanding of the external context in which the MSDR will operate. That context includes the objectives for the business unit or subunit to be managed, as well as the nature of the markets in which the business unit competes, the relationships with suppliers, competitive pressures, and wider economic and industry conditions.

Monitoring the external environment is essential.[7] Shifts in the economy, industry trends, customer perceptions, or competitor reactions will all redefine the means for realizing the company strategy. Indeed, reviewing internal results only cannot allow a clear understanding of the distinction between the influences of luck versus management skill. Basic questions to ask yourself include the following: How did we do compared to the rest of the market? Is our relative position the same or improving? Is this what we planned? To find answers, the system measures the most reliable industry data to determine what environmental characteristics are most critical to the success of the strategy.

Strategy exploits a firm's critical strengths to gain a competitive advantage within its unique environment and often requires it to develop new strengths. The internal system should concentrate on the critical success factors and the core competencies of the firm. The externally focused portion should capture environmental conditions related to the assessed success factors. The effectiveness of strategic implementation is determined by the degree to which the critical core competencies developed by the firm "line up" with external conditions.

Major market or economic changes can have a significant positive or negative impact on results. Although such changes are typically beyond a manager's influence, they usually are not beyond the manager's comprehension. The competent manager has a responsibility to recognize changes in economic and industry trends. Again, an MSDR requires the selection of "matched pairs" of internal and external measures reflecting critical areas of strategic impact and improvement.

Figure 3.2B illustrates some basic relationships among the components of an MSDR. Hierarchically, the MSDR is the servant of the business strategy. Surrounding the portfolio of control measurements in a company's management system are

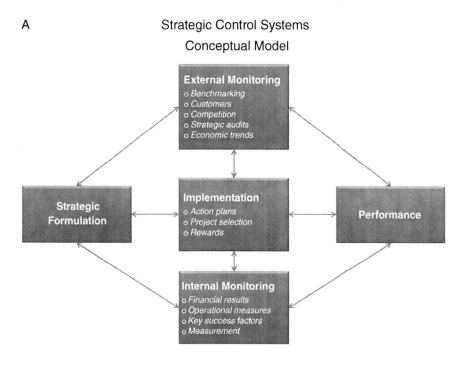

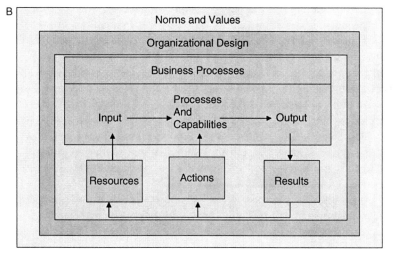

Fig. 3.2 The management system for delivering results: **(A)** external view; **(B)** internal view

the social norms and group values of the organization. This social system determines how groups of personnel interact based on their shared values and objectives. The norms of behavior limit the likelihood of some managerial actions and encourage other kinds. Thus, the organization's norms and values create a kind of performance management system in themselves. Ouchi calls this clan control.[8] Such common values guide the actions of a group defining what results are desirable and what actions are off-limits. This can be a very potent form of control and is probably the primary form of management control in many small business and entrepreneurial operations. Even within large corporations, it is the filter through which specific actions are interpreted.

Just as unpopular laws are apt to be flouted, specific performance measures and SOPs must be in harmony with the shared belief system in order for them to be effective. In some cases, this requires that control systems designers define measures in synch with organizational norms. In other cases, it requires action protocols to be explained in terms of shared beliefs. Or it might mean that no specific control is necessary—since existing norms make an undesirable behavior unlikely. Yet there are times when the culture needs to be changed before the strategy can be fully implemented.

Results measures are especially prone to misuse from manipulation or untrustworthy information. An organization's culture will act as a filter on the interpretation of these measures, their reliability, and their importance. Results measures may be defined a little more loosely where the measures reflect basic tenets of the culture. However, culture can work against results measures too.

The formation of ABB in 1987, at the time the largest cross-border merger in European history, serves as an excellent example of properly knitting all the internal view factors of delivering results.[9] Under the leadership of Percy Barnevik, Brown Boveri (85,000 employees) and Asea (65,000 employees) were combined to form ABB. The new company consisted of 850 separate legal entities in 140 countries. Barnevik moved quickly forming a decentralized matrix organization to leverage the strengths of the combined operations. He believed in individual accountability and clear responsibility. Corporate headquarters staff was reduced by over 90% with decision-making distributed to the over 1,300 separate operating companies. Barnevik, often referred to as the "Jack Welch of Europe," installed a reporting system, ABACUS, which provided reliable ongoing financial and non-financial information on all 4,500 profit centers. It allowed them to aggregate data to show results by segments, countries, and any combination of companies within a country. There was discipline around reporting, and managers came to trust ABACUS as a reliable tool.

A set of policies and procedures were established for all operating units. Managers understood their roles and shared responsibilities in the matrix. Decision-making authority was unambiguous. Standard operating procedures, especially with the operation of ABACUS, were clear and strictly followed. Budgets were managed very tightly in order to gain the economies of scale and provide locally responsive products. This generated sound resource control and kept the organization strategically focused.

One of the key ingredients that made ABB a success was the effort Percy Barnevik and the senior leadership made to building a shared culture and values. They built a policy bible, introduced it to the senior managers at an offsite location, and asked the 300 managers to share the message with their organizations.

The strategy was clear, and the guiding value principles were transparent. A culture of hard work, communications, decisiveness, accountability, and action was established. Most importantly they lived the values so that their actions were consistent with the norms.

We see the ABB organizational and management system fingerprints in many multinational organizations today. ABB often serves as the delivering results benchmark for multinational firms. They paid attention to all of the factors necessary for building a successful company.

When performance measures focus on priorities not already ingrained in the culture, the measures need to be able to stand up to criticisms of their reliability, accuracy, and meaningfulness.[10] Perhaps more importantly, organizational culture will affect the degree to which results measures are seen as reflections of important underlying achievements or simply as ends in themselves. Managers often claim they "beat the system." The organizational culture influences not only the general level to which results measures may be gamed but also the particular areas in which measures will be most likely to be "bent." The Enron collapse is a textbook example of results manipulation to achieve targets.

Performance measures need to help managers balance competing priorities. Improvement in local results may occur at the expense of business-wide results. Furthermore, each business subunit may develop a local variation of the organization's culture. Thus, the same measures may not engender the same managerial reactions in different subunits. This seems to be especially true when the business is organized functionally.

Action measures work closely with the organizational structure and provide the underpinning for the fiduciary responsibilities of managers. Think of these as a kind of infrastructure. They influence the organization's ability to respond to external influences. For example, the Gap and many other multi-site retail operations have a very detailed set of action guidelines. The Gap specifies when the store manager arrives with a sales associate to avoid only having one person in the store. They record what each is wearing to avoid the temptation of theft. Cash register drawers are very carefully counted verifying the count at close the previous night. The manager and associate jointly make the bank deposit at 11 pm. There are many more specific rules that store personnel must follow. These action measures are there to provide a control structure that protects the fungible assets of the business and temptation for the employees.

One final comment about the "flexibility" of performance measures: Measures can be formal or informal. The "official policy" version is generally preferred as the degree of accountability can be clearly understood by all of the organization's players. These official protocols normally set the firm's management tone. They serve as the referenced ethical and compliance standards.

However, an organization cannot function without some degree of individual empowerment. Thus, managers may need to create informal measures for specific purposes from time to time. Unlike measures implicit in the organizational culture, which are also informal, these informal measures are intentional, verbalized, and a constant subject of management discussion.

For example, a company one of us worked with predicated its value on customer service. Each major client had a customer service representative (CSR) who acted as the central point of coordination between the customer and the company's production and distribution operations. The company management came to the realization that each relationship was essentially ad hoc and that this placed a heavy burden on operations to react to a high variety of special requests, which, in turn, frustrated and angered the operations people. The eventual result was trending toward "service with a sneer." Management decided to identify commonalities among the special requests and standardize the best practices for providing those services. In order to execute this idea, a series of meetings among the CSRs, among the operations teams, and across CSRs and operations teams were held. The discussions were allowed to be quite open. Many of the resulting changes were agreed to verbally rather than by issuing new rules.

Informal action protocols can be very powerful, but they are not easily established or maintained. People's behavior can be constrained by social and group norms or by "leading by example." Such informal standards of behavior are a critical part of an MSDR.

We will spend considerable time sorting out these issues in the next several chapters. In the end, we want a portfolio of protocols that will direct attention to the problems and eliminate undesirable actions. Just as importantly, they should leave the details of the actions to the imagination and ingenuity of the members of the organization.

To bring these concepts to life, let's briefly consider how one could build an effective MSDR using a mix of protocol types aligned to, and supported by, the organization's culture. One straightforward example is a firm that has adopted a quality-oriented strategy. The published criteria for quality achievements, such as the Malcolm Baldrige Award and ISO Process Quality certification, reveal the building blocks.[11]

The Baldrige criteria emphasize three requirements. They are as follows:

1) Supplementing financial measures with non-financial indicators. These should be internal for operational quality results and external to judge customer satisfaction and assess customer requirements.
2) Using external benchmarks to gauge performance against the competition. This is a method to monitor the competition and identify competitive threats.
3) Collecting information in order to identify or anticipate changes in the competitive environment.

In a firm deciding on a quality-based strategy, results protocols will measure quality, both internally in terms of error rates and externally in terms relative to the customers' expectations. An effective management system to support a quality strategy implementation will have results measures comparing outcomes with both best-in-class benchmarks and competitors' achievements. And in cultural norms, there will be a strong emphasis on sharing ownership of outcomes and on joint problem solving.

A quality strategy will employ action protocols established through the use of quality-oriented SOPs. These protocols ensure that business and operations processes all adhere to a uniform, best-practices approach. This, in turn, drives down the effects of random variation in the strategy execution process. Continual reduction in unplanned variation is a key ingredient in total quality management (TQM).

A good MSDR in a quality strategy environment will also address resource constraints. Typically, personnel are assigned to work in teams where the pooled knowledge and skills result in greater power to solve problems and constantly improve. Furthermore, these teams are often delegated significant authority in terms of self-management and access to additional resources.

Another hallmark of effective management systems for quality strategies is a focus on the organization's values and beliefs. Organizational leaders will constantly refer to quality, customer focus, continual improvement, and organizational learning in all of their formal statements and memoranda. Their decisions will practice what they preach. In fact, in a truly effective system, those references will also saturate their informal conversations also.

Every manager, consciously or sub-consciously, attempts to develop a balanced portfolio of MSDR components to fit the environment. The key is recognizing the demands of the strategy and the influences in the environment. Once these factors are identified, building a portfolio of complementary measurements to fulfill these requirements can proceed.

Analog Devices, a semiconductor and integrated circuit manufacturer, was plagued with declining quality, poor yields, and delays in customer shipments, poor customer service, and production scheduling delays.[12] The company measures were primarily financial and recorded the accounting results of the above problems. The chairman, Ray Stata, made a bold decision to change the focus of the management team and modify the measurement system. With the help of Art Schneiderman, VP of Quality and Productivity Improvement, he developed a new set of measures that tracked the rate of improvement of on-time delivery, outgoing defect level, yields, lead time, manufacturing cycle time, and time to market. Over a three-year period they saw a two to ten times improvement in all measures of performance. This delighted the customer and freed much needed production capacity. These new sets of measures refocused management and motivated the work force. Some consider the Analog Devices experience as the birth of the balanced scorecard movement.

The Power of Measurement

The appropriate use of performance measures and a structured feedback loop can strongly influence individual behavior and collective unit performance. If the measures used in an MSDR are clear, this will elicit strategically-focused actions and decisions. A change of emphasis on certain measures will also alter behavior. Managers realize that they can use their management system to move the organization in a new direction or reinforce a new set of values. An MSDR is the basis of learning in the organization and can be used extensively as an accelerator of change. Feedback is one of the enduring sources of learning.

In fact, performance measure design, and monitoring, has proven to be very influential in supporting organizational change.[13] The MSDR provides a set of measures and targets important to the firm and the context within which to interpret them. Employees respond to them as reflections of the strategic imperatives. The planning and protocol systems can be designed to promote curiosity and experimentation, either for improving efficiency and productivity or for uncovering entirely new ways to deliver value to customers. The MSDR thus signals the actions and behaviors that are important to the firm.

If new performance measures can help change behavior in a firm, then they can also accelerate improvement in existing strategic directions. The feedback loop of the MSDR is a very powerful learning device. The comparison of planned to actual results, with a solid analysis of the deviations, provides an excellent learning opportunity. This often focuses on operational problem solving, but the technique can also play a role in detecting and reacting to environmental change. The system will reveal if the existing goals and processes no longer match external challenges and signal a need for a new strategy.

Finally, linking performance measures to organizational rewards can enhance the powerful effects of an MSDR. The rewards can be formal or informal, tangible or intangible. It is clear that a control system works best when the individuals are rewarded for accomplishments both specific and apparent to other members. A word of caution however: bonus systems have a tendency to amplify the inherent strategy syndrome. They also raise the stakes for any latitude managers have to "game" the system. Additionally, reward systems create a situation where individual gains are often placed before collective gains.

Conclusion

There are clear linkages between management protocols and achieving strategic results. These connections are the direct result of human behavior being affected by the three types of protocols, results, actions, and resources. In order to ensure the desired behavior, managers need to understand both how the context influences behavioral reactions to specific protocols and how the MSDR can be used dynamically. There is not a single, universal set of "good measures." Rather, managers must carefully select the mix of protocols and system characteristics that fit their organization, their strategy, their management style, and the nature of their personnel.

In the following chapters, we will explore the process of designing, implementing, and employing the management system for delivering results, focusing on measurement systems as the prime feedback mechanism. In the next chapter, however, we examine the role of the control system in "steering" the organization and how the finance and accounting functions act as "keepers" of the management delivery system.

Notes

1. Bellis, Mary, "Inventors of the Modern Computer – The History of the IBM PC – International Business Machines," About.com: Inventors, 2004.
2. There are several articles written on this subject. The first, Nanni, Alfred J., Jr., "Integrated Performance Measurement: Management Accounting to Support the New Manufacturing Realities", *Journal of Management Accounting Research*, Fall 1992, leads to additional research linking the balanced scorecard to strategy. These works include a series of articles written by Kaplan and Norton (1996) and work by Simmons (2004).
3. Mintzberg, Henry, *The Rise and Fall of Strategic Planning*, (Upper Saddle River, NJ, Prentice Hall, 1994). This seminal work on strategy supports the need for consistent management action.
4. Weinstein, Jeff, Editor in Chief, *HOTELS Magazine*, March 2001.
5. Broady-Preston, Judith and Williams, Tegwen. "Using Information to Create Business Value: City of London Legal Firms, A Case Study," *Performance Measurements and Metrics*, (Vol. 5, 2004).
6. For more on behavior in relation to financial reporting, refer to Hagigi, Moshe and Williams, Patricia A. "Accounting, Economic and Environmental Influences on Financial Reporting Practices in Third World Countries," *Research in Third World Accounting*. (Vol. 2, 1993).
7. Simons, R. *Performance Measurement and Control Systems for Implementing strategy*, (Upper Saddle River, NJ, Prentice Hall, 1995).
8. Ouchi, William G. "The Transmission of Control Through Organizational Hierarchy", *Academy of Management Journal*, (1978) and "Types of Organizational Control and Their Relationship to Emotional Well-Being", *Administrative Science Quarterly*, (1978) wrote the seminal work on control within organizations.
9. Harvard Business Review Press has a series of cases on ABB authored by Robert Simons and others.
10. Kellen, Vince, " Business Performance Measurement: At the Crossroads of Strategy, Decision-Making, Learning and Information Visualization," http://www. performance-measurement.net (February 2003).
11. The Baldrige National Quality Award is a quality improvement award passed by the Senate in 1987. Every year the Baldrige Award is given to organizations "that practice effective quality management and as a result make significant improvements in the quality of their goods and services." Many articles have been written about the Baldrige Award and the Criteria required to receive the award.
12. Based on personal interview by one of the authors with Ray Stata, CEO of Analog Devices. Harvard Business School Press case *Analog Devices* (case number 190061) by Robert Kaplan was the first case to introduce the topic (revised edition 1993). Tuck Business School at Dartmouth published a series of Analog Devices cases, *Analog Devices Inc. (A), (B) and (C)*, authored by C. Trimble, V. Govindarajan and J. Johnson (2002).
13. Margaret J. Wheatley and Myron Kellner-Rogers, "Bringing Life to Organizational Change," *Journal for Strategic Performance Measurement*, (April/ May 1998).

Part II
Delivering Results—The Operational Context

Chapter 4
Delivering Results Context

Understanding the context of a situation is worth 20 IQ points. This chapter details the kind of contextual considerations that enter into the design of an MSDR. Some are external forces where the MSDR must be able to cope. Others are more controllable: internal factors that can be managed to increase the effectiveness of strategy execution. We examine both types as well as some processes for analyzing and identifying these factors.

Using an MSDR is akin to piloting a sailing ship. The captain must be aware of critical external influences—the prevailing wind, the current, and the expected weather—and how they affect the course to the desired destination. Similarly, a manager has to be aware of the external business environment and its prevailing economic conditions, supply chain relationships, and competitive challenges. A ship's captain must direct the crew, but this, in turn, is influenced by the design of the ship, its size, and its sails and rigging. So too, a manager's task is affected by the design of the organization, its size, and its available resources.

A ship's captain has two bodies of knowledge to rely upon—physical science and sailing art. A successful manager will need to master both art and science in designing an MSDR, too. We begin this chapter with a few basic theoretical principles for MSDR design and then proceed to an overview of the art involved in the design process. This discussion will serve as the introduction to deeper investigations in later chapters.

The Science of Delivering Results

Our central thesis in this book is that an MSDR requires you to constantly think about what makes sense for your business. There is no mathematical model or academic theory that can be simply applied to create an MSDR. Managing is about human behavior, not physics! However, some science can be applied to guide your thinking. This section of the chapter examines some of those ideas.

The original science behind consistently delivering predictable results grew out of the work on systems control done in the earliest days of the computer and communications industries. In 1948, Norbert Weiner coined the term "cybernetics,"

L.P. Carr, A.J. Nanni, Jr., *Delivering Results*, DOI 10.1007/978-1-4419-0621-2_4,
© Springer Science+Business Media, LLC 2009

taken from the Greek term for "the art of steersmanship," to describe this science of control.[1] Early work in cybernetics emphasized three things: systems are goal-oriented, effective feedback is a major factor related to control, and systems interact with their environments (that is, systems are affected by their environments, but a system's operations also have an effect on its environment).

How do these concepts relate to managing a business? First, the system here is the management system. Its purpose is to guide execution of the business strategy. We saw in Chapter 3 that performance measures are intended to keep strategy execution on track by providing feedback about deviations from the strategic plan. What about the idea of interacting with the environment? Certainly, we expect the management system to lead to actions that improve our firm's competitive position. But there is more to it than that.

Throughout the 20th century, there were various attempts at creating a General Systems Theory—a sort of Theory of Relativity for systems design.[2] In the 1960s, William Ross Ashby published his take on General Systems Theory.[3] One of Ashby's major contributions was his Law of Requisite Variety (1964): In order for control to be effective, a system must have a variety of responses at least equal to the variety of potential disturbances it faces. Ashby used the term "disturbances" to refer to external and internal events that pushed the system off course, out of control. Thus, part of the notion of interacting with the environment is this ability to react to the environment, not simply act upon it.

Ashby's concept of "requisite variety" can provide useful perspective for managers attempting to put together an MSDR. There are many environmental factors and events that could impede the execution of a business strategy. The design of an MSDR, therefore, requires managers to regularly ask themselves two basic questions: (1) What could happen to mess up our strategy implementation? (2) How can we deal with that kind of disturbance?

At one level, this idea is obvious. Of course, managers have to worry about events that could throw their businesses off track. But it is surprising how many potential disturbances companies overlook when creating their management systems. At another level, the whole discussion seems rather vague and hopeless. How could anyone—any organization—anticipate all of the potential problems it may encounter in executing its strategy?

Luckily, Ashby considered this. He didn't believe that a system could respond to every possible disturbing event. Instead, he used the idea of requisite variety to craft three basic principles for systems design:

1. Play the probabilities. Events with low likelihood of occurrence need not be planned for unless the consequence of the event is cataclysmic.
2. Generalize some responses. Where possible, group potential disturbances together under a single broad response.
3. Provide detailed response mechanisms for the rest. Identify the remaining likely and serious types of strategic disturbances and build specific measures to detect them and correct their effects.

Let's put some meat on these bones by specifically relating them to an MSDR.

Playing the Probabilities of Strategic Disturbances

It makes sense that an MSDR should focus on the most probable and most hazardous disturbances. However, Ashby's first principle is really concerned with the flip side of this idea, purposely excluding a concern about unlikely or unimportant potential problems. The nature of a company's external or internal environment will reduce both the likelihood and the potency of some potential disturbances. These environmental regularities need to be explicitly considered when building an MSDR. For example, for many years, Daimler-Benz ignored having specific controls designed to encourage product innovation and functionality. Was this appropriate? Certainly, such innovation was important. However, the firm had a strong engineering culture where the drive for new technology and functional design perfection were part of the culture. Thus, the likelihood that design engineers would fail to improve product features and rely instead on simple cosmetic changes was very low. Many of the safety and drive train features we have come to think of as fundamental requirements for automobiles were first developed by Daimler-Benz during those years.

Assessing the Likelihood of External Strategic Disturbances

The very selection of a strategy is the first and primary contextual influence over any delivery system's ability to do its job. Clearly, some strategies are easier for your firm to execute than others. Some strategies are more naturally suited to your company's strengths and weaknesses. Yet whether that strategy is easy to execute or not, the MSDR must be tailored to support it.

Michael Porter (1980) asserts that "...[t]he essence of formulating competitive strategy is relating a company to its environment." (p.3) Porter created his "five forces" model as an economist's view of industry attractiveness. However, many managers have found the five forces view to provide important insights for managing their companies beyond strategy development. Therefore, it has become a standard topic of study in many MBA programs.

The five forces in Porter's model are (1) the bargaining power of customers, (2) the bargaining power of suppliers, (3) the intensity of industry competition, (4) the ease of industry entry for new competitors, and (5) the availability of substitute products or services (i.e., alternative customer solutions in other industries) in the firm's relevant operating environment. The five forces model suggests that as each of these forces increases, a firm's ability to earn a profit diminishes.

The value of Porter's model for our immediate purposes is that it provides a checklist of sorts for a manager to determine which aspects of the external environment pose little threat and, thus, which kinds of potential strategic disturbances can be ignored without endangering strategy execution.

Consider a company like Starbucks. Clearly, profit pressure from customer power is quite low. Rather than a few huge customers, Starbucks has millions of small individual customers. Thus, they don't need any particular performance measures, standard procedures, or polices related to sales revenue by customer. Similarly, their suppliers, sellers of coffee beans and dairy products, operate in commodity markets. However, the rivalry from other coffee retailers is intense and the barriers to entering the market are low. Thus, an MSDR for Starbucks can focus on specific responses for competitor actions that threaten to upend the execution of its strategy (that is, the ability to detect and counteract such actions).

There are larger-order characteristics of the strategic context also. There are other MBA-program standard models to address these factors. Principal among them are the PEST (Political, Economic, Social, and Technological) model and its more recent derivative, the STEER (Socio-cultural, Technological, Economic, Ecological, and Regulatory) model. Both the design of a strategy and the process of executing that strategy need to address the factors summarized by these acronyms. The execution of a strategy based on supplying coffee-flavored dairy products prepared by a trained "barista" in an inviting, upscale ambience probably faces no threat of derailment from new technology. However, the customer base may be quite sensitive to ecological issues. Thus, the former category can be safely ignored in the MSDR while the latter category deserves attention.

Putting both the five forces and STEER models to work, let's quickly examine Jiffy Lube. At the company's inception, the threat of substitutes for an oil change was pretty low. Automotive engines need oil for lubrication, and that oil has to be removed and replaced on a regular basis. There were many suppliers of automotive replacement parts and fluid. That guaranteed price competition in the supplier markets. The target customer base was comprised of many individual small purchase buyers. Thus, there was no concentration of power among customers, either. The competition consisted of many independent general-purpose automotive service garages. Jiffy Lube could thus focus its MSDR on its customer value proposition (low prices and fast service via low costs from fast, standardized, mass-production-like services) and ecological and regulatory requirements created by used oil disposal.

Different strategies also come with their own hazards. For instance, if your business is pursuing cost leadership, the most serious potential threats may relate to efficiency of operations and utilization of capacity. However, if you pursue a niche strategy, delivering results may hinge on successful market positioning, perceived product quality, and size and share of that niche market. Hence, Wal-Mart's management system will likely have many standard procedures, measures, and controls focused on efficiency and few aimed at potential market size or market share while Neiman Marcus will have a management system with an entirely opposite focus. Note, by the way, that neither organization is likely to *ignore* either operational efficiency or market share. They will simply put more effort and focus on the area where the potential threat of disruption to strategy execution is high and less where it is low.

Managing the Likelihood of Internal Strategic Disturbances

The MSDR must also cope with potential internal disturbances. Such significant factors as leadership style, culture, organizational structure, and incentives can all either support or undercut strategy execution.

In Chapter 3, we mentioned that social norms and attitudes and beliefs create an internal management environment. A company's culture can serve as a powerful barrier to potential disturbances—but not if those norms and shared beliefs are inconsistent with the strategy.

This is exactly why many companies put sustained effort into creating and maintaining an organizational culture that supports their strategy. Motorola, for instance, has been pushing its "six-sigma" approach to quality for over 20 years. Toyota's "no waste" philosophy of high quality and just-in-time execution has been in place for more than 40 years. The benefits of a strategically aligned culture also help many companies determine "fit" when they hire new employees.

Strategies don't always remain effective over such a long time, though. Other environmental factors—competition, the economy, and consumer preferences—can change and require a reformulation of the strategy. In that case, the organizational culture can become the *source* of potential disturbances! This was an unintended consequence of Daimler-Benz's culture discussed earlier. When competitors became adept at quickly copying Daimler's innovations and began to focus on consumer market desires, Daimler's strategic focus on technological advances had to be adjusted to address those consumer issues. But, left to their own devices, the automotive engineers were unlikely to put much weight on cup holder design! Thus, Daimler-Benz had to create new management systems to aim its natural innovative tendencies in a more focused consumer-oriented direction. The organizational culture's orientation toward engineering innovation and perfectionism needed to be actively refocused in the face of adroit competitors.

We can see, then, that a company *can* influence the variety of potential disturbances it has to deal with by adjusting its culture to match its business strategy. But this is not a good argument for making these choices simply to make life easy from a strategic standpoint. Our point is simply that a company must detect and define its strategic-execution "problem spaces" when it chooses its approach to creating value. We examine organizational culture in depth in Chapter 5.

A General Response for Many Potential Problems

Ashby's second tenet was to set a single, general response to an entire class of potential strategic disruptions. There are two primary situations where this approach makes most sense. Both of them relate to the core of the business strategy. First, where threats or opportunities appear that are clearly outside of the strategic direction, the general response must be "ignore and avoid." Second, where threats or opportunities appear right at the center of the strategy, the general response must be to reinforce the strategic effort with a general response.

The strategic threat, prohibited action, is probably the one with which most people are familiar. The vast majority of companies "outlaws" certain practices if they are illegal, conflict with brand image, or violate sound financial practices. Failures of the management system in this area often result in cataclysmic outcomes for the firm. Enron's lack of effective control over illegal subterfuge is a prime example.

Another role of the MSDR is to define what kinds of business pursuits are appropriate and desirable. Indeed, it's important for the delivery system to specifically identify certain inviting business opportunities as outside the scope of the strategy. This is different from behaviors that are "outlawed" by the MSDR system, such as unethical or illegal activity. This is a warning against the pursuit of a course of action that might be desirable under a different strategy, but not under the current one. Among those companies whose management system follows this rule is ADP, a leading computing and information services supplier. ADP employs a strategic "test" for pursuing or divesting business. If the business does not fit under ADP's corporate strategy, it is shunned, discontinued, or sold, regardless of potential profitability. This keeps ADP focused on its strategy.[5]

Identifying and avoiding business temptation is a real issue. Perhaps you recall Ford's catchphrase from the 1980s—"Quality is Job 1." This was a highly visible statement of strategic intent, and Ford made great strides in quality improvement into the 1990s. However, as demand for its highly profitable trucks and SUVs, led by the Ford Explorer, ballooned near the end of that decade, the direct pursuit of volume in that profitable segment may have distracted Ford management from its quality focus. As a result, quality fell and Ford's reputation was tarnished. As you can see from Fig. 4.1, only recently has Ford returned to respectable slots in the J.D. Power quality surveys.

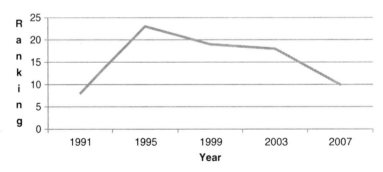

Fig. 4.1 Ford brand ranking on J.D. power initial quality survey

To prevent "strategy creep," the MSDR designer must be able to anticipate how managers might react to a situation and create a feedback system that alerts the manager to danger. For example, most managers believe that it is in the firm's best interest (and that they will be rewarded) if they cut costs. This, however, may not be true. If cost cutting leads to poorer product or service performance, sales may suffer, yielding lower profitability. Similarly, although successfully raising prices may produce improved short-term profits, it may sabotage a strategy predicated on market share growth.

When a manager can anticipate particular temptations and establish requirements that will exclude strategically divergent courses of action, a "don't act" kind of system response can be utilized. The strict "strategic-fit" criteria ADP uses, for example, exemplify this kind of approach. However, this is not the only way to avoid the pursuit of non-strategic courses of action. MSDRs provide guidance for managers. They do not tell them specifically what to do. An effective MSDR encourages managers to be creative in finding ways to pursue the strategy. Thus, many effective MSDRs will head off non-strategic actions through a combination of specific policies, rules, and performance measures. For example, an MSDR could provide positive feedback on an action if it *both* increases profits and improves customer satisfaction. Either one of these outcomes at the expense of the other would be measured as a negative outcome. In some cases, this approach to avoiding non-strategic activity would be both effective and preferable, since it focuses management attention on finding positive, creative solutions rather than emphasizing what not to do.

For strategic threats, a single response might represent a return to fundamentals. An example of preparing this kind of single response comes from EMC Corporation, the world's largest supplier of mass data storage devices. EMC pioneered this market in the 1980s. Its innovative approach was a software-driven array of many small hard disk drives originally designed for use in personal computers into a large box to be used with enterprise-level computers. This "RAID technology" approach is the world standard today. However, EMC's first generation products suffered from reliability problems related to the hard drives it received from its suppliers. These little drives had been designed for pre-Windows computers, where the trade-off had tilted toward low costs rather than reliability. Instead of developing unique management reactions to each type of supplier problem, EMC handled them all in a "blanket" response: It dispatched design and manufacturing engineers to help the suppliers learn to produce better, more robust, and reliable products and to do it more quickly.[6]

In addition to screening out deviations from strategy execution, an MSDR needs to have general alarm responses to looming high-risk situations. When the economy falls, for instance, capital-intense firms need to have measures in place that ensure strong financial positions, with significant liquidity or other access to cash, to let them weather a sustained market downturn. Service firms, or ones without large investments in fixed assets, need to have an early warning system for upcoming changes in the economy. They need to anticipate the need to change course in order to adjust from price enhancement to cost containment if the industry market declines.

Think of a manufacturer of computer chips that has invested over $1.2 billion in a fabrication facility. Its management will focus on making sure there is a sustained demand for the product. The reason is simple enough: The business model calls for 24×7 production in order to realize the volume that will drive unit costs low enough to be profitable at a competitive price. This firm will be quick to respond to changes in market price and will do all in its power to maintain volume. Management will be sensitive to the point of obsession about demand and concentrate their measurements around monitoring and predicting shifts in demand/price relationships. If necessary, prices will be lowered to below profitable levels to maintain volume. On the other hand, a chip design firm that outsources manufacturing for computer chips will take a very different view. Management in that firm will respond to a slowdown by rolling back incoming deliveries.

Specific Responses for Significant Disturbances

Most special potential problems require special controls. Ashby's third principle entails building specific responses to detect and answer specific, important disturbances. Rules, standard procedures, and performance measurements perform this function in an MSDR. In practical terms, it means crafting a system of control to assure that management can actually prevent or detect the effects of the most likely and most serious disturbances. Not all companies do this. Many still employ management control systems focused simply on cost and profit—relics from the era of mass production. This shortsightedness will usually reveal itself.

In the late 1980s and early 1990s, when Johnson and Johnson refocused its corporate strategy, one critical new dimension in many of the J&J operating companies was timeliness of both product development and product delivery. Despite this new focus, however, several of the operating companies continued to use cost-based measures. At one manufacturing division, for example, the only plant measure associated with time was a measure of "dollars shipped per quarter." This was actually a measure of the volume of sales that were shipped out of the factory door. It did not provide any feedback as to whether these shipments were too early or too late. J&J corporate management stepped in to help laggard business units update their performance measures with dimensions like "on-time delivery" and "months to market" and to reorient managers and workers to think in these terms.

The science of delivering results is simply a loosely knit group of control principles and models for scanning the strategic environment. In order to actually build an MSDR, you have to learn to employ these tools with skill and judgment. It's an art. The art of creating an MSDR is in putting these principles together and putting them to work. The rest of this chapter provides some background and orientation on that process.

The Art of Delivering Results

Most of the focus in management systems over the past 15 years has been around aligning delivery systems with strategic requirements and achieving a balance among strategic priorities. Even so, too many companies still do a poor job of connecting their strategies to their management systems. Translating a strategy into realistic causal factors is the first step in the process.

Assessing and Prioritizing Potential Disturbances

Throughout this chapter, we have spoken about fitting the MSDR to the environment, about the variety of potential strategic disturbances. What we have not spoken about is how you decide what are these critical control points. How do you know what controls an environment calls for—and when?

The critical links between the strategy and the environment are a firm's key success factors (KSFs). An understanding of these KSFs is what guides the development of an MSDR. Effective MSDRs concentrate measures and feedback around the KSFs. They measure those things that are important.

Generating an MSDR to fit the strategy and the environment is a three-step process: strategic analysis, KSF identification, and design of the system. There are plenty of methods for conducting strategic analysis. In Chapters 8 and 9, we address how to build sets of measures from an understanding of KSFs. Our concern here is about choosing the method to connect the output of the strategic analyses to your identification of KSFs.

Because each firm is unique in its characteristics and structure, the MSDR will be contingent on the nature of the business, the structure of the firm's assets, the firm's knowledge and skill sets, and the strategy. This is why MSDRs need to be understood within the context of the environment and the distinctiveness of the firm.

Start first with the strategy. Where are you going and how do you expect to get there? The strategy will dictate how the firm marshals and deploys its assets to achieve success. Then you must look at the nature of the business. What is the industry? What is the nature of competition? Who are the customers? Who are the suppliers? Who are the major players? What are their capabilities and desires?

If these questions sound familiar, they should be. Our discussion of Porter's five forces and the STEER analysis models earlier in this chapter raised the same issues. While these kinds of analyses help identify impediments to strategic execution, they also help identify opportunities for your strategic value proposition, critical threats from current and potential competitors, important relationships to forge, and so on. Comparing this list to your organization's competencies and current strategic resources will help determine the KSFs and how they need to be managed. Some KSFs will require the organization to build and develop strengths. Others will need to be maintained and improved. The evaluations become a guide to what to manage, to measure, and to emphasize.

There is no easy way to make this connection. Like most aspects of crafting an effective MSDR, it requires a lot of hard work. However, the whole process works best when there is equal emphasis on logic, communication, and inclusion.

The logic part is straightforward, if not always so easy. Where your analysis identifies a threat, you need to establish control methods that provide a warning. And, if the threat is dire enough, there should be an established set of guidelines for avoiding the threat or mitigating its effects. Where your analysis identifies a weakness, you need to establish protocols that encourage improvement in that strategic resource, either through internal development or through strategic partnering. The hard part here is deciding when a threat is sufficiently dire and whether a strength should be developed as an internal resource or an outsourced one.

The process that works best also improves communication and inclusion: discussion. The best way to get all of the heads in the organization to have the same thing in them is to debate the points of disagreement until a consensus is reached. Discussion is also the best way to assure that all realistic points of view have been considered before any action is taken.

Of course, we do not advocate having everyone in the organization sit in an auditorium and mimic congress. Top management should discuss the strategic analysis, identifying the KSFs in broad terms and setting the priorities in terms of "dire-enough" or internal versus external strategic resources. These broad-term KSFs then need to be interpreted and put into operational terms at lower levels of management. Here again, however, open discussion is important. At some point, when the job gets down to the point of defining specific measurements (how do we actually measure, for example, on-time delivery), inclusion of even lower levels of management and even non-management employees may make sense.

Even in a small organization, this process takes time. It will seem frustrating and inefficient. The process can be moved along a bit more rapidly if chunks of time are scheduled in advance and adhered to strictly. Many companies we have worked with have established management retreats for the top-level employees. However, this is an absolutely critical process. Shortcuts at this point will result in an ineffective management system and, therefore, ineffective strategic execution.

Strategic Choice and Measurement Emphasis

Managers regularly ask us "What is the best set of performance measures?" They assume that guiding strategy execution is basically the same across different firms and condition. But it should be clear by now that different performance protocols work best with different kinds of strategies. This simply makes sense. If a "one size fits all" approach to MSDRs were effective, no one would be concerned about strategy execution! It would be foolish to suggest that there are even a finite number of MSDRs. However, by way of illustration, we can suggest some typical characteristics for MSDRs under a few simple strategy models. Below, we discuss four different kinds of "generic" strategies and highlight some features of their "natural" MSDR systems.

Market Position Defense Strategies

Often called "harvest", "defender," and "low-cost" strategies, market defense strategies aim primarily to protect a strong market position. Firms in this group often have a narrow product range and undertake little product or market development, although this is not universally true. In fact, large multi-product companies like

Procter and Gamble and the PC software businesses at Microsoft are members of this group. Their major characteristic is that they aggressively maintain a prominent position in each carefully chosen product category.

These firms often have substantial experience in the industry and produce reasonably accurate forecasts based on sound historical data. Their products are often mature and, although their main lever for improved profits is cost management, they often dominate their markets in both volume and price. There is a certain degree of stability.

Control systems in these firms tend to enforce narrow ranges of behavior. Budget and financial results are important, and there is a strong emphasis on detailed measures and adherence to standards in production and engineering. The companies are often structured along product lines, markets, or technology specializations. These firms' delivery systems are highly detailed, focused on reducing uncertainty and improving productivity—and place a heavy emphasis on tightening execution by adding protocols to "fix" the system. Employees at P&G are well aware of the fact that their organization is tightly bound by bureaucratic rules and measures. They even refer to themselves as "Proctoids!"

The MSDR for this type of firm is centralized with strong feedback related to identifying deviations from plans and expectations and on providing evidence of corrective action. They tend to rely on budget plans as criteria for success and there are many action protocols—an expanded set of formalized rules and procedures. Porter would call this a cost leadership positioning even though they may not compete on price. Budget, process, and operating control are dominant themes. Efficiency and ongoing cost monitoring are important. Since the tasks are strictly programmed within narrow ranges and budget-type outcomes can be readily measured, corrective actions are often specifically prescribed. Defenders who adopt low cost strategies generally award bonuses for the achievement of budget targets. The focus of results measures and the rewards associated with them is primarily financial in nature.

Growth-Oriented Strategies

Firms with growth strategies are also known as prospectors, differentiators, and builders. Their main goal is "to grow." They choose their strategies to attract new customers. Their distinguishing characteristic is the continual reach for new market opportunities. They are comfortable with uncertainty and actually try to create change. Marketing and R&D are the dominant functions. Maintaining industry leadership and increasing market share are considered much more important than efficiency and short-term profit performance. Researchers have found that these firms have difficulty implementing comprehensive planning systems due to change and uncertainty in their environments. In recent years, Apple has become a high-profile growth-oriented firm.

The MSDRs of these firms concentrate more on problem finding than on devising "canned" solutions. Performance measures provide feedback about critical dimensions of the environment and of organizational performance in order to allow management to determine where to focus its attention.

The organization is usually designed to be flexible in order to allow it to respond to new growth opportunities as they arise. Consider the relationships among technology, consumer trends, and the inexorable growth of Apples "i-products:" iPod, iTunes, and iPhone. This leads growth-oriented firms to the use of a decentralized MSDR whose components may vary among organizational units. Upper-level managers often rely upon personal influence in this kind of organization. Similarly, a distinctly creative and exploratory organizational culture is nurtured to provide another form of management control. Performance measures are used interactively. That is, the performance measurement data are treated as clues to underlying phenomena. There is much active discussion about that data and what it means. This is in contrast to market-position defense strategies where deviations in performance measures represent problems by definition. Here, performance measures are used to encourage debate about potential problems or opportunities. Managers examine measures and consider the meaning and desirability of the reported results. The MSDR places a strong emphasis on coordination.

Porter would term this a differentiation strategy. These growth-oriented firms have a greater reliance on management through coordination and unity of purpose than on using exhaustive lists of formal measures. Nonetheless, they place strong importance on certain aspects of formal protocols, such as accuracy in forecasting data, "reach" budget goals, and careful monitoring of results. They tend to give less attention to cost control. They generally do not have a large historical database to use for forecasting and planning. They want frequent reporting and uniform reports. Good communication and a substantial amount of interaction around measured results are normal. In this case, good control eases the degree of uncertainty and risk. They want to encourage risk-taking, but in a focused way.

Performance rewards contain a large measure of subjective evaluation. Their long-term approach to achieving targets is not compatible with the annual rhythm of financial reports. Building a market position takes place over several years. Apple is actually one of the oldest personal computer companies. It long ago developed a reputation for elegant, simple design and for an alternative, contrarian approach to its business. The company's steadfastness of purpose and philosophy over many lean years underscores its reliance on rewards for maintaining direction over the long haul.

Execution-Based Strategies

Firms using execution-based strategies are highly selective in their choice of competitive sphere. They go where their strengths give them competitive advantage. They are sometimes called "analyzers," because they rapidly copy successful innovations in their markets. They are often very competent at reverse engineering. They also redesign processes or ways of doing business in order to make them more efficient. In either case, the mark of an execution-based strategy is careful identification of customer desires in their target market and focused execution on delivering the desired value. The organization is normally centralized and structured along functional lines. They are, however, willing to change to pursue an opportunity.

Honda Motor Company falls into this category. Honda developed a core competency in making clean burning, efficient, and durable small gasoline-powered engines decades ago. Honda has leveraged that skill from motorcycles to automobiles, then to lawn and garden equipment and power generators. Recently, it put this knowledge and skills into designing and building power generators for their new hybrid cars. Honda was late to enter both the minivan and the SUV markets. However, when their vehicles appeared, they had all of the popular and desirable features, executed very well, with a few new innovations.

Firms like Honda tend to have delivery systems with tight controls around efficiency. They are looking for certainty and stability. However, they are willing to loosen those controls when it enhances effectiveness in pursuit of new, sound ideas. While financial results are important to these firms, their MSDRs focus more on their processes. They pursue continual improvement and learning as a means to "engineering" higher profits.

Response-Based Strategies

These strategies are not so much strategy as simply reactive behavior. The firms may have had well-defined strategies, but they have become obsolete. They may have potentially effective strategies, but disconnected execution. This is the situation we described in Chapter 2 when mid-level managers interpret the strategy as "do what you did yesterday, only better." These firms are constantly running behind the market and behind their competition. Hence, they spend most of their effort "putting out fires." They are often called "reactors."

In this kind of environment, we typically find results measures that are financial in nature. Budgets and profit plans, often extensions of the status quo, are treated as strategic objectives. Nonetheless, the accounting system is seen more as a bookkeeping system than as a source of management information. Action protocols, especially bureaucratic policies and procedures, dominate the mix. The formal delivery system is strongly supported by an organizational culture and "clan control" that emphasizes traditional ways of doing things.

Mature, market-dominant organizations often find themselves in this category. General Motors can be viewed as this type of organization. Credited with inventing the "model year" and masters of mass production, GM dominated the automotive industry for over 50 years. However, GM's success became dependent on high volume to allow utilization of its vast productive capacity. When Japanese manufacturers emerged as a serious threat in the 1980s, GM responded by forming a joint venture manufacturing center with Toyota in 1984—New United Motors Manufacturing, Inc. (NUMMI)—to produce Chevrolet Novas more efficiently. But lower cost wasn't Toyota's only competitive advantage. Over two decades later, GM was still trying to respond to the competition, releasing a new model Chevrolet Malibu in 2008 to compete head-to-head with the Toyota Camry and the Honda Accord. Despite its resources and experience (and technical R&D), GM wasn't first to market in the SUV boom, the "luxury truck" boom, the crossover boom, the hybrid boom, or any other market-creating move over the last 25 years. Instead, it responded when other firms pioneered those markets in order to protect its sales volume.

Changes in the Strategic Environment

The saying goes that change is the only constant. Some changes in a firm's environment are truly external, like the emergence of a substitute technology or the shrinking of the economy. The fact that these changes are external to the firm does not mean that they are necessarily unpredictable, however. The MSDR needs to be maintained constantly. All of the considerations we discussed earlier in this chapter should be revisited on a regular basis. Businesses predicated on freely available credit should have begun to adjust their management systems in early 2008 as the threat to credit markets began to receive active attention in the business press.

There are also internal sources of change. Maintaining compatibility between the system for delivering results and the strategic direction is critical, but many firms neglect to change their management systems when a redirection of strategy, even a major one, is made. However, it is arguably more important to adjust the MSDR when the strategy changes than it is when the execution environment changes. Without a change in the management system, the organization will be executing the old strategy, not the new one! Indeed, in the case of measures designed to encourage improvement and learning in strategy execution, change is imperative. Once the improvements are made, new management goals have to be established.

Even under the most stable strategic models, it is natural and necessary for the strategic focus to be readjusted as time goes by. Figure 4.2 illustrates the four major stages of the life cycle of a product in its journey from initial appearance to extinction. During each stage, different strategies (and, therefore, different MSDR systems) are most effective. Let's examine the typical transitions.

At the introduction stage, the strategic focus is on product/service development and business opportunity. New products, services, or processes are sought that will lead to competitive advantage. Here, measures need to focus on identifying opportunities. The traditional forms of management protocols based on results, task, and actions are less important, though a few, used interactively, make sense. At this stage, there is typically a larger proportion of control via personal interaction and shared norms and beliefs. Controls employing reports and measures are primarily related to operations or project status, often employing a majority of non-financial statistics.

Introduction transitions to growth and a build strategy: offerings are expanded, implementation R&D is emphasized, and production facilities are built. There is a larger mandate for investing capital in projects that build strength. At this stage, the MSDR will seek signals from customers in order to gauge market response to the

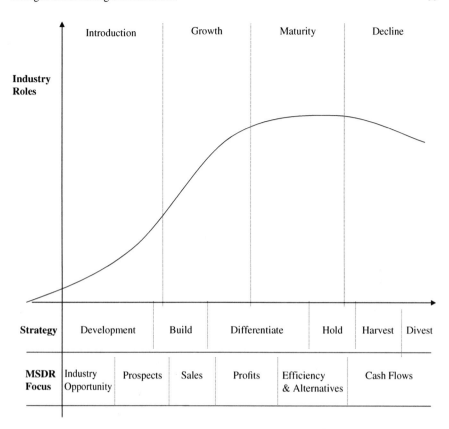

Fig. 4.2 Product life cycle, strategy, and MSDR focus

new innovations. Thus, measures related to sale trends and forecasted sales levels are put in place. The MSDR focuses on improving the predictability of the success of the innovations. It is forward thinking with an emphasis on calibrating the sales growth.

During the latter part of the growth stage, the MSDR focus shifts from predicting sales to reliably estimating profits and, eventually, to building efficiencies to sustain profits. Returns on investment and utilization of working capital and fixed assets are emphasized. Typically, there is a significant increase in analyzing results measures, with careful attention paid to allocated costs, interest changes, and transfer pricing. Depending on the organization's strategy, at this stage the MSDR will sometimes reinstate measures and procedures related to finding opportunities. Unlike the introduction phase, however, the opportunities sought here are more focused and seek alternative applications or markets for the products, services, and internal processes in order to extend their profitable lives.

As the product approaches maturity, the strategic focus turns to profitability. Thus, the MSDR shifts to encompass more efficiency measurements and stricter cash flow budgets. Equipment technology, capacity levels, and defect rates are key concerns. Constant care goes into insuring that the structure of the assets stays proportional to the projected market demand. The MSDR must also address the issue of product or service retirement.

This last assessment leads to the strategy in the decline stage, either harvesting or divesting. Harvesting calls for minimizing cash investment to maximizing cash contribution. Ultimately, there is a divesting and the MSDR emphasis must be switched once more. Here, control is focused on the proper management of costs related to liquidation.

The product life cycle provides a framework for determining an appropriate mix of management protocol types. It also gives an ongoing reference for the contingent application of market intelligence, rules, and measures. Obviously, it is important that the MSDR changes with the firms' changing strategic execution focus as it progresses through the product life cycle.

Conclusion

Management systems are effective only when there is a fit among the measurement system, the strategy, and the environment in which it operates. Misalignment along any dimension of fit can defeat motivation throughout the organization as well as lead to poor execution of the strategy. An MSDR must incorporate external reference points to provide sound context for measuring and motivating performance. Since the MSDR is designed to help execute the strategy, it is important for it to begin by monitoring the implementation of the strategy—and then all the subsequent phases of a product life cycle—and provide feedback to management about the results.

In this chapter, we have mentioned several means to assure that the fit is the best that it can be. One is to maximize the compatibility between the firm's resources and strengths and the environment in which it operates. This simplifies the MSDR system and eases the burden on it. The second is locating the critical control points and designing specific measures to reach peak strategic performance. This is done through the analysis of KSFs. The third is designing the organizational characteristics to simplify both strategy execution and the job of guiding that execution through the MSDR. This entails adjusting the organizational design and fitting the connection between organizational culture and the strategy.

Notes

1. Weiner, Norbert. *Cybernetics: Or Control and Communication in the Animal and the Machine.* (Cambridge, MA: MIT Press, 1948).
2. If you are interested in this idea, there are several authors worth reading. Ludwig Von Bertalanffy was a biologist and cancer researcher whose focus on organismic systems shifted to behavioral science and open systems theory in the 1950s. C. West Churchman, considered to be the father of systems analysis, was a philosophy professor whose range expanded into

engineering, operations research, and administration. His work on "the systems approach" tried to integrate rational thinking with broad human behavior.

Von Bertalanffy, Ludwig. *General System Theory: Foundations, Development, Applications*, (New York: George Braziller, 1968).

Churchman, C. West. *The Systems Approach*, (New York: Delacorte Press, 1968).

3. Ashby, William Ross. *An Introduction to Cybernetics*. (London: Chapman and Hall, 1964). Ashby was strongly influenced by Von Bertalanffy. His focus was specifically on the control of systems. See more at http://rossashby.info/index.html.

4. Porter, Michael E. *Competitive Strategy: Techniques for Analyzing Industries and Competitors*. (New York: Free Press, 1980).

5. A specific example can be found is the following article: Kantrow, Yvette D. *Electronic Data to Buy ADP Unit* (New York: American Banker, Apr 19, 1989).

6. This example was provided to one of the authors by Michael Ruettgers, CEO and Chairman of EMC at the time, during an interview on the Babson College campus. For a bit of background on the initial problem, refer to the following article: Helm, Leslie. "How a Hot Company Overheated" (Cover story) *Business Week* (23 May 1988).

Chapter 5
Organizational Fitness: Culture and Values

Delivering results is the product of human decisions and actions. It is about people working together to accomplish a shared goal. We now explore the internal forces of any group—the people that make the organization. Every firm has its own personality and unique character. Collectively, the members of the organization stand for and represent a certain set of principles. This shapes how they view themselves and the world around them. The culture and values of an organization form the foundation of a management delivery system. Encircling the portfolio of measures as a boundary in a company's strategic delivery system are the social norms and group values of the organization, its culture (Fig. 5.1).

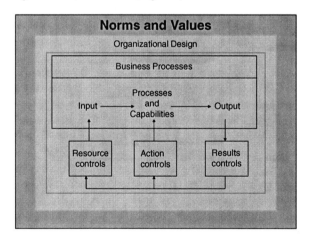

Fig. 5.1 MSDR internal view

This social system determines how groups of people, whether they are stand-alone, a small cluster, or part of a larger group, interact. Their shared values and objectives guide decision-making and the actions of the members. The norms of behavior limit the likelihood of some managerial actions and encourage other kinds of thought and action. Thus, the organization's norms and values create a kind of control system themselves. Ouchi[1] in his seminal work on culture calls this clan control.

L.P. Carr, A.J. Nanni, Jr., *Delivering Results*, DOI 10.1007/978-1-4419-0621-2_5,
© Springer Science+Business Media, LLC 2009

In Chapter 3 we introduced our model of the management system for delivering results (MSDR). In Fig. 3.2B, the internal view, norms and values serve as the border of the entire MSDR model. Norms and values create the context for management. This aspect of MSDR is one that is often overlooked or taken for granted. We find it is not sufficiently addressed by the leadership. More management time is spent with organizational design, strategy, and ERP systems and not enough time on developing a set of shared values. In our opinion, harmonious culture is one of the prime differentiators of firms that successfully and repeatedly execute their strategy. It deserves management's serious consideration and attention. Predictably, we will spend some time talking about culture.[2] MSDR is about behavior and people where culture and conduct can be learned or changed.

Culture can be defined as the norms, values, traditions, attitudes, ideologies, and beliefs shared by a group or organization. It is a collection of shared values that reflect the attitudes and behaviors of its members. Culture is socially created expectation about acceptable behavior. It is a collective shared action. Culture coordinates and aligns our actions especially at times of pressure and anxiety. Under pressure, the common shared values will guide the actions of a group. This can be a very potent form of control. The behavioral norms of the organization define both what results are desirable and what actions are off-limits. In fact, "clan" control is probably the primary (if not only) form of control in many small business and entrepreneurial operations. Even within a large corporation, however, it is the filter through which specific measurements are interpreted. Culture represents the personality of the enterprise, similar to an individual personality. It is unique with specific characteristics and tendencies. Consider the following example from the investment banking industry.

Goldman Sachs, one of the surviving Wall Street investment firms during the financial crisis of 2008, has a very distinct culture. They have a very strong belief in teamwork and the customer. This value system was built during the post World War II era. Sidney Weinberg, the leader from 1930 to 1969, shaped the modern Goldman Sachs. The firm flourished from 1975 under the leadership of John Whitehead and John Weinberg (son of Sidney). Henry Paulson, CEO from 1999 to 2006 and, at the time of this writing, Secretary of the Treasury, continued to foster the core value of team work—"Quite simply, none of us is as smart as all of us." There was a culture of sharing information, working together, and the idea that everyone at the firm represented the entire firm when dealing with customers. Partners and managers freely supported each other and would move to different projects as customer demands warranted. Teamwork was valued, and successful people at Goldman Sachs had a distinct propensity to work in teams. Compensation to partners was based on the overall profits of the firm, not any individual, division, or group. This stands in stark contrast to other investment banking cultures where individuals, generally with large egos, are the dominant focus.

Goldman Sachs' second dominant culture norm was focus on the customer. They believed in very strong client relationships and went to great lengths to know and understand their clients on a personal and professional basis. The mark of success was exceptional client service, not the firm's profits. They expected the profits to come when the clients were served well. There were legends about the senior partners, during the holiday season, attending up to six client parties in a single night to show customer support. There was great pride in becoming the trusted advisor of leaders of major business and world governments. Goldman Sachs employed very smart people to service their government, large municipalities, sizable pension funds, and substantial corporate clients. They were meticulous in pursuing clients. Corporations making more than $1 million per year had a Goldman investment banker trying to do business with them. Many called it the Goldman "machine."

Charles Ellis recently published a fascinating history of Goldman Sachs with many more examples of the power of culture to produce superior performance.[3] Culture contributed to Goldman's survival and transition to a bank holding company during the 2008 financial crisis. Their prime survival tactic, however, was avoiding the sub-prime mortgage financing scandal that sunk Lehman Brothers, Merrill Lynch, and a number of banks and insurance companies. As of this writing, Goldman is cutting jobs and expenses to cope with the difficult financial times. Private equity, real estate, banking, and brokerage will produce significant losses in 2008.

In contrast to Goldman Sachs, the legacy of the Lehman Brothers culture was that of the spirited individual building their book of business and earning the largest bonus. There was internal competitive tension, and it was not uncommon for different individuals to pursue the same account.[4] The CEO, Richard Fuld, who led the firm during the last decade, was recently attempting to change the culture to more of a team play. He recognized his client's preference for dealing with a multinational, coordinated team. Their culture change efforts were too late. The arrogance and individual aggressive actions colored the Lehman image. In 2008, prior to their bankruptcy, they spent $761 million buying their own stock at an average price of $49.60. At the end of 2008, the stock was worth about five cents.[5] Lehman management acknowledged their customers were global, savvy, and well connected in the world. Clients preferred a coordinated team approach to investment banking. The key is matching your enterprise culture to the characteristics of your customers' value. The Lehman CEO was in the middle of a culture change program when bankruptcy hit. He resigned in disgrace. Different cultures operating in the same industry, both were successful in an era of financial market growth. But the culture of team fit the customer's needs better, which provided a buffer Goldman when the markets soured.

Building Culture

Social norms and organizational culture evolve in an "organic" fashion. This does not seem to have stopped managers from trying to manipulate social norms through direct methods of intervention, such as formal discussions, publications, speeches, and mottoes. Nonetheless, culture may be subtly and slowly shaped and reshaped through real changes in organizational design and action. In order to instill "six-sigma quality" values at GE and Motorola, the associated language and concepts have been actively cultivated and regularly discussed for *decades*. Managers there are expected to walk the talk of quality improvement. Command of the six-sigma principles is a vital evaluation point of a manager's performance.

Do not take culture for granted! If you are leading a start-up (or a new organization due to merger or acquisition), setting the tone of the culture is extremely important. Too many leaders do not think about the power they have to influence the personality of their organization. There are consulting firms that can assist with the very important task of shaping the desired culture, or the leader can think about the desired culture and start to reinforce the preferred behaviors. Trust and personal control are based on a set of shared values.

Culture is more than vision and values that senior managers post throughout the company or insist that everyone carry on laminated cards in their wallets. In a perfect world, the vision and values should shape the culture. We always say that the test of a "quality focus" culture is whether the production line will be halted during the last week of the quarter due to some quality issue. Management is pushing hard to make the quarterly numbers, customers are demanding shipments, and the manager must stop the production. This is the true test of values and culture. Fall short of the numbers and reinforce the quality culture or let the culture of quality slip a little (just this time) to make the numbers. Actions speak volumes, and management decisions need to support and reinforce the culture.

The United States Navy SEAL group (Sea Air Land Special Warfare Unit) is the elite unit trained to do some of the most difficult military tasks. Their training is legendary—physically and mentally demanding. Less than ten percent of those volunteers starting the one-year series of programs become certified. One of the core traits of a member of a SEAL unit is teamwork based on trust and caring for fellow team members. They must know the whereabouts of each member of the team at all times, no exception. Their creed is no one is left behind. Their training program puts a big emphasis on teamwork. They run on the beach in unison with twelve SEAL trainees carrying a telephone pole, never to be dropped. Their swimming and underwater exercises are all team-based, using the buddy system. Yet, it is the individual who graduates and becomes a SEAL, an individual who has the culture and belief in teams.[6]

Cultures and sub-cultures evolve when members of the group actively support one another in pursuit of their objectives. It is the disposition of their efforts put forth in solving problems, crafting solutions, and implementing change. The culture evolves as the group carries out the mission of the organization. They map a course of the behaviors that are necessary for success. The characteristics and values of the culture are shaped by the founders and leaders of the group. Their words and behavior send tangible messages as to what is important. The employees observe critical incidents of decisions or actions that often become the folklore of the firm. Consider the culture at Irving Oil Corporation.

Irving Oil Corporation is a privately held Canadian Energy firm operating over 400 convenience stores and gas stations in Atlantic Canada and Northern New England. It is a third-generation, family-run multi-billion dollar operation. They have extended the "Irving Promise" to all their customers. The promise is to have friendly staff, clean washrooms, and well stocked and lit stores to create a pleasing customer experience. Management wants all 400 stores to operate as if a member of the Irving family worked there. The Irving brothers, Kenneth and Arthur Jr., frequently visit the stores. They wait on customers, stock shelves, sweep the floor, and clean washrooms.

The front line employees observe the owners' behavior. They are on a first name basis with them. The Irving family is walking the talk, and the customers are benefiting. They have built a culture of caring for the customer and having pride in their store and operations. Irving Oil regularly publishes extraordinary customer service stories and rewards those associates that go out of their way to delight a customer. Management uses the Irving Promise culture as a competitive weapon to attract customers to their stores. It is working, as they have seen significant market share gains in their served markets. We will come back to the Irving story later, when we cover performance measures and their influence on behavior in detail.

Each of us finds a way to become part of the culture. Culture is learned from experience by anxiety and social trauma or by reward and reinforcement. When you join a new group, there is always some anxiety concerning how everyone will get along and if you will fit in. You want to know what is important and why people think it is important. You want to know what you need to do and say to fit in. You are discovering how things get done. There is uncertainty. Usually the first thing you discuss is common shared experiences and knowledge. The leader will have his or her ways of solving problems. You start to evaluate your fit and gain an understanding of the norms and value of the organization. What does "on time" mean in this organization? Are jokes acceptable ways of communicating? What is the practice around attending meetings, going to lunch, sharing coffee, greeting in the morning, and so on? Behind these surface issues, the company values are communicated and shared.

In order to implement strategy and achieve the goals, a group needs a common language to share the conceptualization of the desired results. There needs to be a set of norms around how people are treated. The allocating of authority, the distribution of power and status must be clear. A method of sharing and coping with crises during unpredicted and stressful events must be clear. When a crisis arises, such as losing a key customer, the team members learn from the experience. Was the leader concerned? How did he or she react? Did they focus on a customer relationship issue or was there a focus on logistics, engineering, or some other department? Was there a necessity to find someone or a department to blame? You learn from the reaction what is important to the leadership and how they handle the problem. This gives you a solid clue to their value system. You then adapt to the norms of the culture. Behavior rules are complex and pervasive.

Culture is the glue that often holds organizations together. The real test of the culture comes in moments of crisis or extreme pressure. The shared group culture sets the tone for actions and decision-making. The classic example is when Johnson & Johnson senior management moved very quickly to pull all Tylenol drugs off the shelf. There was tampering with the packaging and poisoning of the product. The

strong culture of social responsibility and consumer safety trumped financial consequences. The values of Johnson & Johnson were displayed very quickly. At the time,
Johnson & Johnson had a 35% market share. The stock market reaction was a reduction of market capitalization of over $1 billion. Management's decisive reaction won
praise from all. Within a month, they recovered 70% of the loss. They led the new
design of tamperproof packaging for the pharmacy industry. Management was true
to its values despite the temporary financial setback.

You build culture to develop "trust" among the members of the organization.
Think of this as personal control. Consider how often senior managers bring "their"
people into the organization after a takeover or major appointment. You have a relationship, shared values and beliefs, with the potential appointee. You know they
can be trusted. You know their thinking, work habits, skills, and attitudes. You do
not have to worry about discontinuity or disloyalty. These people generally need
very little management. You have a shared language. You understand each other.
You work well together because you share the same values and culture. Culture is
learned from experience and sets the tone for the way things are done in a firm—
quality at GE and 3M, teamwork for the Navy Seals, and customer service for Irving
Oil. Culture makes possible the work of the organization.

Values and Beliefs as Part of the Delivery System

Specific performance measures and standard operating procedures must be in harmony with the shared belief system of the organization in order for them to be
effective. Measures need to align with culture based on business goals. In some
cases, this requires the control systems designers to define measures in terms consistent with the organizational norms. Often, it requires action controls to be explained
or justified in terms of shared beliefs. In some cases, it might mean that no specific control is necessary—the social norms already make an undesirable behavior
extremely unlikely. Sometimes, however, it means that the current culture is a barrier
to the strategic goals.

The management style of the leadership is one of the primary means available
to influence the organization's shared culture and beliefs. Management style affects
the amount of weight that can be effectively placed on the different types of control.
Our experience and our research tell us that management style is a very powerful
force that directly influences the effective (or ineffective) implementation of strategic controls. To be effective, the management system should be compatible with the
leader's personal management style. The leader sets the example and offers a model
for the people in the organization to follow. Enron provides a dramatic example of
how a change in culture with a new leader changed the MSDR.

The Enron Corporation story is about greed, corruption, and eventual collapse.
Some people believed Enron was out of control, but the fact is that the employees
were following the leadership and their behavioral pattern. Why did the delivery
system fail so dramatically, and where were the management controls? In the early
1990s, Jeffery Skilling took over as CEO. He succeeded Richard Kinder, who was
known for his discipline and numbers focus. His Monday morning weekly business

review meetings were grueling and required full explanation of performance. He was demanding but fair. Skilling, with a new management style, took over and set a new tone at Enron.

After three years Skilling successfully transformed Enron from an energy company to a trading company. He established a new culture about completing "deal after deal." Skilling was smart, very competitive, and tenacious. His intensity was plain to see. He micro-managed the reporting and accounting to ensure Enron exceeded the Wall Street analysts' expectations at any cost or with any creative accounting technique. The Enron creed seemed to be "the ends justify the means". With this drumbeat, the traders and dealmakers were under massive pressure to deliver results. Bonuses, status, and even your job were at stake. Make the numbers or else. Skilling made it clear he was willing to bend the rules. Everyone knew it was the end results that counted.

Enron became the "darling of Wall Street" and the shining example of the new economy. They enjoyed favorable business press and were the subject of a number of flattering case studies. Skilling was the star with political and social connections. He built a highly skilled workforce operating in a complex organization using very complex financial instruments. Enron was recognized by the media and various organizations as the most innovative company with the number one CEO in the United States and top quality management. The company had a code of conduct, thorough performance reviews, a risk assessment group, and sound management approval process for deals. They had corporate governance structures and a strong audit partner, Arthur Anderson.

The new CEO transformed the disciplined and orderly MSDR culture to a culture of bending rules; be creative, but get the results or else. Enron shifted from manage to the numbers to manage the numbers. This is subtle but a big jump. You can see how a culture can corrupt. The employees feared for their jobs and were afraid to express their opinion or point out any wrong doings. Blind loyalty was rewarded handsomely. Finally, someone had the courage to blow the whistle, and the house of cards collapsed. Many are now serving jail time, but many more employees and investors lost everything.

In the end we want a portfolio of specific controls that will direct attention to the problems and eliminate undesirable actions from consideration, but otherwise leave the details of the actions to the imagination and ingenuity of the members of the organization. The culture of fraud and corruption at Enron provided the green light for the individual actions taken by the leadership. Skilling's style and values were the growth medium for corruption. On the other hand, Lincoln Electric offers us a very different set of values and beliefs that set the tone of operation. It is an excellent example of using the firm's values and beliefs as an integral part of the delivery system.[7]

Lincoln Electric is a 113-year-old provider of quality welding and cutting equipment. With sales at $2 billion, they enjoy a dominant market share by focusing on the customer and offering value with quality products. Management believes they can build quality products at lower cost and pass on the saving to the customer. The company founder, James Lincoln, had faith in the individual, competition, and incentives. Lincoln is credited with many innovations in the work place including incentive bonuses, employee stock ownership, employee suggestion system and advisory boards, piecework pay, and group life insurance. They have a no lay-off policy and people are guaranteed a job for life. They have no paid holidays or sick days and people willingly accept overtime to meet spikes in demand. The company shares a large portion of the company profit with the employees. This encourages an entrepreneurial environment in the plant. The Lincoln employees manage themselves based on the pay for performance compensation system. They are paid for what they produce. Defective work has to be corrected by the employees on their own time.

The compensation system consists of wages based on piecework output and year-end bonus based on their merit rating (equal portions quality, adaptability, flexibility, productivity, dependability, team work, and safety). About 60% of the compensation is variable. Workers' bonuses average around $25,000 per year and, in a good year, could be double that. Each individual manages his tasks and is given the autonomy for solving problems and reporting their results. The control system is a great example of clan control based on peer pressure. There is a strong trust between the management team and the production workers. Both parties share ideas that improve quality, productivity, and customer delivery.

Lincoln has a policy of promoting from within; very few people enter the company at middle or upper management levels. They do not have a formal organizational chart, and the hierarchy is very flat. The administrative portions of the business operate in a similar lean fashion with a concentration on productivity and value-add activities. The employment lines are long at Lincoln with people seeking the job for life. After the first year the employee turnover rate is very low. However, the turnover in the first year of employment is very high. The culture and value system at Lincoln Electric sorts out those who would thrive during the first year of socialization. In both Enron and Lincoln Electric, the culture was the critical part of their delivery system. The corrupt Enron culture led to its demise. The thriving Lincoln Electric culture continues to serve as the bedrock of the MSDR system.

Fitting the MSDR System to the Culture: When Culture is Critical for Control

Cultures and values play a major role in delivering results in small entrepreneurial organizations. These firms often have no formal reporting or information system and rely on informal guidance from the leaders. In this case, the prevailing culture sets the work tenor and often serves as the primary method of insuring the execution of the strategy. The leaders establish the tone, and employees quickly adopt the melody playing. There is normally close proximity and considerable personal interaction. The use of trust and personal control is extensive. Management style and individual values guide the actions of the firm. In this case, the MSDR is in the organizational culture. As the firm grows and the organization evolves, more structure is added to the MSDR system.

Culture is the silent part of the organization that serves as the undergirding of the MSDR system. In a centralized command and control environment, with close and constant supervision, culture and values play a less critical role. Culture is there and provides the atmosphere where work gets done. The functional structure of the organization permits management to monitor the tone of the decision-making closely. There is little room for individual leaders to make their own interpretations of the prevailing culture or to adopt a completely different set of values. Managers use a healthy mix of results, action, and resource controls to coordinate the specialized knowledge of each operation. For example, the coordination of manufacturing, marketing, and engineering for a new product launch is guided by the consistent interface of each of the functions in a command and control centralized environment.

Decentralized organizations allocate the decision-making to the operating units. The business unit managers have a greater degree of freedom on how their entity will operate. Culture, in this case, plays a much larger role in helping decentralized organizations implement strategy. Decision-making authority is well distributed, and profit and loss responsibility is given to an array of managers. A business unit is responsible for all the functions involved in their product line. They are encouraged to develop their business under the policy standards umbrella of the corporation and need to manage their business unit within the corporate guidelines. The leaders have a greater degree of freedom in establishing their culture with autonomy in decision-making. How do you ensure that the decentralized decisions are in the best interest of the business unit and the corporation? How do you know the manager will make the decisions consistent with the culture guidelines? These issues are the trade-off of having the business unit closer to the markets and customers able to respond quickly to changes.[8]

In addition, decentralized business units are normally separated geographically and operate in different parts of the corporate value chain. In conglomerates, like GE, they could be in totally dissimilar business value chains. In the business unit structure, shared culture and values are critical ingredients for an operating MSDR. GE tolerates a large amount of decision-making freedom with their business units. But they have a very powerful culture that is followed and continually reinforced. Their passionate six-sigma quality program and their regular internal management development training reinforce the strong GE culture and values in the business units.

Business units pursuing their own agenda with different leadership and strategy ideas can be very problematic. A strong strategic thrust requires consistency in agenda and execution. For example, a large Belgian intermediate chemical company shifted from a centralized hierarchal organization to a decentralized business unit structure. They were benefiting from their centralized structure to achieve economies of scale for their large-scale production operations. Sales growth, however, was slowing and they were not penetrating markets outside their local served area. The global market was untapped and offered the needed growth.

They opened a number of business unit subsidiaries in countries throughout Europe. Local, entrepreneurial-minded managers were selected to lead the various subsidiaries. These business unit managers were encouraged to develop their markets, and corporate committed to build local production if the volume warranted. The company shifted from economies of scale strategy to a differentiation strategy as they expanded globally. The change in strategy was communicated, but the culture remained focused on insuring full production capacity. The functional headquarters managers felt the role of the new business unit subsidiaries was to find orders to fill plant capacity. The business unit leaders, on the other hand, saw their role as developing markets with a variety of new and old products. They brought an assortment of new proposals for their countries. Some included new production facilities, and others went to market using very different supply chains. Most of these innovative proposals were rejected at corporate review despite meeting all the financial hurdle rates. They were counter to the corporate culture of consistency and predictability with little risk.

The culture to support the new strategy was not sufficiently developed. The business plan proposals were analyzed against the economies of scale standard of enhanced capacity utilization. Over time the talented subsidiary managers left the firm totally frustrated. Corporate functional mangers were not supporting their business plans, and new business was lost due to the unresponsive headquarters managers. Senior management felt they had a sound strategy for growing the company. They employed the best and brightest business unit mangers. Only after a series of capable subsidiary managers left the firm did they realize they had a culture problem with the execution of the new strategy. For the successful implementation of strategy, the appropriate culture is required. In this case, the shared values did not support the new strategic approach. In decentralized organizational structures, fostering a consistent culture is a continual challenge but critical to the coordination of activities.

A clear and strong organization culture is important in situations where financial measures are difficult to obtain. Delivery comes from culture control, which guides decision-making and sound judgment. The professional medical community in major hospitals uses professional values and culture to heavily augment financial measures. It is difficult to measure the results of a doctor's professional judgment, insights, and sense of caring for the patient. The patient outputs can often be out of their control, but their profession and organization desires a proficient and qualified approach.

Today there is an increased emphasis in medical schools on teaching professional standards. The simple Hippocratic oath loses meaning in today's managed care world. This training and professional culture development is continued throughout internship, residency, and specialty training. Doctors have control over diagnosis and treatment, decisions about which test and examinations are appropriate, the drugs and procedures to use, who to refer where, and the nature of follow-up care. They are encouraged by their professional associations to uphold the highest standards despite the ever-increasing economic pressures around the cost of good medical care. The professional culture is very important and provides needed guidance for the expert whose judgment is critical for our health.

Building a Sustained Culture

The desired culture and norms that provide clear guidance and focus attention come from reinforcement and constant examples from the leadership. You develop a culture by employee involvement, management support, signals from others, and reward systems. People need encouragement to participate in building a specific culture. To maintain a strong culture you need to continually keep the message coming. Without the proper reinforcement cultures can shift and drift.

In a quality-focused firm, engagement through formal programs (such as quality circles, six-sigma black belt training, or quality advisory boards) or informal approaches (such as social gatherings, rallies or conversations with management) is essential. Give people choices of how to get the work done with the idea of taking responsibility for their actions. Recognized quality programs (GE, Motorola, and Toyota) have a critical feature of very active employee involvement from all levels of the organization. The quality literature tells us this is how you build a culture of quality excellence. An example of how not to build a culture of quality is a company we know that encourages employees to become six-sigma black belts on their own time and at their own expense. The message is clear: quality is of secondary importance to productivity and cost reduction management. In this case the desired culture of excellent quality was, as you might expect, not achieved.

Culture, our set of shared beliefs, is about people living up to expectations. In order to develop the desired culture, managers must be clear about the specific attitudes and behaviors desired. They need to set the norms. Firms such as 3M, Intel, Hewlett-Packard, Johnson & Johnson, and others are recognized for their emphasis on innovation. In a survey of over 500 managers from these industries the lists of norms most frequently cited were as follows: risk taking, rewards for change, openness, shared goals, autonomy, and a belief in action.[9] Without these underlying cultural traits, innovation would not prosper. 3M's stated goal is to have 25% of the annual sales come from new products less than 5 years old. Management credits the 3M corporate culture and norms as the key ingredient for their product innovation success. The norms are powerful because throughout the organization executives at all levels are reinforcing the culture message and living by the norms they created.

At Lincoln Electric the quality focus is properly reinforced when the production workers are given freedom to design their work but the responsibility to fix quality problems on their own time. This is why firms with strong cultures have a rigorous selection process and an elaborate orientation program to help new people get assimilated into the culture. In the 3M innovation culture, every employee is given time and encouragement to pursue their creative ideas. They promote networking and communication of new ideas; recognizing new ideas can come from anyone in the organization. Employee active involvement helps solidify their beliefs. The Post-it note discovery is a legendary example of the participation factor in the 3M innovation culture.

Dr. Spencer Silver, a 3M scientist, discovered the sticky material in 1968; but there was no commercial use for it. It did not bond like the other 3M adhesive products. Art Fry came up with a practical use of the material as a way to hold the markers in his hymnbook, which kept falling out in church. Fry, under the 3M "bootlegging" policy, used a portion of his work time to develop the solution. The Post-it note product line was launched in 1977 and today is a well-recognized global product.

A culture thrives only when the leadership supports the values by their actions. Speeches, posters, and slogans help communicate a culture value, but management actions and decisions are the signals of the real values in an organization. As stated earlier, stopping the production line to ensure quality rather than reach production targets sends a very powerful message. People are looking for consistent patterns. Managers must be careful about their actions as a communicator of values. On occasion this may involve some symbolic activities or even some acting to convey a value. One of the authors was CEO of OSRAM North America, a lighting company. He wanted to build a strong work ethic culture. He made it a point to be the first one in the office and the last one to leave. With an East coast location, many of his early morning activities were phone conversations with the European parent (six time zones ahead) and the early evening activities conversations with his California operations (three hours behind). He would have preferred to do this from home but wanted to send a strong work ethic signal to the people. The signal was well received, and the work ethic culture blossomed.

Many companies say the customer is number one in priority. Watch the manager's actions to see if that is true. An executive was staying in a hotel in Denver. When she went to her rental car the first morning, she discovered a dead battery. The hotel manager heard her make a desperate call to the rental car agency and heard them tell her it would be two hours before they could come out. The rental firm should have had in place a system for faster response time. In lieu of that, the rental agency manager should have had the foresight to offer other options such as suggesting the guest take a taxi to the meeting and offering to reimburse the fare. They offered no other option for her to get to her meeting. The hotel manager, on the other hand, volunteered to lend her his personal car saying it would simply be parked in the lot all day, and he had no use for it. The hotel manager sent a powerful culture message of what is important to his staff at the hotel and secured a customer for life. The rental car agency also sent a powerful message of poor customer service. They lost a customer for life.

Signals from coworkers are just as important as management signals. Peer acceptance is very influential, and we often look for cues from others when we are uncertain of what action to take. We want acceptance by the group. At W. L. Gore there are no titles or organizational charts; everyone is an associate or leader. At Honda and Nissan all managers and production workers wear uniforms at the plant. These policies support the culture of equality, equal treatment, and team. A stable culture rests on stimulation and communications among group members, the feelings the members have for each other. Southwest Airlines is acknowledged for its culture of fun. The flight attendants and pilots are known for playing jokes, dressing in costumes, and having a light banter with the flying customers. The airline offers a distinctive experience for the customer. It is one of their competitive differences. The company screens for personality traits and looks for those who will fit in. Each flight team is different, and their interaction and mutual support creates the fun flying experience for the customer. [10]

Another company where the strong culture plays a pivotal role in their success is FedEx. They are passionate about the image that the package must make the flight and be delivered on time. People are given wide latitude in operational decision-making within their system. They want people to react properly to the many different customer delivery challenges. The FedEx teams at airports and distribution centers regularly celebrate innovative individual action that allowed the package to be delivered on time. Sometimes it even involves breaking the FedEx rules. The people have tenacity and a sense of urgency to move the package to the intended location. There is the FedEx corporate principle that every customer query is answered that day. Can you imagine the peer reaction when, at the end of a shift with packages still in the queue, an employee says, "OK we will get to it first thing tomorrow?" The norm is just the opposite. FedEx employees will track the customer down to her cell phone to let her know that an important legal document is on its way.[11]

Shaping the desired culture comes from rewards, recognition, or positive feedback. Managers have a wonderful opportunity to reinforce the desired behavior by recognizing acts and decisions right after they happen. Other techniques like certificates, awards, special parking, time off, dinners, or money are strong behavioral reinforcers. These give you the opportunity to shape the attitudes and culture you want inculcated in your company. Reward the attitude and behavior (action). We will discuss rewards in depth later in the book.

Conclusion

Building a set of shared values that represents the norms of the organization is a very powerful tool for implementing strategy. It takes time, consistent messaging, and management attention to fabricate a culture. Culture motivates behavior and provides a degree of freedom for people to do their job. It is more critical in decentralized and start-up organizations.

Culture is learned by repetition and consistent strong signals. This is the leader's job. Set the example and continue to repeat and reinforce the culture and value message. Look for symbolic action and the opportunity to send the culture message. The theme of the examples in this chapter, Goldman, Navy SEAL program, Irving Oil, Lincoln Electric, J&J, 3M, OSRAM and FedEx, is one of clear and constant signals sent to the enterprise employees unmistakably stating the firm's values. Each of the examples represents a cultural training event that produced learning. Strong cultures require many and consistent learning episodes. Remember, in the absence of a formal MSDR, the shared culture will serve as the guidance system.

Notes

1. Ouchi, W.G., "A Conceptual Framework for the Design of Organizational Control Mechanisms," *Management Science* 25 (Sept. 1979) pioneered the use of social control to guide and manage organizations.

2. There is a very large body of literature on culture. They offer definitions, benefits, and methods of defining, building, and assessing culture. Some of the seminal works are the following: Tushmann, M.L. and O'Reilly, C.A., III, *Winning through Innovation: A Practical Guide to Leading Organizational Change and Renewal*, (Boston, MA: Harvard Business School Publishing, 2002); Kilmann, R.M., *Managing Beyond the Quick Fix*, (San Francisco, CA: Jossey-Bass, 1989); Kilmann, R.H. and Saxton, M.J. (eds.), *Gaining Control of the Corporate Culture*, (San Francisco, CA: Jossey-Bass, 1985).
3. Ellis, C.D., *The Partnership, The Making of Goldman Sachs*, (New York: Penguin Press, 2008).
4. Auletta, K., *Greed and Glory on Wall Street: The Rise and Fall of the House of Lehman* (New York: Random House, 1986).
5. Sloan, A., *Fortune*, "The Deal," Dec. 8, 2008.
6. There are many books on the US Navy SEALs. *Lone Survivor* by Marcus Luttrell (New York: Back Bay Books, 2007) offers a good insight into the SEAL training.
7. There are over ten case studies published by Harvard Business School Publishing. The Lincoln story has been used as an example of innovative human resource practices and taught in many MBA programs.
8. Chandler, Jr., Alfred D., *Strategy and Structure* (Cambridge, MA: MIT Press, 1962) wrote the seminal work on organizations structures for implementing strategy.
9. Tushman, M., O'Reilly, C., and Nadler, D. (eds.), *Readings in Management of Organizations: An Integrated Perspective*, (Cambridge, MA: Ballinger, 1989).
10. Gittell, J.H., *The Southwest Airlines Way*, (New York: McGraw Hill, 2002). There is a continuing steam of Southwest Air stores; Stephen Hopson has an interesting blog, Adversityuniversityblog.com
11. There are numerous published Fed Ex stories with many benchmarks for business. Two complete stories are Basch, M., *Customer Culture: How Fed Ex and Other Great Companies Put Customer First Every Day*, (Upper Saddle River, NJ: Prentice Hall, 2002) and Frock, R. *Changing How the World Does Business: FedEx's Incredible Journey to Success – The Inside Story*, (San Francisco, CA: Berritt-Koehler, 2006).

Chapter 6
Internal Strategy: Governance Structure

We are told solid foundations are necessary for strong structures. Configuring the ownership and governance, the platform of a firm, is critical for creating a well-built MSDR system. The home foundation contains the critical sources of water and power so necessary for a well-functioning house. The governance structure establishes the pathways and control of an organization. It directly affects how the organization functions and how the agents manage the firm. Just as architects must consider the building configuration when designing the operating systems, MSDR designers must consider the nature of the business, the structure of ownership, and the strategic intent. In this chapter, we explore the governance structure, and in the next chapter we look into the organizational structure.[1]

Governance Structure

The organization's structure has everything to do with the execution—and ultimate success—of strategy. Starting with the stockholders, it is extremely important that they are in harmony with their agents, the managers of the firm. The board of directors, elected by the stockholders, serves to ensure that these parties have the same expectations and goals. Figure 6.1 outlines the traditional governance structure. A category of business literature, called agency theory, explores this topic. Suffice it to say, a critical element of an MSDR system is to align goals and personal rewards between owners and agents. This helps ensure that managers are motivated to do the best thing for the corporation and not, necessarily, only the best thing for themselves.

What will the governance structure look like? What is its blueprint? Let's examine the foundation of structure with a closer look at agency theory.

Agency Theory

This body of literature looks at structures and systems that allow agents (management) and owners (stockholders) to work toward mutual goals. Much of the research looks at the sharing of available information, the measurement systems, and the motivation of each group. The underlying theory is that the managers will

L.P. Carr, A.J. Nanni, Jr., *Delivering Results*, DOI 10.1007/978-1-4419-0621-2_6, © Springer Science+Business Media, LLC 2009

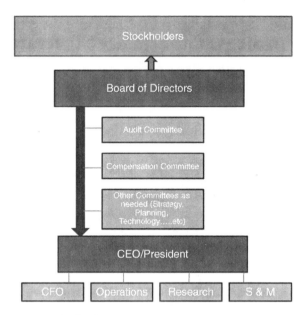

Fig. 6.1 Governance organizational structure

naturally take those actions or make those decisions that will benefit themselves first and stockholders second. The trick is to find a structure and system that promote mutual benefit. The procedure is building an agreement on the strategic direction and balanced incentive compensation.

Stockholders are absentee owners, if you will, and need proxies to serve their interests. They originally invest in corporations because they like the product or service proposition, believe in the strategy, and have confidence that the management team will properly execute the strategy. What keeps things on track is an underlying MSDR system that constantly reminds managers of the strategic goals. Management gets stockholder approval through the board of directors who represent the stockholders and the authority to invest in capital assets or to seek other financing to fund the strategic opportunities.

Managers are encouraged to increase the wealth of the stockholders. A growing trend is the use of stock or stock options for sharing the wealth created for the stockholders and motivating the agent to work in the best interest of the owners.

Yet, this practice has led to some very serious abuses, which create the demand for additional MSDR tracking systems beyond such things as insider-trading reports. Indeed, movement in a firm's stock price is not always the result of company performance. "Irrational" markets do the same thing. During the dot.com boom, stock prices would rise despite reported significant financial losses. The excitement around the future possibilities of some technology masked a rational view of the financial results. Many of these high tech firms failed after the dot.com bubble burst. There are also many short-run techniques agents can employ to raise the stock price. A common practice, for example, is extending the terms of sale from 30 days to

120 days to increase the top line revenue now. But this has a negative effect on the top line revenue of the less-immediate future. You borrow from tomorrow for today. Further, the management team can choose certain accounting techniques to boost reported earnings. Sadly, recent events have shown that the temptations are there.

So, simply offering stock incentives does not create a goal congruency between stockholders and managers. There needs to be much greater agreement on the strategic direction of the organization along with improved measurement systems that will help ensure the strategy is properly executed. We will explain the use and structure of incentive systems in Chapter 9.

While the MSDR system must fit the organization like a well-tailored suit, there are numerous choices management must make to ensure a good fit. Now we want to talk about the rules of engagement. How can good governance adaptation work to your advantage in implementing strategy? How do you make the right choices in governance that fit the nature of your business and your competitive situation?

You need to start at the top and look at the governance configuration. The formation and structure of enterprises is often viewed as a legal task.[2] There is not sufficient thought given to how these entities will operate and who will have the responsibility for delivering results. Starting with the dot.com bust, followed by the Enron failure, and continuing today with the global financial crises, people are asking about the oversight of companies and government agencies that have produced so much failure without warning.[3] There is a loud cry for accountability while firms scramble to address their corporate governance structure. Good governance allows active participation of the shareholders to facilitate sound corporate decision-making and the achievement of strategic intent.

The demise of Enron put corporate governance in the forefront of business issues. Founded in 1985 to develop a nationwide gas pipeline company, Enron became the largest gas merchant in the world in 2003 with 21,000 employees in 40 countries. They held the number seven spot on the FORTUNE 500 list. Enron diversified its portfolio through the use of special purpose entities (SPEs). This "creative accounting technique" allowed the firm to pursue risky ventures without reflecting their costs on their balance sheet. In October 2001, Enron reported a large loss after taking a $1 billion charge against earnings. They restated their earnings for the prior five years, and by November of that year their debt rating was classified as junk. Bankruptcy quickly followed. What were the fifteen distinguished outside board members doing?

As we described earlier in the book, Enron's leaders managed the numbers to meet Wall Street expectations. The board tolerated a conflict of interest with the compensation and the structure of the SPE units. Outside directors' pay was considered by many as excessive at $350,000 per year in compensation and stock. They attended four meetings a year and talked with the management team on occasion. Many directors had consulting arrangements or benefited from generous donations by Enron to their organizations, a conflict of interest. They were anything but independent directors. The congressional investigations, numerous books, and research articles explored the many details of the collapse. While there were numerous reasons, poor governance stands at the top of the list.

Rules of Engagement

We discuss the governance rules of engagement under the following categories: *Independence, Structure, Lack of Knowledge, Compliance, Independent Auditor, and Individual Roles.*

Independence: A proper set of incentives is the key to finding governance alignment between the owners and the managers. Do not assume management will act for the benefit of the stockholders. Self-interest will prevail. The recent emphasis on governance is the attempt to find good stewardship with balance and reason on boards. Too many boards are made up of friends, family, and supporters of the CEO. With this composition, board members are indebted to the CEO. Honest and unbridled stockholder representation is difficult. The Richard Grasso pay disaster is a good example.

Grasso was the chairman and CEO of the New York Stock Exchange (NYSE) from 1995 through 2003. The details of his excessive compensation package of $187.5 million became a major issue in 2003. Grasso hand-selected members of the board and the composition of the compensation committee. The directors followed, almost blindly, management's recommendations. These same directors approved Grasso's pay in the prior year, 2001, of more than $30 million, the same amount as the total net income of the NYSE that year.[4] As the story played out in the press, many of the directors of the NYSE claimed no knowledge of the situation despite approving the pay package. After the exposure and protests from NYSE members, government officials, and leaders of major pension funds, some directors changed their minds on the compensation decision.[5]

SEC chairman William Donaldson said that approval of Grasso's pay package "raised serious questions regarding the effectiveness of the NYSE's current governance structure."[6] The NYSE directors offered little oversight and let Grasso, to whom they felt obligated for their board seats, run the operation. Since this incident, the quest for outside board members with industry or financial knowledge has increased. Embrace the outside critical view. It can benefit you and the shareholders.

Structure: The Sarbanes–Oxley Act (SOX) specifically addressed the composition, structure, and reporting relationships of board of director committees. Boards are paying closer attention to the configuration and responsibility of the board committees, especially the roles of the audit and compensation committees as noted in Fig. 6.1. Prior to SOX legislation many firms were very lax and casual with the role of board committees. It is essential, and now required, for audit committee members to have financial experience with the acumen to work more closely with outside auditors. The relationship of management with the outside auditors is no longer the responsibility of the management team. SOX rules have transferred audit oversight to the Board Audit Committee, where it rightfully belongs. The audit committee members must be independent directors with no consulting or professional relationships with the firm. Now, qualified independent directors are in high demand for audit committee assignments.

The compensation committee regularly seeks help through consultants and/or competitive data sources when structuring senior executives salaries and bonuses.

Compensation committee recommendations today are put under greater scrutiny. Public outcry on the size of bonuses and golden parachutes (termination agreements) is growing louder. Michael Ovitz, president and COO of Walt Disney Co., received a $140 million severance payment after less than two years on the job. Robert Nardelli, CEO of Home Depot, received over a $200 million severance while the stock price dropped 6% during his short tenure. The Lehman Brothers board approved more than $100 million in payouts to five top executives as the firm went bankrupt in 2008. The business media and press rightfully continue to question the value of these packages. Compensation committees are starting to listen and take their fiduciary duties more seriously.

If you ever serve on a compensation committee or interface with this committee there are several caveats to remember. First, committee members must perform good due diligence. Make sure you fully understand the employment contract, especially the termination clauses. Second, outline the long-term sustainable performance criteria. Construct long-term incentives for delivering results and make provisions for not delivering as promised. Third, be very careful using compensation consultants' recommendations. They will tend to find the highest comparable comp levels and report their results in quartiles. Most directors view their CEOs operating in the top quartile, thus, further bending the comp upward. Avoid the "Lake Woebegone" result. Everyone cannot be "above average." Fourth, get stockholder buy-in. Solicit input from the major investor groups. Finally, apply the rule of reason. Is the compensation package reasonable and proportionate to the value created? Have the directors done their fiduciary duty for the stockholders?

This is primarily a US problem as compensation practices are much more realistic in other parts of the world. The United States' ratio of CEO pay to the average worker pay is a factor of 474:1. In other countries it is on average 40 times less (Germany 12:1, France 15:1, Japan 11:1, Canada 20:1 Britain 22:1, Hong Kong 41:1 and Mexico 47:1).[7]

There is a growing trend of using non-financial performance measures as a basis for incentive compensation. A study of 317 firms using financial and non-financial bonus programs found an increase in the use of non-financial metrics when:

- There is "noise" in the financial numbers;
- The financials are not trusted;
- In regulated industries such as power companies where there are limits on pricing and returns;
- In differentiator strategies where the financials do not always reflect achievement;
- In quality-orientated firms which are comfortable with using non-financial measures to judge performance.[8]

The researchers found that financial measures predominate with firms using stable defender strategies and those with "powerful" CEOs, as defined by the number of board members appointed by the CEO.

Lack of Knowledge: One of the biggest challenges for board members is getting sufficiently robust firm data and information. Management supplies the data, but the board members must consider the nature of the information. Does the reporting represent the true economic model of the business? Can you trust the integrity of the data? Are there black holes of information? The academic world tells us that there is imperfect and asymmetric knowledge between the managers, who know more, and the owners who are dependent on them for their data. Management creates the information the owners see. The owners do not have direct access to the underlying data. The challenge for the board members is getting good information that provides insight into the performance of the firm and where the firm is heading. Stockholders invest based on future expected performance, so the business data must look forward and not just backward.

In order to approve the enterprise strategy and financial decisions to properly fulfill their board responsibility, the members must know the firm's technology, products, and process. Directors should be familiar with the industry and the competition and need to recognize the capabilities of the management and workforce. Directors must take the time to learn the business, and not just the financials.

One of the authors served on the board of a venture-backed high technology firm in California. The board was comprised of representatives of the major stockholders, three venture capital firms, a large individual stockholder, two firm founders, and the author. He was the only outside board member and was familiar with the firm through consulting and the industry through experience. The firm manufactured and distributed specialized high-tech lighting products used in motion picture projectors, circuit boards, medical instruments, rear projection TVs, and other technical products.

During the early stages, board meeting reports focused on cash burn rates, explaining the technology, manufacturing process, and key customer interest in the products. With minimal sales revenue, the prime concern was the monthly rate of invested cash use. The three venture capital board members, holding the majority of stock, were not familiar with the industry or the technology but were experts in financing. Those familiar with the technology and industry were excited about the future potential and attempted to communicate this enthusiasm to the venture capital firms. The assessment of the firms' future expectations varied widely. In order to help focus on the future, the author and the management team developed a business scorecard. In addition to the typical financial metrics, they tracked progress along the manufacturing development curve, the number of new adoptions, the number of new and repeat customers, the number of new products made, the progress of the work force talent development, and movement along the business plan time line. This bundle of non-financial data helped the board to understand the firm better, monitor its progress, and project its future results. The experienced venture capital members were amazed by the insight the non-financial data offered. At the early development stage of a firm's growth, the knowledge and understanding gained from the financials lag significantly. In early stages, the financials are not good predictors of success. There is a clear need for non-financial leading indicators.

From our experience we suggest that board members get to know the key members of the management team. Look for consistency in information and possible omissions. If you vary your sources of information, oversight and inconsistency will become apparent. Develop sources of knowledge about the industry and the competition. With SOX regulations, the lack of knowledge is no longer an excuse for fraud or non-compliance. As an employee or manager, you can help educate the board members about the business. The deeper their knowledge the better they can provide advice and counsel.

Compliance: Today boards are being held accountable for management's lack of compliance to financial, government, environmental, legal, and ethical regulations. Risk management is taking more of a front seat for firms and their directors. The board needs to ensure there are proper counter measures and hedges to mediate the consequence of negative events. They need to make certain that there are adequate controls with good checks and balances in the firm. The Sarbanes–Oxley Act of 2002 places a strong emphasis on internal controls. Directors must monitor management's compliance to SOX and ensure adequate risk management processes are in place.[9] Some boards have created a Risk Management Committee to oversee the risk mitigation process.

The mission critical role of the board members is to set the tone for risk management. The directors signal management on the importance of compliance, including ethical behavior, firm reputation, and franchise value. The atmosphere for risk is set at the top. If board members do not take risk seriously, then do not expect management to manage the firm's exposure. Test the risk compliance controls occasionally. This may reveal some weakness in the system that is not detected with ongoing monitoring. Finally, make sure there is a program that provides the escalation of unresolved risk exposures to the board of directors. This is achieved through open communication and access. The managers and the directors own the enterprise risk.

We always advise members of volunteer boards to make certain they have directors' insurance. Director and officer insurance provides financial protection for directors and officers of the organization in the event they are sued in conjunction with the performance of their duties. Depending on the nature of the organization (a community play company, a social agency, a religious group, an environmental group, and so forth), there are compliance risks. A community social help agency had a small full time professional and administrative staff along with a large number of volunteers. During a routine tax audit, it was discovered that the agency had failed to pay withholding tax for a significant number of employees over a number of years. The agency did not have the money and protested the IRS claim. The all-powerful IRS held the volunteer directors (with no director's insurance) personally responsible for the tax debt. Imagine receiving this notice in the mail! Directors have a fiduciary responsibility for the organization.

Independent Auditors: In the recent spectacular failures of Enron, Tyco, World-Com, Lehman Brothers, and others, one must ask the question, "Where were the independent auditors?" One of the cornerstones of governance is the use of independent auditors, reporting to the board of directors, usually through the board finance or audit committee. They serve to verify the financial reporting and compliance to government and accounting rules. On paper, this looks reasonably acceptable. The reality, however, is quite different. The accounting firms are selling their services to the companies and generally work closely with the CEO and CFO of the firm.

The audit firm negotiates the scope and cost of the audit with the firm and then presents the arrangement to the board. The day-to-day details and confirmations are done between the finance function members and the audit team. The CFO and audit partner oversee the operation.

The firm's CFO demonstrates the accuracy and appropriateness of the financial accounting to the outside auditors. Those auditors were engaged to review the company's operation by the board, but the details of the engagement were screened by the CFO. Do you see a real potential for conflict? What an embarrassment to the CFO when the audit firm cannot confirm or validate the firm's financial reports and practices to the board. None of the spectacular failures mentioned above were discovered by the audit firm. Discovery came from individuals blowing the whistle. We believe that the CFO can fool the auditors with a success rate of about 95%. Certified financials really say we certify the data we are shown as correct and the firm followed generally acceptable accounting practices. The close relationship between the Enron management team and Arthur Anderson, the auditors, led to Arthur Anderson's blind acceptance of management's accounting. This failure of oversight led to the collapse of Anderson.

Individual Roles: A potential major structural flaw in some firms is when one person fills the job of Chief Executive Officer (CEO) and Chairman of the Board (COB). This is a common practice in the United States with 55% of listed firms. The same individual is acting as the lead agent and as the lead owner (stockholder) of the same firm. This is a concentration of power that works if flexibility and quick response are needed. But power can corrupt if unchecked. Richard Grasso, filling both the CEO and COB roles, is blamed for compensation abuse at the NYSE. Are the stockholders' interests better served with the dual role structure? Many academics maintain that division of the roles is better for the shareholders.[10] In the United Kingdom, separation of the roles is encouraged and is the common practice.

Conclusion

Governance structure and operation sets the tone for the organization's ability to execute the strategy. The lack of attention to details or opaque structures will encourage the same in the firm. The role of the board of directors is critical in reviewing, evaluating, and approving the strategic direction. A set of well-structured checks and balances ensures that management leads the firm to the intended target. Pay attention to the rules of engagement. Board members must be independent and have the ability to freely challenge management. Compensation and Audit Committees have very serious fiduciary responsibility that can no longer be delegated to management.

Directors must know the industry, markets, the competition, and the firm. Use a combination of financial and non-financial metrics to diagnostically evaluate management's performance. In today's world, compliance necessitates clear separation of duties and active participation by directors. Board seats are no longer honorary positions. They come with serious responsibility and serious consequences if not properly executed.

Notes

1. There is a very large volume of work discussing governance. The issues are more about execution. The concept is rather straightforward. Here are some of our favorite works in this area: Lawrence, P.R. and Lorsch, J.W., *Developing Organizations: Design and Administration*, (New York: Addison-Wesley, 1969). This is a classic on the subject. Epstein, M.J. and Hanson, K.O. (eds.), *The Accountable Corporation* (4 volumes), (Westport, CT: Greenwood Publishing Group, 2005). This is an excellent comprehensive reference. Salmon, W.J., Lorsch, J.W., and Donaldson, G., *Harvard Business Review on Corporate Governance*, (Boston, MA: Harvard Business School Press, 2000). Lorsch, J.W. and Tierney, T.J., *Aligning the Stars: Organizing Professionals to Win*, (Boston, MA: Harvard Business School Press, 2002). Carter, C.B. and Lorsch, J.W., *Back to the Drawing Board: Designing Corporate Boards for a Complex World*, (Boston, MA: Harvard Business School Press, 2004). Charan, R., *Boards that Deliver*, (San Francisco, CA: Jossey-Bass, 2005).
2. For a complete technical overview of agency theory, see Jean-Jacques, L. and David M., *The Theory of Incentives: The Principal-Agent Model* (Princeton: Princeton University Press, 2002).
3. Bethany, M. and Peter, E., *The Smartest Guys in the Room* (New York: Penguin, 2003), p. 410.
4. Kelly, K., Craig, S., and Dugan, I., "Grasso Quits NYSE Amid Pay Furor," *Wall Street Journal* (Sep. 18, 2003)
5. Gasparino, C., *King of the Club: Richard Grasso and the Survival of the New York Stock Exchange*, (New York: Harper Collins, 2007) recounts the story in excellent detail.
6. From the testimony of William H. Donaldson to the United States Senate Committee on Banking Housing, and Urban Affairs Concerning Improving the Governance of the New York Stock Exchange (Nov. 20, 2003).
7. Chattman, J., "The Orgy Continues: American CEOs pocket billions more in pay and perks," www.wsws.org (Apr. 14, 2005).
8. Ittner, C.D., Larcker, D.F., and Rajan, M.V., "The Choice of Performance Measures in Annual Bonus Contracts," *The Accounting Review*, vol. 72, No. 2 (Apr, 1997), pp. 231–255.
9. COSO, the Committee of Sponsoring Organizations of the Tredway Commission provides excellent guidelines and frameworks, the COSO model, for managing risk.
10. Lodere, C.F. and Waelchli, U., "Protecting Minority Shareholders: Listed versus Unlisted Firms," ECG-I Finance Working Paper No 133/2006.

Chapter 7
Internal Strategy: Organizational Structure

Modernist architects coined the maxim that form follows function. The emphasis on essential supporting structures applies equally to designing an effective MSDR. The various parts need to elegantly support, and facilitate, the underlying organizational structure and institutional way of thinking. There's nothing prefab about this. Structures directly affect the contextual nature of delivering results. System designers need to consider the nature of the management team, the reporting relationships, the motivation of the managers, the relevance of geography, the nature of the products, the segmentation of markets, and the flow of feedback information. The key to structure is to align the organization's parts to achieve the corporate strategy. The MSDR must serve as a flexible framework for strategy implementation.

Organizational Structures

The organization's structure has everything to do with the execution—and ultimate success—of the strategy. Whether small startups or large multinational corporations, firms impose an organizational structure to get the work done. These range from a simple functional hierarchical structure to a complex matrix organization. How do the operating units need to be organized to deliver value to the target customers? What structure will support that organization? What is its blueprint? As mentioned earlier in Chapter 4, centralized structures are usually best for defender strategies and decentralized structures work well for aggressive-leader strategies. Let's examine the foundation of structure with a closer look.

Managers with whom we deal often think of their organization's structure as the organizational chart—the set of formal reporting relationships and the hierarchy of authority. It is important to recognize, however, that this set of formal relationships doesn't always capture the pathways through which tasks are defined and work gets done. Since we are centrally concerned with strategy implementation and execution in this book, the way work gets done is important to our discussion. The MSDR must acknowledge and adjust how the parts of the organization fit together and work together to achieve strategic results.

There are really only two basic approaches to structuring a company—a functional approach or a market-oriented, value-chain approach. In a functional approach, the primary distinction used to divide up the work is an internal view of the type of activity to be performed. Thus, groupings like manufacturing, marketing, and administration are the major separate "components" of the organization. These functional areas are then further broken down into smaller, more specialized task areas.

Figure 7.1 provides a general functional organization chart. Note that the functional approach closely corresponds to traditional business majors (like finance and operations) and professional designations (like salesman or accountant).

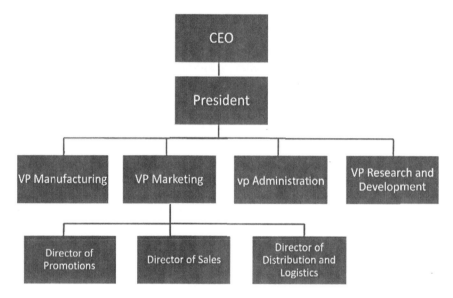

Fig. 7.1 A simple functional organization structure

A market-oriented organizational structure divides work units by their external focus, that is, their value chain links beyond the company boundary. In its pure form, this is a teamwork view, where the tasks are the products, services, or market segments. Note that, for the employees' specialization to be about the market, every person in the organization would have to be a functional generalist—taking orders, producing the goods or providing the service, purchasing the inputs, shipping the product, and billing the customers. It is difficult to conceive of this kind of "pure market-orientation" form of organizing to be applied to any company but a small entrepreneurial business, like a "mom & pop" convenience store. Instead, we typically see a version of this sort of organization in a larger company that has multiple business units. The entire operation is divided into several market-oriented sub-units, but each business unit has its own internal structure that is functional. Figure 7.2 illustrates an organization chart for a simple market-oriented structure applied to a multi-unit company.

Very few large businesses can operate on a purely functional basis. Imagine Hewlett-Packard or Bank of America organized on a purely functional basis. While

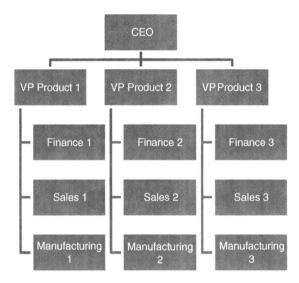

Fig. 7.2   A typical market-focused organizational structure

it is natural that there would be some functional specialization, it is equally natural for these companies to be split up into separate groups based on product type (PC versus printer) or market segment (retail banking versus business loans).

In practice, the vast majority of companies must use a combination of both the functional and the market-oriented approaches. The functional approach allows for greater efficiency and technical expertise, but the market focus encourages greater effectiveness and market expertise. In the early 1990s, Johnson & Johnson was still a loose amalgamation of separate businesses. In fact, the company referred to itself as "a family of companies." This approach was clearly effective. Among the separate J&J's companies, MacNeil Consumer Products was a leader in over-the-counter medications, like Tylenol; Lifescan was a market leader in medical devices related to diabetes; Johnson's was a leader in baby products, like it's "No more tears" shampoo. Each of these business units remains a leader in its respective field today. However, many common "back room" functional operations were consolidated in the mid-1990s. This allowed J&J to markedly improve the efficiency, for example, of its receivables and payables management. The trick to such a reorganization was that a distinction had to be drawn between the critical market-focused specializations and the critical efficiency-oriented functional specializations that did not distinguish one business unit from another across their markets. Thus, in the end, the primary consideration in determining the mix between functional organization and market-oriented organization is strategy.

There is a third form or organizational structure that is a full hybrid of the functional and market-oriented approaches. This is called a matrix organization. Unlike the form depicted in Fig. 7.2, a matrix organization implies that each person in the organization is simultaneously a member of a market-oriented team and a member of a specific company-wide function. The key characteristic is that everyone has a joint set of responsibilities—one to the product, project or business unit and another to the corporate function. Figure 7.3 illustrates a simple matrix structure.[1]

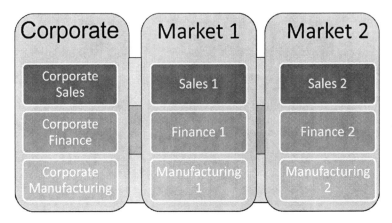

Fig. 7.3   A simple matrix organizational structure

Organizational Structure and Strategy

Each strategy essentially needs its own business unit. This is not to say that there is a single way to organize for any strategy! Recall that we have already established that the organizational culture and external context (including, for example, competition and customer power) will influence how the strategy will be best executed. What we mean by the statement that each strategy needs its own business unit is that a starting point for coming up with an effective and efficient organizational design is to be clear about how many strategies your company has.

In Chapter 3, we argued that strategy was about market positioning. Thus, it makes sense that if your company has a particular market position it is trying to establish and maintain, it would be appropriate to have a market-oriented business unit to support that focus. If a company has only one business strategy, then the whole company is that market-oriented business unit. But many companies actually have multiple strategies that are hierarchically related. That is, there may be several business units each with its own business unit strategy focused on different products or markets. These will all operate under a general strategic umbrella, the corporate strategy.

Corporate Strategy Versus Business Unit Strategy

Corporate strategy refers to the selection of businesses that the firm pursues and the allocation of corporate resources to those businesses. The challenge of corporate strategy is to determine the advantageous strengths that the corporate body can bring to bear across different markets and then come up with a way to exploit those strengths. At one end of the spectrum, a company may focus its energy and resources on a single industry and market segment. You are most likely to have run across a firm like this in a local market, like a small chain of restaurants.

At the other end of the corporate strategy spectrum, a company will spread its resources across many businesses in many different industries and markets. These are conglomerates or holding companies. Berkshire-Hathaway is an example of this kind of firm. It operates in businesses as diverse as insurance and home furnishings. Furthermore, it is even diversified in those industries, owning separate and distinct company units that serve different markets within each industry.

Business unit strategy refers to how a business competes in its industry. A business unit strategy addresses four questions:

1. What is the product or service you sell?
2. What is the target market for this product or service?
3. What is the customer value proposition (why would those customers buy what you offer)?
4. How do you make money selling that product or service to those customers for that value proposition?

As implied above, not many large businesses can operate under one business unit strategy for long. Even apparently single-focus businesses like, for example, Staples or Starbucks, soon find that they have developed skills and resources that can be applied to new market segments or new businesses altogether. In Chapter 4, we mentioned ADP as a company that made a concerted effort to remain focused on its core data-processing business. But over time ADP discovered that it made sense to segment its activity into businesses focused on different-sized customers and different kinds of customer services.

When the variety of products or services becomes large enough to require different business unit strategies, it makes sense to establish different business units. When more than one target market is established, implying that a new value proposition is required, it also makes sense to establish different business units. When we speak of centralized versus decentralized organizations, we are really talking about the number of business units in the organizational structure. The more business units there are and the more autonomous their decision-making is, the more decentralized the firm is.

Note that "different business units" is not the same as different businesses! Hewlett-Packard sells many different types of laser printers and will have a "node" on its organization chart for each printer product family. These are not different business units. However, the main business division that manages those laser printer lines, the Imaging and Printing Group, does contain multiple business units.

Let's take a look at how a company like HP could configure its organization structure to map to its various business units strategies. Figure 7.4 depicts a segment of an organizational structure like HP's, which contains three major market-oriented business groups (Personal Systems, Imaging and Printing, and Technology Solutions) in addition to several functional groups which provide "across the organization" service and support (Finance, Marketing, IT, HR, R&D, etc.). Each of the three major market-oriented business groups can be viewed as a different business, although they are certainly related and complementary. Within the Imaging and Printing Group, there are five business units. Figure 7.4 shows the business units within the Imaging and Printing Group to be entertainment, digital photography, laser printers, inkjet printers, and printing supplies. Each of these arguably has its own target market and customer value proposition. Drilling down further into a business unit, it makes sense to establish additional organizational units (shown as nodes on the organization chart) for each product type. This shows up as color lasers and monochrome lasers within the Laser Printers unit at HP. It is unlikely that those two nodes on the organization chart would be viewed as having different enough target markets or value propositions to be treated as different business units. Nonetheless, it will be useful for HP, from the point of view of managing the activities, to have people specialize in one area or the other. In fact, it may even be valuable to specialize at a finer level, perhaps even at specific inkjet printer lines.

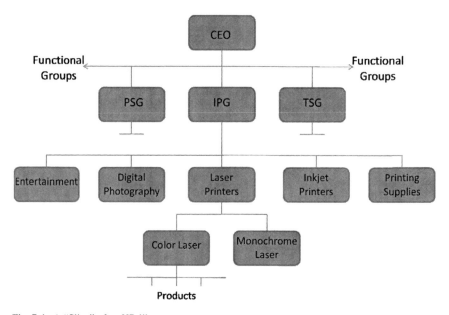

Fig. 7.4 A "Slice" of an HP-like structure

Administrative activities often parse into functional departments. Their jobs are to support the corporate strategy—building skills and competencies that can be exploited throughout the various business units. For example, marketing efforts at HP are separated into a matrix combination of value chain and functional departments. That is, marketing is distinct from sales, but market promotion and sales for a particular product line are formally linked through some kind of reporting and work relationship.

So, if the organizational structure is designed to reflect the variety of business unit strategies, this raises two fundamental questions for the MSDR. First, how does the MSDR coordinate efforts to execute the business unit strategies? Second, how does the MSDR provide feedback about the effectiveness of those efforts?

We focus on the first question in Chapters 8 and 9. Over many years, we have been observing and advising firms on the mechanism for coordinating strategic work across organizational units. While the organizational structure makes some strategic work easier to execute, it also creates problems for coordination.

As to the second question, it makes sense that, at a minimum, there are some financial outcome measures related to each organizational unit. We spend the remainder of Chapter 7 on that topic.

The Effect of Structure and Financial Performance Measurement

A theme of this book is that MSDR systems encompass far more than financial metrics and performance targets. Nonetheless, every business will have a set of financial measures that managers watch. Regardless of the intended use of those financial measurements and the accounting techniques and definitions used to compile them, the accounting data will affect how managers throughout the organization perceive problems and how they try to solve them.

Accounting numbers do have a pivotal role in the evaluation of company performance. After all, the final test of whether or not the organization has succeeded is its ability to earn a profit. If only for this reason, accounting is the ultimate organizational measurement system. It is a pretty safe bet that your company puts some serious effort into assessing whether it is going to "hit the numbers" and, if not, why not.

More than that, though, accounting provides trailing-edge measures for analysis of wider strategic issues. Reflection on what led to quarterly results, for example, can be used to determine new courses of action. That is, the accounting results can be used as very general feedback—red flags really—that help keep activities oriented toward company goals. They are "final scores" on the effectiveness and efficiency with which those goals were pursued, if not a play-by-play analysis.

One company we know performs this kind of profits-to-strategy review on each quarter's results. One line of enquiry is feedback on the strategy execution. Did profits fall short because of a shortcoming in market penetration or quality improvement? Such a result points to the need for increased focus on execution. Another line of enquiry is feedback on the strategy itself. Did the expected profits materialize? If so, were there causative factors other than good execution of the strategy? Are those factors likely to be repeated? Do they represent new opportunities for which the strategy ought to be adjusted? If the expected profits did not materialize, was the execution of the strategy on target? If so, maybe it is not an effective strategy!

Beyond simply measuring a business unit's performance, accounting numbers can be used to evaluate the job the unit's management is doing. Managers perceive (often rightly) that accounting results are prime measures of their performance, their management scores. Insidiously, managing the accounting results (as opposed to operational outcomes) can sometimes become the focus of managerial efforts itself. This, of course, defeats the purpose of performance measurement.

Accounting-based controls were originally devised in environments where management could be more directive and prescriptive than it can today. Back then, competition, product life cycles, and the knowledge needed to execute business plans were more stable. The roles played by various members of the organization were well defined (under functional specialization). Think of this situation as General Motors in 1958. With high volumes of uniform products produced for mass consumption, most manufacturers were concerned with low production costs over long product lives. Thus, it was possible, in many cases, for senior management to know what needed to be done and to devise accounting control measures that both directed subordinates' attention toward those things and encouraged them to take action. Of course, few companies today would characterize their operating environment as stable and predictable. Furthermore, the competitive battleground has become more and more about standing out from the pack on dimensions other than (or in addition to) low price. Thus, low cost is not the primary objective across the organization today. Profit cannot be programmed.

Even if we believe that financial measures are no longer sufficient for the task of delivering results within an MSDR system, we do not believe that they are passé. On the contrary, everyone knows how important the bottom line is.

The trick to updating these systems is to increase everyone's focus on how they contribute to just that—the bottom line.

Delivering Results and Responsibility Accounting

Responsibility accounting is a means to accomplish that connection between managers and the bottom line. Responsibility accounting is the name given to the traditional idea that the delivery system should only measure things that the manager of the business unit can control or influence. We are still talking about accounting here, so the basic reports are about financial outcomes. Generally speaking, those financial metrics can be revenues, expenses, and assets. Traditionally, responsibility accounting systems are classified into three different groups. Where a manager's direct financial influence is limited to costs (as in a production department), the straightforward set of financial metrics is costs. That department would be called an expense center in responsibility accounting terms. Similarly, if a manager's direct financial influence is limited to revenues (as in a sales department), his or her department would be considered a revenue center. Revenue centers are often considered the same type of responsibility center as expense center, since they employ the same type of financial reporting mechanisms. Moving up a level in breadth of responsibility, managers with responsibilities that include both expenses and revenues are said to manage the second basic type of responsibility center, a profit center.

Finally, the broadest set of managerial influences includes authority over the investment in business unit assets. Managers at this level are said to oversee investment centers.

Note that an independent business is, by definition, an investment center. There is a general assumption that the kind of decision-making freedom and attendant authority and responsibility associated with an investment center encourages entrepreneurial behavior—motivated, creative, opportunity-seeking action. Expense or revenue centers, on the other hand, are viewed as constraining environments, where managers are forced to behave in a bureaucratic and politically motivated way. Thus, there is a tendency in many firms to "elevate" expense centers to simulate profit centers and to redefine profit centers to resemble investment centers. We examine the three different kinds of responsibility centers below.

Expense Centers

The standard measures of expense center activity are, as you would expect, departmental expenses, expressed both in total and in relation to planned or budgeted amounts. A great deal of thought has gone into how to analyze those differences from budget (budget variances) so as to separate the effects of purchase price, consumption efficiency, and demand volume. Measurements of this sort are, for the most part, focused simply on efficiency of execution, not issues related to strategic choice. Even worse, some budget-based measures encourage managers to contribute to overall inefficiency by measuring their departmental spending in isolation. We won't spend any time here reviewing those techniques.[2] We will focus, as always, on delivery of strategic results.

If a business unit's processes must map to strategy, then all parts of the firm should focus on achieving the strategic intent and every manager should understand the role they must play to produce the desired strategic results. But for managers who are basically responsible for expenses (or, in a sales organization, for revenues), financial measures do not do a good job of reflecting strategy execution. Simply monitoring and measuring only the inputs consumed (or generated) in their departments will not necessarily help them stay on track to achieving the overall strategic goals. That is, how much you spend tells you little about either the strategic results you have achieved or the effectiveness of your strategy implementation. The gross sales you booked tell you little about the strategic penetration of the target market or the delivery of the customer value proposition.

Figure 7.5 illustrates some expense center tasks. Note that the available financial measurements reveal little about the results of strategy execution or even, for that matter, about whether the strategy was executed. In fact, the only thing clear about the strategic results of these support activities is that they are challenging to identify! In these situations, an MSDR will go beyond financial reporting and create a set of non-financial measures to reflect the strategic contributions. Even so, it is very difficult to measure effectiveness when activities are not directly related to strategy.

Department Type	Input $	Output $
Support Activities		
Accounting/Finance	Expense $	Collections $?
Human Resources	Expense $	None
Law	Expense $	Legal awards $?
Development	Expense $	None
Procurement	Expense $	None
Primary Activities		
Inbound logistics	Expense $	None
Manufacturing	Expense $	None
Outbound logistics	Expense $	$ value of Shipments
Marketing Sales	Expense $	Revenue $
After Sales Service	Expense $	Warranty expense $

Fig. 7.5 Financial measures in expense/revenue centers

As we will discuss in Chapters 8 and 9, balanced measurement systems can be developed to evaluate these often-nebulous types of activities.

Let's illustrate this discussion with some numbers. Assume the annual total expenditure for outbound logistics in Exhibit 7.5 was $100,000. Of course, this number means little by itself. Management might want to compare it to the budgeted expense of $75,000. Under such a comparison, the expenditure for outbound logistics would look bad and there would be pressure to reduce expenditures for outbound logistics in the future. However, perhaps sales were higher than budgeted. Now management would want to compare the expenditure to a budget that would have been in place for higher sales. Maybe that revised budget would be $85,000. The cost of outbound logistics still looks bad. But suppose the increase in expenditures was related to an initiative to gain market share by offering a rapid replenishment system for customers that would allow them to order in smaller amounts, but more frequently. Since outbound logistics costs are driven by number of shipments, not dollar value of units shipped, the total for this category of costs rose dramatically. However, this initiative might have been the reason that sales increased beyond the original budget. The increase in volume may have resulted in lower average production costs and in lower inventory needs at the factory. Overall, profits may have increased specifically because of the actions that resulted in a higher expenditure for outbound logistics. Perhaps a profit number might have captured all of the interconnected parts, but a narrowly focused expense number does not.

Simple expense reporting is irrelevant to strategy execution and encourages political game-playing rather than motivating strategic behavior. If this is true, how should financial results measures be incorporated into the MSDR? MSDRs employing a responsibility center approach often attempt to deal with this problem by imputing profit or investment center status on business segments that are not "natural" profit or investment centers. For example, by defining simulated selling prices for their internal services and charging those rates to the user departments, companies often turn their corporate information technology departments into profit centers. We will incorporate this idea into a discussion of the formulation of profit center measurements, in general.

Profit Center Measures

Business units that have influence over both expenses and revenues are natural profit centers. Think about a copy center that is part of a large chain. The manager of that center oversees direct contact with the shop's customers and production and delivery of goods and services. That manager may not have much influence over asset management, however. Corporate management may determine the number and type of copiers, the furniture and fixtures, and even the paper stock inventory replenishment schedule. That's a prime example of a profit center.

But the copy center manager described above does not have complete control of either costs or revenues. Once again, decisions about promotion and advertising are probably made at corporate headquarters. Likewise, the expenses for building rent and machine depreciation are results of corporate decisions. Nonetheless, it is arguably more strategically motivating for that manager to think about the shop's "profit" than simply the costs that manager can control. That manager is much more likely to consider the overall implications for the copy center's business if a customer makes a request for an emergency copy job late on Sunday for delivery on Monday. On an expense measurement basis, he or she might be only influenced by the expense of overtime. Under a profit center basis, consideration of the incremental profit, customer satisfaction, and, ultimately, repeat business would be included in the decision mix.

If a profit center approach works for a copy center, why wouldn't it work for a factory too? Conceptually, it would make sense, but there is typically one big problem—often, the factory and its management do not actually sell anything and generate any revenue. Instead, that factory's productive output joins other products produced at other factories to be sold by a general sales force. In short, the factory and its management are responsible for product costs, but not revenues. The sales organization is responsible for revenues, but not product costs. Of course, the factory may not sell anything, but that doesn't mean it does not have an effect on sales. Product quality, on-time delivery, and responsiveness to the final customers' design needs are quite critical to generating sales revenue in the final analysis. Thus, both for reasons of motivation and focus of attention, the preferred structure here is the profit center. It motivates a mindset that matches the corporate point of view and directs the manager to consider the strategic consequences of his or her decisions.

So, how do you turn the factory (an expense center) into a profit center? You "simulate" it by creating a hypothetical transaction between the factory and the sales organization! This may sound a bit strange at first, but the vast majority of the profit centers we have seen over the years are of this latter type—a simulated profit center. As academics, we can talk about these arrangements as simulated profit centers, but, in the world of business practice, these are perceived as very real profit centers by their managers.

The reason for "creating" a profit center is straightforward. Driving strategic awareness deep into the organization requires the creation of a "matching mindset" in mid-level managers. Just like corporate managers at the top of the corporation, departmental managers are asked to compare and match expense inputs with revenue outputs to create a kind of simulated version of profit.

Another term for a matching mindset is goal congruence. Generally speaking, goal congruence is thought to be enhanced when managers are evaluated against profit. That is, if managers get a better evaluation when profit goes up, then the manager's goals match the company's. Thus, designers of financially based control systems are likely to try to create artificial profit centers when the manager can influence costs but there are no direct revenue measurements available, as in a factory. The same goes for parts of the business where managers influence revenues but simply *inherit* costs from other parts of the company, as in the case of the sales organization that sells the goods made in the factories. Both kinds of business units will often be redefined as profit centers using some artificial measure of revenues or costs. Let's talk about how this is done.

Simply put, you cannot have a measure of profit unless you have both some measure of revenues and some measure of expenses. The critical link between a department that is primarily a producer and the department which takes its output to sell is a price for the transaction where the goods are moved from one group's responsibility to the other. This simulated price is called a transfer price. The transfer price multiplied by the volume of goods quantifies the sales for the department producing the goods. The same number quantifies the costs for the selling department. Once we have crossed this conceptual divide, we can apply transfer pricing throughout the organization. Parts produced by one manufacturing plant might be sold in an internal transaction to a subsequent plant that uses the component to make another product. Transfer prices can even be applied to internal services that never reach an external customer, such as IT. Often, the reality of this transaction is reinforced by establishing a policy that allows the business unit on the purchase side of the transaction to get price quotes from external suppliers.

Note that transfer prices do not reflect real independent financial events. Since we are examining business units and not complete businesses, these measures of revenues and expenses will not show up in the final numbers used for external financial reporting. Under a profit center approach, business *unit* income is not a real "bottom line," but the managers of the business unit are likely to act as if it is.[3]

While we are on the subject, we should recognize that profit for a profit center can also be simulated through the use of departmental "bottom lines," other than net income—gross margins, or even contribution margins. Often, two measures of profitability will be used. One is a dollar target; the other is a percentage margin (e.g., business unit return on sales).

The use of transfer prices turns expense centers and revenue centers into profit centers. Since managers are evaluated against their business unit profits, they can become quite sensitive to the transfer price in use. A higher transfer price yields more profits to the "seller" and less to the "buyer." A lower transfer price cuts into the seller's profit and increases the profit reported by the buyer. In a situation where a profit center has some real market transactions and some "transfer market" transactions, managers are led to consider the trade-off between efforts to support transfer sales and efforts to develop external sales. The choice of transfer price policy, therefore, can have quite an impact on how managers behave.

A few years ago, a major telecom equipment manufacturer had a huge contract for establishing an extensive telecommunications system in the Middle East. The company employed a transfer pricing system to allow measurement of the contributing departments and divisions. But transfer prices for transactions across political boundaries also often affect taxes. A major goal of this company's transfer price system was tax minimization. Thus, transfer prices were set to record "profit" across international borders in such a way that more profit showed up in the lower-tax jurisdiction and less in the higher-tax country (International laws permit this, but they typically set some criteria for justifiability of the transfer price.)

The equipment manufacturing for this company was based in the United States, but the business unit installing the system was based in the Middle East. In between, there was a European unit that acted as a wholesaler and distributor of the equipment. As a result of this company's transfer prices, the profit from the US-to-Europe transaction was shifted to the European division. That division then added a margin to set the transfer price to the Middle East business unit. As a result, when the Middle East business managers went to buy equipment, prices for the company's high-end equipment in the Europe were higher than those for (inferior) equipment produced by an Eastern European competitor. Because the company's transfer-price system allowed the project team in the Middle East to source its own components, the competitor's equipment was purchased. This enhanced the reported "profit" of the business unit with the Middle East project. The managers of that business unit did what they were supposed to do under a profit center approach. However, it also diminished the profit of the corporation as a whole. Less internally produced equipment was sold, sacrificing potential profits at the producing business unit in the United States. Worse, the actual cost of producing and shipping the equipment internally would have been less than the external supplier's price! By improving its own profits, the Middle East business unit lowered profits for the corporation as a whole. But there is more! In this particular case, there was another casualty. The use of the competitor's equipment soon led to implementation difficulties and system performance problems which required major rework in the Middle East.

Since transfer prices are "made up," they can be anything management desires. As implied above, many companies consider tax and "local content" rules to influence their choices for transfer prices. Another typical approach is to use a cost-based measure, that is, book cost on the production side plus some percentage markup. This often leads to a lack of motivation to reduce costs; so many firms try to employ a market "price" as their transfer price. The transfer price is often adjusted in some way or based on some market-simulating method. Finally, some organizations leave their business units free to work out a solution for themselves, often called a negotiated transfer price.

Economic analysis indicates that the best theoretical transfer price for overall company profit maximization is the opportunity cost of the supplier. In accounting terms, this means that it should be the market price (perhaps less some savings in transaction costs) if one exists, or the variable cost of manufacturing if no market price exists. However, whether they are cost-based, market-based, or some negotiated price, transfer prices should encourage strategic goal congruence. Thus, in the end, the system should be set up not for financial reasons but for how it affects manager behavior.

If using a market price for transfers is best, why don't companies just do that? The fact is that a good external reference price is often very difficult to come by. In a sense, the "product" being sold across business unit boundaries is a function of the organizational structure. It may not correspond to any externally available product or service. Even if it did, there might be a need to get a competitive bid from the outside. This is especially true when the item under negotiation is a unique product or service tailored to the buyer's specifications. Seeking an outside bid comes with some caveats. Sometimes a bidder may set a low price to get a foothold in the market or to use up excess production capacity, or it may toss out a fictional bid, knowing that the work is likely to go to the buyer's sibling division. Even with a market-based transfer price, then, setting a transfer price is not a simple matter.

In the final analysis, there are plenty of reasons to use a simulated profit center format for reporting financial results within an organization. Basically, all of them come down to motivating and directing strategic behavior. However, simulating that profit is often problematical and comes with its own set of executional difficulties and problems.

Investment Center Measures

Another beneficial organizational structure measure tracks the amount and use of the balance sheet assets against the overall output measure to gauge asset-use effectiveness. This is called an investment center approach, where accounting output measures—such as return on net assets, return on capital employed, or return on investment— motivate a manager not only to make a profit through matching expenses with revenue but also to use the assets wisely in achieving a return on investment.

For example, Intel manufacturing facilities (called fabricators or "fabs" in industry parlance) sell their product to the Intel sales organization at a set transfer price. The fab manager is expected to make an internal "matched" profit and a return on the assets employed on that sale. The fab manager must consider the fab expense, the product demand, the transfer price, and the asset utilization of the fab to generate the best return on net assets. Corporate managers are measured on a similar ROI basis and will encourage the fab manager to make the best decision for the manufacturing facility—which should also provide the best results for the corporation. In Intel's case, this generally means using the assets at capacity. The challenge is to make sure managers at the operating level are held responsible for the balance sheet assets.

The use of investment centers grew with the trend toward decentralized organizations, which reached its zenith in the 1960s. The idea was that, especially in a conglomerate, top management could not know enough about any one of its major business units to do a good job of directing them. Instead, corporate headquarters executives set strategic priorities and goals and handed over the direct control of the division to its internal management.

Today, organizations tend to be more focused. Far fewer companies try to operate divisions in many different industries, with a few notable exceptions. For example, General Electric continues to make microwave ovens and jet aircraft engines as well as run a finance organization. Berkshire Hathaway owns insurance companies and furniture retailers. Still, most large companies "divisionalize" to the extent that they identify strategic business units that operate quasi-independently.

There is a bit of faith involved. Top management devises strategies and formulates goals, but often doesn't know the actions that lead to achievement of these ends. Middle and lower management are left to discover those actions for themselves. Thus, the principal problem of delivering results in the modern business organization has become to motivate and direct subordinates to learn ways to execute the strategies on their own.

Divisionalized, decentralized organizational structures would not be so popular if the benefits did not clearly outweigh its costs. The costs of decentralization are that some economies of scale are given up, that some degree of "command" control is given up, and that the divisions must be coordinated using methods other than direct orders. The benefits are basically in the area of managerial behavior. First, division managers have much greater knowledge of their business unit's market(s) and can get information about business operations more directly. Thus, they can make better decisions about each business unit's operations than managers with a wider scope of responsibility. Second, since they are closer to the action, these managers can respond more quickly to market challenges and opportunities. Third, and perhaps most important, managers with more autonomy—and rewards—are likely to have more entrepreneurial spirit and a greater motivation to make their business units perform. In a phrase, their performance is highly visible.

It is the job of investment center measurement systems to both minimize decentralization's negative aspects and capitalize on its strong points. The challenge is to "sweat" the assets employed by the business unit to generate ever-greater free cash flow. Given the "portfolio" nature of the conglomerates of the 1950s and 1960s, it is not surprising that return on investment (ROI) became the measure of choice for investment centers.

In its simplest form, ROI is net income divided by investment. The use of ROI as a performance metric dates back to the early part of the 20th century. Unlike external financial analysis using ROI, internal performance measures cannot rely simply on data in financial statements. Thus, "net income" is strictly related to the business unit under examination. As with profit centers, there must be some surrogate measure of business unit profit. All of the noise inherent in the previous discussion of profit center measurement applies in investment center measures, too. In addition, there is the added complexity of defining "investment." Should the investment include all divisional assets? Should it include only current productive assets (e.g., not those under construction)? Should it include a percentage of current assets managed by the central corporate administration that is used to support the division? Should it exclude the business unit's debt?

Once again, this is a matter to be decided based on the context in which the firm is operating. And to repeat, the objective is to ensure goal congruence. The challenge is to parse assets so that the manager and the unit performance is properly evaluated based on accountability matched to responsibility.

Measures of investment center performance, at least in the United States and Europe, are overwhelmingly limited to a simple ratio of business unit income to business unit investment. The way the numerator and denominator are defined, however, tends to be almost unique for each organization. An alternative to ROI for investment center evaluation is residual income (RI). RI is defined as follows:

RI = Pre-interest business unit profit – (investment base × hurdle rate).

Under an RI measurement, we add another management-determined variable. The hurdle rate is some measure of the cost of capital for the organization. It may be an explicit calculation of corporate cost of capital or it may be a standard set by company policy. Frequently, this is more of a stretch goal than a carefully analyzed one. Hence, we frequently see round numbers used in hurdle rates, like 10%, 15%, or 20%.

RI has a conceptual advantage over ROI as a measure. Since ROI is a ratio measured in percentage terms, it does not, in fact, indicate whether a business unit is contributing more profit to the corporation. That is, under ROI a manager can create a high score by "cherry picking" projects and focusing the investment base to only those very profitable projects. This keeps the return high, but may exclude perfectly good business opportunities that have an ROI well above corporate requirements, but less than the business unit's current ROI. Which would the corporation rather have, a business unit with an ROI of 50% on an investment base of $1 million or a business unit with an ROI of 25% on an investment base of $100 million? Although the manager's actions may not result in such a huge difference, ROI-based evaluation may lead a manager whose business unit has a 25% ROI to reject a new project expected to have an incremental ROI of "only" 20%. The new project would lower the manager's "score." However, if the corporate cost of capital is 15%, the new project would provide incremental income to the company as a whole.

RI takes this effect into account. The hurdle rate indicates the minimum acceptable ROI to the company. Any project with an ROI above the hurdle will result in a higher "score" for the business unit. Use of RI is consistent with most project analyses based on some measure of net present value.

So why don't more companies use RI? Frankly, nobody knows how common the scenario described above actually is. Furthermore, there is already so much arbitrariness in the measures of income and investment that the additional precision of RI may seem wasted. Finally, RI requires a good measure of the long-term cost of capital. Most companies have a hard time estimating this value. If they estimate too low, then investments with negative cash flow will result. If they estimate the hurdle too high, then good projects will be rejected.

A *trademarked* version of RI, EVA (economic value added), has gained a following among large companies. This is the version of RI promoted by the consulting firm of Stern Stewart & Company.[4] It is characterized by special adjustments of accounting income to approximate cash flows, as well as adjustments to the investment valuation and the definition of the hurdle rate. For our purposes, the details of those adjustments are unnecessary. What is important is that the concept of RI has been given a boost in popularity by the ascendance of EVA.

There are financial measurement alternatives to simple expense, profit, and investment center models. One of us saw a rather interesting demonstration of such an alternative in a research study conducted nearly 20 years ago.[5] At the time, US manufacturers were obsessed with the success of their Japanese competitors. Many US firms tried to copy a long list of typical Japanese behaviors. These included not only smart practices like "just-in-time" inventory management but also some rather bizarre activities like morning calisthenics for the production workforce! Nonetheless, US firms persevered in their use of ROI as a measure of divisional success. Interestingly, the research study found that the large majority of the Japanese firms used profit margin, a percentage measurement of a profit center performance. Subsequent analysis revealed that those Japanese firms believed in the importance of ROI, but felt it did not provide clear signals to appropriately motivate and direct the business unit managers. Instead, those manufacturers relied on the combined effect of several policies and measures to drive the desired outcomes. Market planning drove the investment in plant assets, so the top managers did not want the business unit managers to play with that variable. JIT and zero-waste programs "in the trenches" managed down the need for current assets. Target costing was used to plan strategic returns. Thus, the only critical variable that the business unit managers needed to focus their attention on was achieving the return on sales in the plan!

Conclusion

No one should be held accountable for things outside their control. That's why MSDRs scrutinize managers' outcomes only based on resources they actually manage. That is also why a sound organizational structure will partition the organization into work units based on the range of resources a manager needs to bring to bear on achieving the business unit strategy. An effective organizational design pays very close attention to ensuring that accountability is equal to responsibility for each of the units and that there is a real focus on measuring the outputs. Managers are quickly frustrated when they are held accountable for results when they are not responsible for the resources employed to generate the results. Conversely, the strategy is defeated when the measurement of business unit performance introduces irrelevant variables or obscures the underlying set of relationships across organizational unit boundaries. MSDR system keepers must pay very close attention to this simple equation. Managers must make sure they coordinate the activities of the various business units so that the total organization works as a single delivery unit.

   This is particularly challenging in a matrix organization where there is a shared responsibility for results. For example, the product line manager is responsible for the sales and profits across all sales territories for the product. She or he looks at the business from a product point of view. The sales manager, however, is responsible for the sales of multiple product lines in a specific territory. He or she looks at the business through another set of eyes: the customer's. Both are responsible for sales. When targets are not achieved there is often finger pointing, with one blaming the product and the other the sales effort.

   Organizational structure and the related accounting measurement have a profound effect on the execution of strategy. However, it is quite impossible to find a perfect organizational structure that balances effectiveness and efficiency on its own. Likewise, it is impossible to devise an accounting framework that provides sufficient accurate feedback on the execution of strategy. The structure and reporting approach provide the final bit of context to the heart of the MSDR's workings. We now turn to those workings as we discuss the system of measures that provide balance among the activities of the various parts as they align themselves with execution of the business strategy.

Notes

1. As we imply here, matrix organizational structure has become more popular in recent years, given its potential to deliver the "best of both worlds" of organizational structure. We cannot do much justice to the topic here; it's a complicated enough subject for a book of its own. Here are some such books:

   Davis, S.M., Paul R.L., and Michael B., *Matrix*, (Lebanon, IN: Addison-Wesley, 1977).

   Galbraith, J., *Designing Matrix Organizations that Actually Work*, (San Francisco, CA: Jossey-Bass, 2008).

   Gottlieb, M., *The Matrix Organization Reloaded*. (Westport, CT: Greenwood Publishers, 2007).

2. If you are interested in the mechanics of calculating and reporting budget variances, libraries are full of informative literature. Here is a place to start—a section of a book written by colleagues of ours:

   Livingstone, J.L. and Theodore G. *The Portable MBA in Finance and Accounting* (3rd edition) (New York: John Wiley and Sons, 2001).

   Here are a couple of references you can access through the Internet.

   A "primer" type article: http://articles.bplans.com/index.php/business-articles/growing-a-business/plan-vs-actual-part-3-understanding-variance-analysis/

   And an extensive bibliography: http://maaw.info/VarianceAnalysisArticles.htm

   Also, you should be aware of a growing rejection of the idea of managing through annual budgets and budget variances. A primer reading for this is

   Hope, J. and Robin F., *Beyond Budgeting: How Managers Can Break Free from the Annual Performance Trap*, (Cambridge: Harvard Business Press, 2003).

   You can find more about this from many organizations and web sites that have been fostering development of this idea. Here are a couple of them: http://www.themanager.org/knowledgebase/Finance/Beyond_Budgeting.htm

   http://www.juergendaum.com/bb.htm

3. This is another area that has received lots of examination by business researchers and practitioners over the years. There is a rich trove of background reading available. Here are a few to get you started. First, a classic article on the issue:

Goetz, B.E., "Transfer Prices: An Exercise in Relevancy and Goal Congruence," *The Accounting Review*, Vol. 42, No. 3 (July, 1967), pp. 435–440.

Here are some more recent books on transfer pricing:

Abdallah, W.M. *Critical Concerns in Transfer Pricing and Practice*, (Westport, CT: Greenwood Publishers, 2004).

King, E., *Transfer Pricing and Corporate Taxation*, (Brookline, MA: Springer, 2009).

4. If you have an interest in learning more about EVA as an evaluation method, here are two places to start:

Stern, J.M., John, S.S., and Irwin, R., *The EVA Challenge: Implementing Value-Added Change in an Organization*, (New York: John Wiley, 2003).

Stern, J.M., Irwin R., and John S.S., *Against the Grain: how to succeed in Business by Peddling Heresy*, (New York: John Wiley, 2003).

5. Scarbrough, D.P., Nanni, A.J., Jr., and Michiharu S., "Japanese Management Accounting Practices and the Effects of Assembly and Process Automation," *Management Accounting Research*, Vol. 2, (1991), pp. 27–46.

Part III
Measuring What Matters

Chapter 8
Performance Measurement Systems

Over time, performance measurement metrics have evolved. Departments and people found it hard to relate performance to finance and accounting results alone. And they wanted more specific, actionable data: measures that were predictive and motivated certain actions, systems to monitor external factors such as customers, competition, and markets. Some wanted to track the progress of the firm's degree of innovation. What emerged was a comprehensive measurement and feedback system most commonly known as balanced scorecards. There are many versions of scorecards. We focus on the proper use of measurements and the critical design consideration necessary for successful scorecard implementation.

Recognizing the Power of Non-financial Measures

With an increasingly complex business environment, financial metrics alone were not capturing true performance. Managers encouraged by the use of such non-financial measures as productivity, speed, quality, on-time delivery, and customer satisfaction were quick to roll out other innovative measurement programs. They rightly believed that workers could relate their activities to operational measures. Financial metrics were backward looking, often complex, and rarely directly related to an individual or group's actions. Meantime, the total quality movement demonstrated that quality and operational measures were good predictors of business outcomes.

Front-line managers, particularly, realized the value of better metrics to record performance data and to motivate behavior. Traditional financial accounting measures, however, have remained highly relevant to those at the top of the organizational pyramid.

Today's balanced measuring systems include a mix of results indicators, direct operational measures, and other metrics that capture the key success factors of the firm. Balanced does not mean an equal proportion of measures from all possible measurement categories. Rather, it refers to a mixture of financial and non-financial metrics. Outcome measures are normally expressed in various financial terms and ratios. But firms now include measures such as customer satisfaction and on-time

L.P. Carr, A.J. Nanni, Jr., *Delivering Results*, DOI 10.1007/978-1-4419-0621-2_8,
© Springer Science+Business Media, LLC 2009

delivery. Some refer to these as lagging indicators, since they are not predictive. To create balance, another set of measures was added to capture and explain how certain results were achieved. These leading indicators now include cycle time, defects per million, number of customer calls, number of service requests, and shipments per day. Together, indirect financial outcome measures and direct performance measures capture the key success factors for strategic success. This is the heart of managing what matters.

The Evolution of Performance Measures

Today's balanced performance measurement environment has many fathers. Thanks go to such academics as Eccles, Kaplan, McNair, and Nanni[1] as well as practitioners like Keegan, Lynch, and Cross[2]. They developed a balance of operational and financial measures to evaluate business unit performance. These researchers and consultants were strongly influenced by the quality movement, observing that managers who were focused on results had introduced an array of operational and statistical measures, along with innovative financial-assessment techniques. To these, they added new tools and integrated quality measures such as failure rate, defects per lot, yield, statistical process control (SPC), six sigma, and cost of quality. These measures had a powerful influence on people's behavior, as they were more easily understood than financial measures. Further, they gained management support and often complemented the firm's strategic key success factors. Balanced measurement systems created a common language throughout the firm and contributed to improved performance. With such results, many firms have adopted this popular measurement schema.

Among patriarchs of the movement, Lynch and Cross[3] created the architecture and logic for balanced measurement systems with their "smart performance pyramid", as depicted in Fig. 8.1. The triangle demonstrates how corporate visions, as articulated by senior management, drive the attainment of the objectives through the organization to all levels—from business units to business operating groups to departments and work centers. The measures of strategy achievement percolate up through the organization from operations, including staff and line departments. The measures consider both internal and external metrics as a way to calibrate the internal results.

More tools for measuring operational effectiveness came from just-in-time (JIT) procedures and activity-based costing and management (ABC-M). Like quality management, these techniques employ clear physical indicators to manage performance. Simple and clear linkages occur between each level of performance indicators. Such operational measures as high yield, low defect rates, short cycle time, on-time delivery, and high capacity utilization have all helped firms achieve strong financial results. Management just had to pick the key success factors linked to the strategy.

During the same time, management accounting underwent a renaissance. There was a renewed focus on relevant measures and a call for innovative thinking[4].

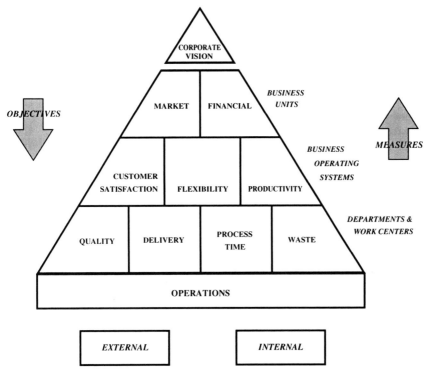

Fig. 8.1 The smart performance pyramid
K. Cross and R. Lynch, "Accounting for Competitive Performance," *Journal of Cost Management for the Manufacturing Industry*, Spring 1989, pp.20–28.

Creative cost management paradigms such as activity based costing (ABC) better linked the operational process with cost or resource consumption. It focused managers on the activities that cause cost and provided relevant data easily addressed by all levels in the organization. Managers studied the cost drivers of their process or business and the size of their cost pools. They identified the value and non-value added activities, isolating those resources not consumed by the service or product process. The data were presented in innovative financial and operational measures that everyone understood. Most importantly, it revealed actions managers could take to improve their operational and financial performance. Both types of measures were used to gauge strategic attainment. For example, one of the key measures for semiconductor manufacturers is the book-to-bill ratio. This is the best predictor of the relationship between demand and supply. It reports whether the industry has more semiconductor orders that it can deliver (a ratio > 1). The ratio is widely published to show the industry production capacity.

Strategy development, meantime, underwent its own metamorphosis. As mentioned, Michael Porter advanced his five forces method of assessing strategic position.[5] He introduced yet another set of non-financial measures to determine the attractiveness of industries. Widely adopted since, his model offered managers a more meaningful method to arrange and analyze the data from the industry and their firm. Porter recognized the importance of a firm's financial configuration with his structural and executional cost drivers. These considerations, coupled with the five forces assessment and a SWOT analysis, provided management the individualized data sets necessary for intelligent strategy formulation.

Porter's work was, in turn, extended by efforts to harmonize strategy with the right management decisions and firm actions. One of the first efforts to shape this linkage came when John Shank and others built the concept of strategic cost management (SCM) from the Porter model.[6] They linked cost systems and expense structures with the firm's strategy through the analysis of both the industry and firm-level value chains. They recognized that actions require resources and they sought clever measures that linked the firm's spending and cost structure to their chosen strategy. This management breakthrough created more meaningful ways to use finance and accounting data to support decision-making.

The expanding power of information technology facilitated all this data scrutiny, making its collection, arrangement, communication, and analysis much easier. Managers realized the value of using a mixed measurement system and moved quickly to adopt a set of measures that fit their organization. As the movement grew, many consulting firms started offering various balanced scorecard programs and software, making adoption even easier. But as we shall see, real difficulties remained.

Balanced Measurement Systems

As companies struggled to develop their new and robust measurement systems to support the delivery of results, management consulting firms experienced a boom. Such systems were codified and given titles, and academic papers explained their benefits.

Balanced measurement systems came in many flavors: balanced scorecard (BSC), dynamic business scorecard (DBS), and strategic performance gauges (SPG) became the best known. As touted by their promoters, they were designed to trace the short-term and the long-term goals of the organization based on the strategy. Typically, there are six performance areas: market (customers, consumers, competitors), environment (communities, regulatory), people (employees, partners, suppliers), operations (process, technology, systems), adaptability (innovation, learning), and financial (stockholders and regulatory requirements). The group of measures reflects a "holistic" or integrated way of evaluating the implementation of strategy. The emphasis is on balancing, not maximizing one measure, which sometimes comes at the cost of another measure. Management's challenge was to select the measures that best reflected the key success factors of the unit being measured. Corporate, division, and department key performance indicators would probably all be different, but each would reflect the outputs that had to be delivered to achieve strategic goals.

In a series of Harvard Business Review articles and the publication of five books, Kaplan & Norton popularized the concept of balanced measurement systems They offered a specific framework for a measurement system in the implementation of strategy. Called the "balanced scorecard," this framework gives managers and employees a brief, yet thorough, view of their business by complementing traditional financial measurements. They used four structured categories: measures on financial results, customer satisfaction, internal business processes, and the organization's innovation and improvement activities.

They pointed out that financial measures alone cannot indicate whether a company is meeting its long-term strategic goals. For example, what if a company's mission is "to become our customer's most valued supplier?" No financial measure can adequately capture that mission. Other quantitative and qualitative measures must be used. These operational measures, or leading indicators, predict whether the firm will create value for shareholders. Kaplan & Norton's structured framework provides the platform from which these other measures can be articulated and translated into specific goals for management and employees alike. We will use the classic Kaplan and Norton balanced scorecard model as a basic reference point to explain scorecards in general. The critical factor for scorecards and an MSDR system is the design and implementation of the measures. Later in this chapter we address the implementation issues and in Chapters 9 and 10 we focus on the critical element of aligning your measures to the strategy.

To further explore that framework, let's examine the four measurement categories recommended by Kaplan & Norton. Exhibits 8.2 and 8.3 show how the system works—going from vision/strategy/goals; to key success factors; to measures (what you measure); to measurements (how you measure) (Fig. 8.2).

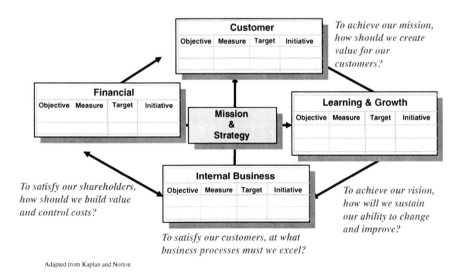

Adapted from Kaplan and Norton

Fig. 8.2 Structure of a Typical Contemporary Balanced Scorecard

1. *Financial Perspective: "How do we look to shareholders?"*
   Although Kaplan & Norton stress that other measures are important in measuring success, financial measures are still a central focus for companies. If a company's strategy and mission are not creating value for its shareholders, then they must be re-examined. Traditional balance sheet, income statement, and statement of cash flow measures capture the financial performance.
   Example: A company sets a business unit goal to double market share while becoming its customer's primary supplier. This goal can be financially measured by completing a market share analysis and comparing it with the economic value added (EVA) of the firm.
2. *Customer Perspective: How do customers see us?*
   The customer perspective is the second view at which a business must consider. A company will prosper only so long as it provides value to its customers. Kaplan & Norton suggest that customers have five primary needs: cost, time, quality, performance, and service. By focusing on these customer needs and measuring whether they are being met, companies can meet their financial objectives.
   Example: The company that wants to double market share while becoming its customer's primary supplier has to find a way to measure if it is attaining the goal of becoming the number one client of its customers. A survey of customers can generate the data to determine if that goal has been met.
3. *Internal Business Perspective: What must we excel at?*
   The company must scrutinize internal processes to meet financial goals and customer needs. Certain internal business measures like cycle time, defects per million, quality control, employee skills and training, and productivity can be used to measure these goals.
   Example: Continuing on the previous example, suppose that the business unit believes that it will reach its goals by being a high-quality manufacturer. The internal business perspective may look at TQM (total quality management) advances and defects per million to measure the unit's success at reaching these goals.
4. *Innovation and Learning Perspective: Can we continue to improve and create value?*
   The competitive landscape demands that companies focus on innovation and learning. Without these advances, financial, customer, and internal process measures cannot be improved and shareholders will not receive the increased value they expect.
   Example: A company's goal to be a high-quality supplier will improve as manufacturing learning occurs and its workforce becomes more skilled (Fig. 8.3).

The ultimate mission of this framework is to make the company's balanced scorecard a transparency of the company's mission statement that is directly applicable to every employee in the organization.

A good example of the BSC at work can be seen at Cigna Casualty and Life, which successfully used the BSC to provide direction at the company, to measure

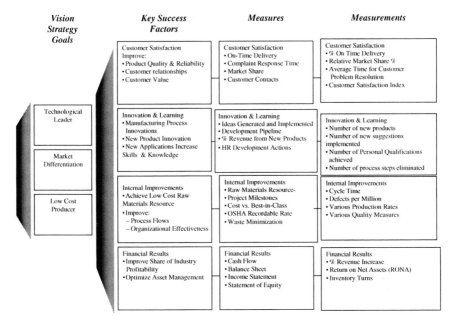

Fig. 8.3 Strategic measurement framework: a generic example

performance improvements, and to motivate managers. Cigna's BSC included the following measures:

- *Financial*: shareholder expectations, operating performance, growth, and shareholder risk.
- *Customer*: producer, policyholder, and regulatory relations.
- *Internal Business Process*: business growth, underwriting profitability, claims management, and operating productivity.
- *Innovation and Learning*: upgrading competencies, information technology support, and support organization alignment.

Cigna's metrics were unique to the company. They moved from losing money with the exclusive use of only financial measures, such as RONA, ROI, EBITDA, and EPS, to making money using a set of financial and non-financial measures. In essence, the firm developed a family of measures that fit their organization and competitive situation and changed the business model. The Cigna success story is held up as the positive benchmark for adopting business scorecards.

IBM was an early adopter of the scorecard measurement system. Its management referred to their categories as portfolios of measures and urged managers to achieve success or balance in each category. IBM's portfolios were ranked in the following order: customer satisfaction, quality, employee satisfaction, and financial results. Management believed they had to make the organization much more customer responsive and sensitive and placed prime importance on measures in this portfolio. They adopted a six-sigma approach to quality and knew this was the hall-mark reputation of the firm. The last portfolio, financial, had once been the only portfolio of performance measurement. The new balanced measurement system had a profoundly positive effect on the IBM management culture and aided the resur-gence of the company. Over a four-year period the stock price increased 80%. In the banking industry, Chemical Bank followed the four Kaplan and Norton per-spectives rigorously. They retained Dr. Norton's consulting firm to develop their balanced scorecard. The chief of retail banking, Michael Hegarty, was concerned with merging the cultures of Chemical Bank and the recently acquired Manufactur-ers Hanover bank. The balanced scorecard created a common goal and supported the culture change. On the other hand, Citibank, an industry leader, developed a bal-anced measurement system for all four of the bank's strategic business units, using seven unique categories of measurements. In both bank cases financial measures were only one of the categories.

In another case, a well-known full line computer company struggling with the technology and distribution changes in the industry used the balance measurement system to help change their culture. Managers were quite skilled in managing finan-cial results. This led to a myopic focus on short-term results and insensitivity to the changing market and competitive actions. This company added such non-financial measures as customer satisfaction, geographic distribution of sale, number of sales calls, and number of new products to their regular reporting system. All the non-financial measures were custom-developed for each of the 14 business units and linked directly to their key strategic success factors. To reinforce senior manage-ment's mandate for change, an incentive system was developed based on the new measures. One senior executive of this firm observed the following: "We are con-siderably more transparent. Much of the mystery of the financial performance is removed. Best of all our unit managers can now relate their performance to mea-sured results." This is the very essence of scorecard measurement systems: They serve as both a historical performance report and a predictor of the future. In gen-eral, the financials tell what happened and the operational measures point to future performance. Indeed, the underlying theory is that if you take care of the operational results the financial results will take care of themselves.

Many firms also use this new approach to performance measurement as part of their culture change program. They recognize the power of measurements to influence the desired behavior and want managers to think and act more strategically.

Balanced Scorecard Insights

Not all managers are believers in the balanced measurement system. In fact, some companies have experienced excellent operational performance results but have not seen corresponding improvement in the financial results. Managers rightfully wonder why good leading performance indicators do not translate into good finan-cial results indicators. Frustrated, they wonder why a shorter cycle time, improved quality, and higher customer satisfaction while achieving sales targets do not result in improved ROI. Why, indeed? This question challenges the basic logic of the balanced measurement system.

Judge for yourself: Going back to one of the 14 business units of the full line computer company mentioned previously, the imbalance between operational results and financial results was very apparent. Despite achieving all operational goals—the targeted customer satisfaction level, the product quality level, the order to invoice or average time for order fulfillment level, and the amount of partner or indirect channel sales percentage—the unit's financial performance showed a significant loss.

Upon investigation, it became apparent that the idle production capacity due to shifts in demand had a very negative impact on the financial performance. The unit was not able to adjust its significant fixed costs to the decreased industry demand. The balance sheet was bloated and the carrying charge expenses to the income statement were significant. Managers maintained they did the best they could, given the industry changes. Corporate management was very dissatisfied with the loss and a greater than 10% miss for the financial targets. Was this a scorecard or a management failure?

The use of non-financial measures in reporting routines presents a number of challenges. The primary questions are as follows: How are they linked to financial performance? Can non-financial metrics predict future financial performance? A number of researchers have challenged the effectiveness of balanced measurement systems.[7] The core of the concern is the selection of the non-financial measures. They often lack an explicit causal model. Are the non-financial measure linked to the key success factors of the strategy? We devote two chapters to this critical issue as this is where most balanced measurement systems break down. The other concern is a simplistic fixation on the "four buckets" of the Kaplan and Norton balanced scorecard. As if they were ordering from a menu in a Chinese restaurant, managers, are choosing measures from column A and measures from column B and so forth, not considering their link to the key success factors of the strategy.

Characteristics of a Good MSDR Reporting System

The concept of a feedback and measurement system is elegantly straightforward. Why, then, are some people frustrated and dissatisfied with the measurement systems they live with? A big part of the reason is that certain aspects of the system are distorted. To avoid scorecards that are out of whack, one needs a set of stable, easy-to-understand characteristics.

Easy to Understand

Simply put, MSDR measurement systems provide feedback to managers, departments, divisions, and individuals with the intent to stimulate the desired behavior. Management wants a certain set of actions and decisions that are consistent with the strategic intent. But in order to get the behavioral effect of a measure it must be clear and easy to understand. This is one of the fundamental problems with the exclusive use of accounting measures. They were not easily understood. Operational metrics such as on-time delivery or product yield percentage are abundantly clear. Operators instantly understand what behavior they need to change to improve the measurement. Ergo, keep the measures simple so that those being measured do not have to ponder the meaning of the measure. Also, it's best to use objective measures that can be expressed numerically. You want a clear line of sight from the measure to the desired behavior. In addition, the data used must be accurate and reliable. Why use the "cost burden rate," a difficult to understand financial measure, when you can use "product yield" data to show the effect on cost performance.

Actionable, Reflect Causality

In the design phase of building a balanced measurement system, managers are inclined to select measures that they are good at or where achievement is accomplished 100% of the time. This does not provide constructive feedback on performance. But it does reflect human nature: If we had a choice, we would prefer not to be measured. Measures, however, should build in a set of expectations that can be calibrated to quality or quantity of performance.

Further, managers and individuals should be held accountable for the area of performance for which they are actually responsible. When we measure performance factors outside the control of the individual or group, frustration and distrust of the measurement system develops. An MSDR system must strive to achieve the formula Accountability = Responsibility (A = R). This is easy to say, but hard to accomplish.

Time to Correct

Learning comes from feedback based on experience. A balanced scorecard compares performance to some agreed-upon standard. Based on the results, we develop an understanding of how we missed our target. We make changes to achieve the measured target. An integral part of the development is to establish the time required to make the changes. Managers need to ask the question "when?"

Frequency is another time component. How often should the measurement episodes take place? In many data-rich environments, continuous measurements are possible. Call centers and telemarketing operations are particularly sensitive to this. There should be sufficient time for the corrective behavior. For example, production yield reports and on-time shipments are done daily. Actions can be altered immediately to improve the results. Customer satisfaction surveys are normally done on an annual basis. There are many factors that influence the customer's experience and it takes time for certain customer improvement programs to make an effect on employee behavior.

Another important consideration is to provide the feedback as close to the event as possible. For example, many firms have pushed the monthly financial reporting to as close to the end of the month as possible. Typically, it takes five days before the monthly financial results are made available to operating units. But some companies, such as Johnson and Johnson, do it in one day. Managers want the results measures close to the event so that they can make corrections for the next period. They want to learn from the previous experience and apply their learning immediately.

Dynamic

Time does not stand still. Strategies change, roles of units change, and individual goals or assignments change. MSDR measures should be reviewed on an annual basis at a minimum to ensure their relevancy and linkages to the key success factors. Measures also have a life span. They can become obsolete or irrelevant. When the target is hit 100% of the time, is it providing valuable feedback for learning and performance? For example, a microchip firm found it was making on-time delivery as measured against the customer requirement 100% of the time. They continued to use this measure but realized a better measure was the ability to meet emergency customer orders, not the regular orders.

The dynamic nature of the measures and the lack of the ability to combine measures, like accounting consolidations, from the lowest unit to the total corporation take some adjustment. Managers are used to looking at comparisons of the same measures, this year's results versus last year's results for any category of cost, revenue, or budget, etc. It is important to ensure the measures are relevant and can influence behavior. Managers must instead consider whether the measures have real meaning.

Limited Number of Measures

It is critical to measure those things that are important and not create a collection of measures. Social science research indicates that humans can only process up to seven simultaneous measures at one time. Beyond that, an individual cannot clearly determine the appropriate action based on the measures. With too many measures, the line of sight from the measure to the behavior is lost. Studies have shown that, eventually, too many measures produce confusion and overload as managers take actions they think appropriate, as if there were no measurement system.

Linkage

A gas pedal needs a connecting rod to the fuel injectors to make the car move forward. Similarly, the various portfolios of indicators should firmly link performance to strategy. The choice and number of measurement categories vary, but should directly connect to the firm's key success factors. It is imperative that senior management ensures the categories are appropriate and actually linked to strategy. There is no real mechanical check on the linkages. Rather, it is based on management judgment and knowledge of the strategy and key success factors. There should be total agreement on the meaning of the goals and measures and what actions people need to take to succeed. Figure 8.4 provides a general outline of the horizontal linkages (strategy → key success factors → what you measure → how you measure) and the vertical linkages which are thematic in nature but connect measures throughout the organization's layers.

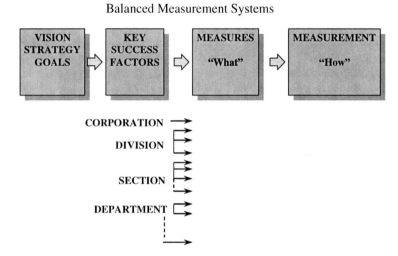

Fig. 8.4 Balanced measurement system linkages

Infrastructure

When launching an MSDR reporting system, adequate resources need to be employed. Typically, accounting software and data are already available in abundance, but a business scorecard uses multiple sources of data. Operational, point-of-sale, customer, and other data sources are also required. Many firms install a data warehouse system like Oracle and attach a reporting system like Hyperion. Several consulting and software firms offer a complete balanced measurement system. Data collection, however, costs money and each firm must determine how much data they really need to run the firm and what they are willing to spend. It is very possible to develop an MSDR system using a set of Excel spreadsheets. In order to keep cost down and reliability up, it's desirable that data collection not be labor intensive.

To get their arms around key data, many firms are using enterprise-wide reporting systems (ERP) to coordinate and mine their various functional and legacy systems. The more popular systems, SAP, People Soft and Oracle, have a business scorecard feature imbedded in their system. Today, we are operating in an information and data-rich environment. The challenge is to obtain sufficient Information Technology (IT) support for the MSDR system.

A critical consideration that needs to be addressed up front is who or what function takes responsibility for managing and maintaining the MSDR reporting system. In many organizations this is the responsibility of the accounting and finance department. However, because of the mixed nature of the measures, in some firms the systems management has fallen to IT, or Strategy, or Knowledge and Information, or a separate "scorecard" department. We believe that the accounting and finance function, working as strategic business partners with line management, should maintain this decision support system. Accounting is responsible for providing sound information for decision-making. The data can be both financial and non-financial in nature.

Method of Reporting

First impressions are lasting. How an MSDR reporting system "looks and feels" is very important. We want to build trust and credibility with any system that provides feedback on performance. Employees want consistent, unbiased, timely reports with a clear distribution. The idea is to create transparency and use the information to manage, not broker the information for power. Typically, this requires good systems discipline. The reports become trusted with a user-friendly format, the distribution is clear, and the availability is uniform throughout the organization. Further, there is data control on the use and accuracy of numeric reports. The intent, like the measurements, should be simple: We want to trust the accuracy and reliability of our instruments.

Organizations that do this well have a sound set of procedures that prevent "gaming" of the facts. They offer a wide distribution of the reports with clear graphical displays. Often scorecards are posted on an internal website with a set of access regulations. The data are made available to everyone. The use of graphics and warning lights (red, yellow, green) make the feedback information quickly understood and require little time to understand.

Implementation

Launching a comprehensive MSDR system is no trivial matter. By its very nature, the system will have a powerful influence on the behavior of people—behavior that management wants to be consistent with the strategy. Managers must therefore make sure that sufficient resources and time are devoted to the implementation. This includes developing an internal marketing and information plan so that all the people in the organization understand the purpose and format of the MSDR system.

We recommend piloting the system so that you can calibrate the instrument. If you are going to use the system for incentives, make sure you baseline the measures so that you can calibrate your measuring device. One of the biggest issues is that the organization must provide the infrastructure to achieve and sustain goals, and not just implement the system. One of the pitfalls for many companies is that they set and communicate goals, and how objectives are to be measured, but then management does not give the front-line workers the tools and resources they need in order to achieve these goals. As an example, production is told to increase capacity by 30%, while capital equipment spending is frozen.

Utilization Rate

An MSDR system acts like a drive system of an automobile. From the engine to the wheels, a car has another set of linkages: the transmission and drive train. Something similar must take place between the operational performance indicators (leading indicators) and the financial indicators (lagging indicators) for a performance measurement system to be both a results tabulator and predictor of performance. The MSDR measurement system is built on this premise.

The financial results are the product of a well-executed set of activities. The linkage between the financial and non-financial measures is critical in establishing the effective relationship between operational metrics and financial metrics. Like a transmission gear, the more direct the linkage, the more the power of predictability. The utilization measures, a third group of metrics for the MSDR measurement system, predicts the degree of linkage between achievement of operational results and improved financial results. It provides an estimate of the effect of improved non-financial measures on the financial results. Utilization measures are defined as the degree of capacity utilization: the amount of process waste, plus fixed cost and working capital utilization. In other words, it is a measure of how well, or efficiently, the balance sheet of the measured business unit is being used. This determines the linkage between operational performance and financial performance. The logic is quite simple: Investors or lenders provide money or capital to managers to invest in a business. The business unit obtains, through the capital budgeting process, fixed assets (such as production facilities and equipment) and builds net working capital, (inventory and accounts receivable minus accounts payable) as the business grows. A satisfactory return on the investment in the business is obtained if adequate profits are made and the invested fixed and working capital is sufficiently used. This is the basic principle of return on investment (ROI) where ROI = profit/investment. Managers want to create the most value (profit) with the given resources (assets or investment). The return on investment is a function of both profit earned and the balance sheet turnover or utilization. If a production facility is running at half capacity there is significant amount of plant and equipment idle and not operating. Fixed assets are not used or working to generate a return. For example, a sporting goods store has an excessive amount of running shoes (6 months supply). This is an increase in working capital, which requires more profit to produce the desired return. From the formula ROI = profit/investment, the investment increases (denominator), but with the same profit, the return decreases.

Utilization measures focus the manager on how effectively he or she is using purchased assets. For example, is the recently acquired printing press that cost $5 million being used more than two hours per shift? The capital budget plan called for six hours' use per shift usage. Managers know that as this equipment sits idle the depreciation or lease payment is still accumulating. Another manager just purchased a $5 million computer network server for the sales and marketing department. If the department does not use the network due to inadequate training or fear of conversion, it is hard to reap the designed productivity gains. These gains are often key to the justification for the capital investment. In both cases, investments were made in a business that is not being properly employed to deliver a unit of service or a product. These firms may have excellent quality and top rated customer service, but the idle and unused resources will not allow improvements in return on investment.

Utilization is a very tangible concept when assessing current assets, such as inventory and accounts receivable. A build-up in these accounts consumes a firm's cash. Many firms have adopted policies and systems such as just-in-time (JIT) to help manage the utilization of these assets. Companies operating in very competitive markets often build systems to produce only on a customer's order, to avoid the costs and risks of holding finished goods inventory. This is becoming the standard practice in the PC industry.

An exact utilization measure is elusive, but can be quite valuable in predicting the effect that operational improvement has on financial results. Precise measurement difficulty arises from the fact that measuring waste or non-value activities or the cost of a firm's unused capacity is quite difficult. It is clear, however, that a firm's resources must be matched to achieving the current and future market opportunities.

The measurement problem starts with defining the baseline capacity. Is it theoretical, practical, normal, budget, or actual capacity? The best reference is the practical capacity. Some, however, recommend starting with theoretical capacity. The next step is to determine what part of the capacity is being utilized. This includes an assessment of the planned idle capacity. Figure 8.5 offers a list of the various available measuring tools.[8] The CAM-I (Consortium for Advance Manufacturing-International), a non-profit cooperative memberships organization, also provides an excellent guide for measuring capacity.

The semiconductor division of a major computer company recently started a balanced measurement system. In addition to financial measures, they adopted many quality measures such as defect rates, percentage yield and process measures such as cycle time and wafer starts per day. The division controller lamented, "These new measures are helping us understand our business better. The product line managers are learning to integrate the financial and non-financial measures. We still, however, need to develop the understanding that profit is directly linked to factory (FAB) utilization. It cost about $1 billion to build and fully equip a FAB. If we are not operating the facility 7 days a week 24 hours a day we cannot make money. This is a very asset intensive business. I am trying to impress this upon the product managers."[9] Because the semiconductor industry is so sensitive to FAB utilization, it is no surprise that industry observers watch closely the "book-to-bill" ratio. This is the industry surrogate for utilization. Executives and industry specialists want to make sure new orders ("book") are arriving at an equal or greater pace than the shipments ("bill") from the facility. They know the key to profitability is factory utilization. If the ratio falls below 1 there is real concern.

Features Model	Capacity Baseline Emphasized	Primary Time Frame of Analysis	Organizational Focus
Resource Effectiveness	Theoretical Capacity	Short- to Long-Term	Process/Plant/ Company Levels
Capacity Utilization	Theoretical Capacity	Short- to Intermediate- Term	Process/Plant/ Company Levels
Capacity Variance	Theoretical Capacity	Short- to Intermediate- Term	Process/Plant Levels
CAM-I Capacity	Theoretical Capacity	Short- to Long-Term	All Levels (Potential)
CUBES	Theoretical Capacity	Short- to Intermediate- Term	Process/Plant/ Company Levels
Cost Containment	Implicit Theoretical Capacity	Intermediate-Term	All Levels (Potential)
Gantt Idleness Charts	Practical Capacity	Short-Term	Process Level
Supplemental Rate Method	Practical Capacity	Short-Term	Process/Plant Levels
Theory of Constraints Capacity	Practical Capacity Marketable	Short- to Intermediate- Term	Process/Plant/ Company Levels
Normalized Costing Approach	Normal Capacity	Intermediate-Term	Process/Plant Levels
ABC and Capacity Cost Measurement	Normal Capacity	Short- to Intermediate- Term	Process/Plant/ Company Levels
Integrated TOC- ABC	Various	Short- to Intermediate- Term	Process/Plant/Value Chain Levels

Fig. 8.5 Tools and techniques for measuring the cost of capacity

At Intel, the company recognizes the power of FAB utilization by concentrating on design for manufacturability. It also closely monitors and ensures that the "book to bill" provides a sufficient continuous volume of orders to support production. One of the reasons for the famous "Intel Inside" advertising campaign was to lessen the sole dependence on sales volume to third parties. They wanted to create demand for their products by end users. Management knew the volume of demand was critical to filling the FAB and producing the financial results required by investors. Because of the very high capital investment and the extreme sensitivity to production volume, the "book-to-bill" ratio was used extensively by Intel to forecast their financial health.

There are numerous other examples where the utilization rate serves as a predictor of the financial effect of operational improvement. The link can be at the plant, SBU, corporate, or industry level. Managers from each segment of the organization

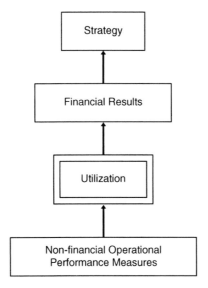

Fig. 8.6 Utilization Rate

use operational numbers to measure performance, and their ability to translate these operational figures to financial results is based on capacity utilization.

Conclusion

Measurement systems are critical to the successful implementation of MSDR systems. Incorporating the appropriate non-financial metrics linked to the key success factors of the business is the heart of the measurement challenge. The development and acceptance of the scorecard concept by managers offers a better set of metrics to measure their path of strategy implementation. The necessary workforce actions and management decisions become clearer with a scorecard. There are numerous published success stories but there are many more accounts of firms troubled with scorecard program implementation.

We offered a number of insights and characteristics of a good reporting system. These guidelines, we find, are more central to the successful implementation of an MSDR system than the choice of scorecard frameworks. There are many ways to foul the implementation of a measurement system: The measures are not easily understood; managers are held accountable for performance with many critical factors outside their control; there are far too many measures blurring what is really important; supporting infrastructure is lacking, or senior management does not fully support the scorecard program. The two most important factors for successful implementation of a scorecard system are ensuring the measures link to the key success factors and the utilization of the firm's assets.

There is a wide array of non-financial measures from which to choose. Managers must focus on the critical few measures that directly link to the key success factors of the strategy. We need a concentrated beam of light (measures) that stimulates action, not a broad beam of defused light unable to focus on and illuminate the central issues. Choosing measures is very tricky. Left to our own devices, we will choose the things we are good at, with the measures readily available. These measures may or may not be important.

Non-financial metrics are reasonable predictors of financial success if the asset utilization rate is reasonable. If there is significant excess of capacity or very sloppy management of the balance sheet resources, good non-financial metrics will not predict good financial results. The connection between the two types of metrics is weakened. We will next look at how you can use the business scored measures and process as a strategic alignment tool.

Notes

1. Eccles, R.G., "The Performance Measurement Manifesto" and R.S. Kaplan and D.P. Norton, "The Balanced Scorecard – Measures That Drive Performance" were both published in the January-February 1991 edition of *Harvard Business Review*. Nanni, A.J., Jr., Dixon, J.R., and Vollmann, T.E., "Integrated Performance Measurement: Management Accounting to Support New Manufacturing Realities," *Journal of Management Accounting Research*, (Fall 1992) served as the basic research for other contributions to the topic. Kaplan, R. and Norton, D. have written extensively about their technique of strategy mapping.
2. Keegan, D.P., Eiler, R., and C.K. Jones, "Are Your Performance Measures Obsolete?" *Management Accounting*, (June 1989); McNair, C.J., Lynch, R.L., and Cross, K.F. "Do Financial and Non-financial Performance Measures Have to Agree?" *Management Accounting*, (November 1990) followed by Lynch, R.L. and Cross, K., *Measure Up: Yardsticks for Continuous Improvement* (Cambridge, MA: Blackwell, 1991) provided guidelines for developing balanced measurement systems.
3. Lynch, R.L. and Cross, K.F. *Measure Up: Yardsticks for Continuous Improvement* (Malden, MA: Blackwell Publishers, 1995) pp. 125–129, 148–149 outlines the development of this clear model.
4. There were many authors encouraging this movement. The work of Johnson, H.T. and Kaplan, R.S., *Relevance Lost: The Rise and Fall of Management Accounting* (Boston, MA: Harvard Business School Press, 1987) was the central rallying point.
5. M.E. Porter's seminal works *Competitive Strategy* (New York: The Free Press, 1980) and *Competitive Advantage: Creating and Sustaining Superior Performance* (New York: The Free Press, 1985) significantly influenced the character of strategy development.
6. Shank, J.K. and Govindarajan, V. *Strategic Cost Analysis* (Boston, MA: Irwin 1989) started the movement of relating cost analysis to strategy.
7. Ittner, C. and Larker, D., "Coming up Short," *Harvard Business Review*, November 2003 and Scneiderman, A. "Why Balanced Scorecards Fail," *Journal of Strategic Performance Measurement*, (January 1999).
8. Certified Management Accountant Management Accounting Guideline 42, *Measuring the Cost of Capacity*, (Hamilton, Ontario: The Society of Management Accountant of Canada, 1996).
9. Based on interview notes from a consulting engagement with a semiconductor manufacturer by one of the authors.

Chapter 9
Aligning the MSDR Measurement System with Strategy

The best strategy in the world will go no place unless the organization agrees to focus on the objectives. Creating that critical buy-in until now has been the job of "communication," training, and often brute force. But there's a better way. This section illustrates how to use the MSDR scorecard as a strategic organizational alignment tool. This provides the critical linkage between the firm strategy and the measures of the key success factors necessary for implementing the strategy.

There is a hierarchy of alignment around goals and means. On the largest scale, alignment is achieved when all parts and functions of an organization's value chain work toward the same purpose. On the human level, it means that all members of the organization can identify their personal values and objectives with those of the firm.

Strong alignment gives people a clear and shared sense of purpose. Inspiration and energy run high, and both individual and team effectiveness increase. This is (or was) the case at many "dot-com" startup companies. People exhibited a strong sense of dedication and intense personal engagement. Commitment could be measured, literally, in long workdays and personal sacrifices willingly given for the "good of the firm." Such a pumped-up group may burn itself out over time, and so the challenge is to continue the alignment as the firm grows in size and complexity.

Weak alignment causes people to work at cross-purposes, decreasing effectiveness and enthusiasm. Insidiously, functional or individual objectives begin to take precedence over the needs of the larger organization or the customer. Morale and productivity diminish over time, and the organization becomes more vulnerable to competitors and market forces.

Misalignment can take several forms:

- A group believes its members are aligned but, in fact, individuals have different goals;
- Individuals share goals but have unstated disagreements about how those goals should be reached;
- Warring camps exist, ensuring that overall commitment to any chosen strategy is weak;

L.P. Carr, A.J. Nanni, Jr., *Delivering Results*, DOI 10.1007/978-1-4419-0621-2_9,
© Springer Science+Business Media, LLC 2009

- Active opposition does not exist, but many group members are unconvinced of the need for, or the likely efficacy of the proposed action;
- People don't know what the goals of the organization are.

To the last point, it is no surprise that a survey of 293 organizations in the United Kingdom showed that in poorly performing organizations, two-thirds of employees did not have a good understanding of overall organization goals. Even in high-performing organizations, fully a third did not understand the organization's goals.[1]

But an MSDR scorecard approach can at least get everybody on the same page. For example, Colonia Insurance, a diversified German insurance company and part of the AXA group, decided to create a Customer Care Center (CCC) to provide better customer service and to stem increasing customer defections. The CCC would provide a single telephone number to handle all customer questions and problems related to its insurance products. Conceived as a 24×7 operation, the goal was to handle 90% of all customer problems on the first call.

Senior management required directors of the various insurance groups (health, auto, life, property, and casualty) to fund this new central service department. However, they didn't uniformly agree with the concept or the operation. They raised concerns about costs, productivity issues, the CCC staff's capabilities, the existing information technology, and the system's potential to resolve customers' problems. This sounded like trouble ahead for the CCC manager, who knew that his department, by itself, was not the solution to stopping customer defections—and worried that this would be the measure used to judge his performance.

But instead of mission impossible, a balanced scorecard was developed to resolve the CCC manager's measurement concerns—to assure the directors that the CCC was operating effectively and efficiently. In other words, the agreed-upon measures, such as lapse rate trend and number of calls solved on the first try, were linked to the strategic intent of the CCC and answered the various concerns of the directors. The CCC manager breathed a sigh of relief and was able to use the scorecard to manage and motivate his department. Meantime, the funding group managers were just as comfortable with the revised set of measures, which gave them assurance that the CCC would actually perform as designed. Their scorecard is outlined in Appendix A, Item I.

In today's data-rich world there is an abundance of possible measures. As noted in the previous chapter, we need to be careful and selective with the number and types of measures we choose. Measures have a purpose and do influence behavior. The key is getting the organization to work toward the agreed strategic target. As stated earlier in the book, the noted authors Robert Kaplan and David Norton developed a strategy mapping methodology to help firms align their balanced scorecards.[2] In addition to the major consulting firms, there are numerous boutique consultancies that concentrate on helping organizations with measurements and alignment.[3] In this chapter, we will discuss the process of gaining alignment, outline the necessary conditions for alignment, and offer a number of caveats to make sure that your MSDR system is designed correctly.

Strategic Alignment

For obvious reasons, new programs and initiatives are aimed at eventual failure when alignment is lacking. Even when they produce quick results, such initiatives frequently fall into disarray over time. The history of the quality movement offers many examples. Without constant urging by management, the commitment to quality typically deteriorates, even in firms where quality provides an obvious competitive advantage. However, consistently successful firms somehow manage to maintain alignment around Total Quality Management (TQM) or other strategic dimensions. At General Electric, for example, everyone is continuously indoctrinated in the critical importance of quality and educated in the six-sigma tools of quality. Moreover, infrastructure systems such as training, career development, and hard-to-ignore rewards and compensation plans all support the central message. Likewise, DuPont enjoys one of the best safety records in industry largely because its entire global workforce is aligned around this issue. At DuPont, safety is *the* strategic imperative. Their Safety Training Observation Program (STOP) is a behavioral-based program that brought DuPont positive recognition. It was so successful that other companies wanted to buy the service. DuPont earns about $100 million selling their STOP program to others.[4]

The foundation for gaining alignment is individuals agreeing on goals and measures as GE and other examples demonstrate. But the strategic alignment process starts at the top level of the organization and cascades down, unifying direction for units and functional teams and, ultimately, individuals.

Tying performance measures to overall goals is what makes these cascading steps real and able to support the strategy. Without meaningful measures, many organizations fail to get the attention of employees, and the cascading strategy falls flat. All too often, strategic plans and goals are simply filed away with the supporting data, assumptions, and logic used to create the strategy. To avoid this failure, managers need to make the strategy tangible with quantitative measures that produce rewards or penalties.

The General Motors European strategy board took all the right "steps" when it sought to improve organization-wide alignment with their scorecard. Rather than leave each area of the company to its own devices, scorecards for each of the 8 business units and 12 separate functions in different countries were developed according to a common process and format. Each unit and function had to set strategic objectives that aligned with GME's corporate scorecard. In addition, a common scorecard template was devised and cascaded for all 25 national sales companies in GME, though they select their own objectives according to their business circumstances. Thus, the board's strategic direction cascades down to and guides the manufacturing, sales, marketing, people, process, and systems capability of each entity.

At Mobil Oil Corporation in the United States, the balanced scorecard served as a model for individuals' "personal" scorecards. They migrated from a corporate scorecard to a business unit scorecard to a division scorecard. At each level, the local personnel developed their metrics to fit their key success factors. The New England Mobil scorecard was different from the West Coast Mobil scorecard.

Different regions have different market challenges. The company is continuing to cascade the scorecards down the organization. Explains Edward T. Lewis, Jr., Americas M&R Business Specialist, for the Marketing and Refining Division: "One of Mobil's major groups is doing the personal scorecard with notable success. There is a clear benefit to getting people to understand how their behavior drives results in the business unit. The next step is to get more leverage and benefit from each individual, to see exactly what they need to accomplish to drive exceptional business unit results. The personal scorecard concept might be the answer."[5]

The scorecard is a statement of strategic intent. For example, at the SBU level a firm is determined to improve the overall new customer acquisition rate. As the scorecards are deployed at the unit level, they also focus on unit new customer acquisition, cascading as depicted in Fig. 9.1. At the team functional level, they assess the ratio of new customer revenues to sales and marketing expenses as a measure of supporting the unit strategic target. At the operational or individual level sales calls/week on prospects is the metric used. In this case the measures are different at each level, but the theme or strategic intent is consistent. The business is aligned to the strategic intent.

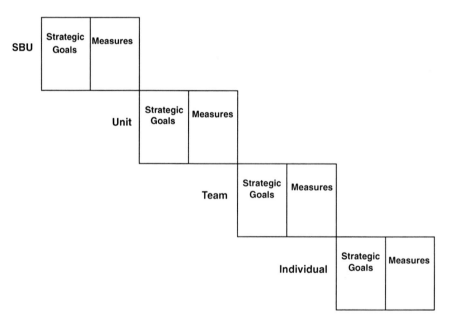

Fig. 9.1 Cascade alignment

Three Effects of MSDR Scorecard Alignment

Alignment is tightly bound to the concept of a performance measurement system. The measurement system can serve as an excellent tool to cascade the firm's strategy. Indeed, measurements signal to all levels what is important in the organization. And this is manifested in at least three ways:

1. Performance measures aligned with the organization's strategy measure the right kind of progress;
2. The scorecard, itself, becomes a powerful mechanism for aligning the organization with the strategy;
3. Executives help institutionalize strategy as they align around the performance measurement system; employees, too, become ingrained with the belief that the system is "part of the way we work."

Again, "you get what you measure." Put another way, people tend to live up to expectations. Codifying those expectations against solid metrics has many advantages. Among others, it allows managers to

- translate vision into operational and quantifiable measurements;
- reduce a strategy to its critical success factors;
- identify and align the action steps needed to accomplish strategic goals;
- establish a clear link between strategy and functional tasks;
- compare actual performance to planned performance so that corrective actions can be taken;
- analyze and manage strategy.

Serono (now part of Merck) was a $1 billion (US) Swiss biotech firm. It put these precepts into action. Over the past 10 years, the company successfully shifted production from conventional pharmaceutical methods to biotechnology. Since assuming the reins in 1995, Ernesto Bertarelli has been shaping and developing his management team, as well as forging his biotechnology vision. In the process, the company has transformed itself from dependency on a single product family, infertility drugs, to multiple products. Serono was building the infrastructure to support a worldwide marketing effort.

To start the process, Bertarelli boldly proclaimed a five-point strategic intent:

1. As a provider of specialty pharmaceuticals, we will focus on niche markets where we can contribute with innovative products.
2. An entrepreneurial and pioneering spirit will be fostered throughout the firm.
3. We will strive to be the partner of choice for patients, physicians, and payers in our chosen fields.
4. We will expand R&D efforts worldwide to create a global presence.
5. We will attract, develop, and train the best talent in the pharmaceutical and biotechnology industries.

Bertarelli developed a balanced scorecard system to monitor the company's performance against each strategic intent and then set about building a scorecard as an aligning mechanism for the entire organization. His purpose was to keep the five elements of strategy in front of departments and people at all times. Moreover, he believed that the scorecard would help people to coordinate their efforts. In addition, Bertarelli used the scorecard to report his firm's advancement to the stockholders. This proved very valuable, as the development cycle in biotech is quite long with financial results lagging behind new product launches. He could report development progress with the scorecard and attract investors looking to the future.[6] In late 2006, Bertarelli sold Serono to Merck for 10.6 billion Euros. Appendix A, Item II, outlines the scorecard used by the Serono US operation.

In the past, organizations often tried to do the same thing with behavior or development interventions. However, experience shows that most failed. Employees frequently interpreted these isolated programs as "the flavor of the month." Often tied to themes such as waste reduction or productivity improvement, they tended to create employee skepticism or, worse, fears around job security.

In response, more and more senior managers began rallying employees behind a single big idea, such as "customer satisfaction," "shareholder value," or "economic value added." Though laudable, the problem with these approaches is that although alignment may be created around the goal, the organization is typically misaligned around the means to reach the goal.

Getting functions or business units aligned with the overall strategy is never easy. As a result of the way the parts of the organization developed (opportunistically), many organizations today are made up of fiefdoms, each unwilling—or unable—to share power, resources, information, or ideas in the interests of the greater good. Trapped in their heritage "stovepipes," business units or functions may find it difficult to see how actions at their level can lead to greater achievement for the total organization.

At Serono, CEO Bertarelli set the example by using the scorecard to measure his own performance. This action provided proof of his support for the use of the tool, thereby assuring its acceptability for other parts of the organization.

Roberto Fuentes, a senior manager in the Finishes Division of DuPont Mexico, observes that the very act of creating scorecards for the business—and each of the three strategic business units within the Finishes Division—was a powerful experience. The exercise clarified strategy, both overall and for each business, and clearly identified the strategic links and synergies across the division.

For example, achieving alignment between what HR does and what corporate strategy requires has been a critical issue at Universal Music Group after a late 1998 merger between Universal and PolyGram. The combination created a global enterprise whose strengths combine international economies of scale with a local entrepreneurial market focus. It does so in over 40 countries with such record labels as MCA, Decca, Island, DGG, and Mercury.

A central HR team in New York determines HR strategy to guide managers and HR practitioners across the business. They provide the guidelines on HR solutions for the business managers and serve as the internal consultants. The local HR practitioners understand their company operation and needs. Central HR takes the approach of helping others achieve their strategy.

In effect, in this example, the key issue for the local and central HR practitioners is strategic alignment. To enable linkages between HR and business strategy, practitioners use a framework called the HR Strategy Contribution Matrix. There are three steps:

- Working with the strategic planning function, HR identifies the three-to-five critical high-level strategies that support the long-term business vision.
- Decisions are taken on two or three key HR contributions for each strategic priority, which may yield 10–15 opportunities for interventions.
- Three-to-five strategic HR goals are prioritized from these contributions, which will have significant impact.

What makes this all work is individual commitment, which begins with getting everybody on board up front. The experience of a group of managers in the Microelectronics Division of IBM shows how not to create consensus. After considerable time and effort the team succeeded in devising a simple scorecard that was rooted in the division's vision and that identified critical success factors for the business strategy. The scorecard also encompassed customer and innovation measures previously lacking. However, the team found it difficult to obtain top management buy-in, largely because senior managers were not involved in the scorecard's creation. The team also encountered resistance in deploying the scorecard to the division's business units. In time, the initiative's champion left the organization, and the saga ended with the division reverting to its original financial measures.

In the 1990s, Lucent Technology boldly embraced the balance scorecard concept. The Global Financial Services (GFS) operation moved quickly to implement their scorecard system. This shared services group provides payroll, accounts payable processing, accounts receivable billing, cost accounting, and other accounting services for all of the $30 billion revenue global operations. The use of non-financial measures to evaluate performance of GFS had great appeal to management. There was the general concern that GFS was too expensive and error prone. Scorecards could address this problem.

Their scorecard design and implementation were excellent. They followed many of the guidelines and caveats outlined in Chapter 8. The GFS division managers participated in the design process, and senior management supported the program. Despite the sound design and good socialization of the scorecard system, it was abandoned within a year. The problem was that the general manager continued to use the budgets to manage the shared services operation. He supported the scorecard concept but only referred to it as an afterthought during the monthly budget review meetings. It was clear through management actions that the budget counted and the scorecard measures did not. The challenge for companies is thus two-fold. First, is to make sure that a strategy exists and that it is appropriately communicated and understood. Implicit in this step is the full support of senior management. If they do not support the strategy, how can you expect the workers to execute the strategy? Second, is to put in place mechanisms and processes that direct and steer alignment. The remainder of this chapter will describe how to do this.

Building Alignment for Scorecard Development

In an ideal world people prefer not to subject themselves to any kind of measures. It takes the pressure off the expected performance. With the increasing notoriety of scorecards, there are many groups convinced of the value of performance measures and committed to the development of such a system. More frequently, though, executives have only lukewarm interest in performance measures or scorecards. The latter group politely discusses the idea and typically appoints a member or a staff person to gather more information about the concept. But executive enthusiasm often wanes even further by the time the preliminary data are gathered. Scorecard managers know they will be facing an uphill battle. There are three steps to building buy-in:

- Assess the state of executive alignment around the strategy;
- Build executive commitment;
- Drive commitment down and across the organization.

There are no shortcuts to developing alignment and commitment for a measurement system. The first step is to determine if the executive team shares a commitment to the strategy. Are they aligned and in agreement? If the senior leadership team is not in sync, then a measurement system is a waste of time. Often consulting firms are engaged to perform this assessment. Third party intervention can more easily detect the passive-resistant players; those that verbally support the strategy but whose decisions and actions are often contrary to their words. Lucent's GFS operation would have benefited from this kind of intervention. A good example of the assessment process is the techniques used by Bernstein Associates. The *Executive Group Alignment Process (EGAP)*, developed by Dr. William Bernstein of Bernstein Associates, is useful in determining whether executives are not only willing to begin building measures, but able.[7]

EGAP is a technique for assessing and promoting alignment among senior executives around their organization's strategic plan and its implementation. With interviews and surveys, EGAP probes team members on both their commitment to strategic goals and their perception of "strategy relevant ideas."

The process begins with surveys that

- Quantify individuals' commitment to the strategic goals or to the new initiative;
- Identify the conditions required for effective implementation of the strategy or initiative;
- Measure how well executive team members work together.

The results of the research are fed back in an initial group meeting, which is designed to

- Identify areas of strong, weak, and variable commitment to strategic goals;
- Rally the team around areas of strong commitment;

- Explore the underlying causes of variable commitment to goals;
- Assess the team's willingness to work together toward implementation.

Strong commitment to strategic goals can engender strong feelings or longings in people. Weak commitment to goals is associated with low energy and non-action (Fig 9.2).

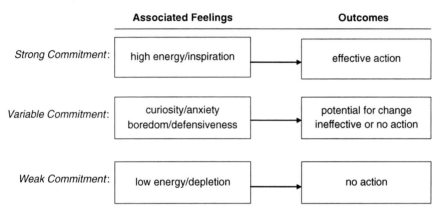

Fig. 9.2 The relationship of commitment to strategic action
Source: Bernstein Associates

When commitment is strong, the team is aligned and can move forward without hesitation. But when the opposite is true, the odds of successful implementation are very low. Therefore, the strategic element should be dropped, or at least shelved, until the causes of the weak commitment are dealt with. Understanding the cause of the uncertainty is central. It may stem from factionalism. Or it may be caused by indecision or ambiguity. Teasing out the reasons allows groups to actively engage on the issues and, ideally, build common understanding and a new consensus.

Tactics used by many firms to gain this essential support include the following:

- Recruiting a high-level person to serve as a champion or sponsor for the idea;
- Preparing a business case that demonstrates the need for the initiative;
- Providing executives with educational materials, guest speakers, or seminars and scheduling benchmarking site visits to high-performing companies;
- Finding a business unit in which to conduct a demonstration pilot.

Among these tactics, perhaps the most active means to gain and maintain executive support is to find an effective champion or sponsor for the measurement initiative. A champion may be a senior staff person but ideally should be a member of the senior executive team. Such a person should have the following:

- Peer credibility;
- A persistent nature;
- Good influence skills.

Equally convincing on an intellectual level, a strong business case helps focus discussion on benefits. Traditionally, a business case is framed in financial terms and includes a multiyear estimate of a future project's costs and revenue benefits. However, business scorecards are very difficult to quantify from a return on investment perspective, especially as predictors. A performance measurement system is, after all, a tool to reach an end, not an end in itself. Such systems are thus best presented in terms of usability and benefits.

For instance, Bama Pies, Inc., a wholesale bakery products company supplying a number of large national restaurant chains and a Malcolm Baldrige National Quality Award winner, couches its scorecard as a means to

- Communicate the strategic direction of the company;
- Link individuals, business units, functional areas, and departments across the organization;
- Focus measures on key drivers of performance to ensure the organization is working toward the same goals.

Air Products and Chemicals, which sells a portfolio of atmospheric gases, materials, and equipment to industrial, technology, and health-care markets, defines its scorecard as a way to

- Build the vision into "key result areas";
- Show where problems are and how to change them to meet corporate goals;
- Cascade the targets and measures established by the senior management team through the organization;
- Obtain agreement and support for key result areas across different departments and business units;
- Link results to compensation.[8]

Once the strategy is set, other key decision-makers and influencers throughout the organization must be aligned around the need for performance measures. This requires communicating down and across the organization. Firms can accomplish this in a variety of ways, including

- Distributing books, articles, and videos on the subject;
- Hosting motivational speakers;
- Holding in-house workshops, seminars, and presentations;
- Attending public seminars, conventions and exhibitions;
- Assigning coursework at universities, colleges, and institutes;
- Retaining consultants and software vendors;
- Staging benchmarking site visits to organizations noted for world-class performance measurement systems.

Remember, however, to select and screen elements so that a consistent point of view is presented.

For those "from Missouri," however, showing rather than telling will be most compelling. This can be effectively accomplished by creating a pilot project to demonstrate the viability, uses, and benefits of performance measures. A pilot cannot only demonstrate value, it can provide a ready-made "recipe book" for others in the organization. What's more, pilot pioneers can become consultants to spread the concepts to the rest of the organization. They can also uncover and correct issues, problems, and obstacles before performance measures are set in concrete for the larger organization.

An Example: TransCanada Pipelines Ltd.

Gordon Masiuk, a performance measurement consultant, accepted the role of corporate organizational and business effectiveness consultant with TransCanada. He had read a description of an improved version of the balanced scorecard called the "Dynamic Business Scorecard" (DBSC)[9] and discussed the concept at length with William Fonvielle, its originator. Masiuk saw that the attributes of the dynamic scorecard were completely consistent with quality precepts. Shortly after the merger, the executive leadership team (ELT) began a strategic planning process, thus providing an opportune time to integrate measures with strategy. Masiuk started using the dynamic scorecard framework in sessions with executives to show how different areas linked up. Soon, he began working with the Transmission Business Unit, developing the scorecard there, along with an organizational, business-process, and employee-focused performance management approach dubbed the "Integrated Performance Framework (IPF)." The combination of these concepts provided a holistic model for integrated planning, goal setting, performance measurement, leadership, culture, performance management, and incentive compensation. By conducting frequent workshops, meetings, and presentations, Masiuk began to build support for these concepts. Eventually, he gained agreement to pilot the cascading of goals and measures from the corporate strategy down to the business unit strategy, then down to a functional area (customer service) and to individual teams. With the process ongoing, Masiuk turned his attention to selling the ELT on this big idea.

"I had to find someone on the ELT who could embrace the concept. I was fortunate enough to spend some time with Sarah Raiss, who is the Corporate Vice President of Human Resources and also my boss's leader. Sarah is new to the company. She has a very open mind, is receptive to new ideas and is supportive of her people."[10]

"When I took her through the IPF and Dynamic Business Score Card concepts," Masiuk goes on, "she was convinced that these approaches were exactly what our 'New TransCanada' needed. Sarah excitedly said, 'We need to get you in front of the ELT as soon as possible!' Within a few weeks I had delivered to the ELT a 45-minute presentation of the model with sample goals and measures. It was Sarah's sponsorship and support that 'got me in the door.'"

Nor did Masiuk get bogged down there. "Following the presentation," he says, "I received a go-ahead to work in partnership with the HR vice presidents and their business unit presidents to develop their business unit goals and measures."

Masiuk found that he didn't need to write a business case in order to persuade the ELT of the soundness of his approach. "I think that one reason a business case was not needed was that the DBSC and IPF intuitively make a great deal of sense," he asserts.

"They help to simplify, focus and integrate the business planning process, and this integrated approach is adaptable to whatever business environment we are currently in or will be moving towards in the future."

As Masiuk learned, once acceptance is gained at the executive level, the next step is to gain support and commitment throughout the organization. Some of the same tools and methods used to align executives may also be useful with other employees, especially educational materials, in-house workshops and presentations, and successful demonstration projects.

However, many employees may be predisposed to dismiss measurement initiatives as yet another management fad or, more ominously, a management tactic to monitor employees. The very fact that measurement involves the gathering and manipulation of numbers may be off-putting to some. This is when the company leaders must clearly signal their commitment to using the performance measurement system to manage the company. They need to demonstrate how the measurement system is useful for everyone wanting to improve their performance.

Using the MSDR Performance Measures to Create Organizational Alignment

A fully functioning MSDR performance measurement system is inherently an aligning mechanism. The trick is to make certain that it becomes "the way we do business." But a preliminary step is to make certain that the system is indeed strategy relevant.

Measurements help achieve vertical alignment. They inform workers how they are achieving their goals in key strategic areas such as customer service and quality. A good measurement system makes obvious how each part of the firm, and in some cases, individuals, impacts the financial results. For example, a firm's strategic goal is to improve overall new customer acquisition rate. The business unit adopts a measure of new customer acquisition rate. The sales department adopts a measure of the ratio of new customer revenue to sales and marketing expenses. The sales force is measured on sales calls per week on new prospects. The measures are thematically linked but different based on level in the firm.

Beyond the development and operation of the performance measures lay two system considerations: communications and rewards recognition. Communication is critical to every measurement-related activity. Without the ability to transfer information from one person to another, alignment would be improbable if not impossible. The U.S. government's 1997 benchmarking study, *Serving The American Public: Best Practices in Customer-Driven Strategic Planning*, reports that among the most successful companies "effective internal communication" was necessary for successful development and deployment of strategic and business plans. Internal communication was seen as the linkage between planning and practice. The entire workforce has to fully understand its role in achieving success and what is expected throughout the process. Leadership's strategy must be clearly understood at all levels of the organization."[11] Performance Measurement Associates provide a communications checklist and a list of communications principles for its scorecard clients, as below.[12]

Performance Measurement Communications Checklist

- Build enthusiasm for and commitment to the performance measurement process.
- Demystify the subject of measurement.
- Give all employees information vital to their understanding of the performance measurement system and the business case.
- Ensure that relevant information is provided at a level of detail appropriate to the recipients' positions and roles.
- Help minimize the disruptive effects of change by preventing unpleasant surprises.
- Provide two-way communication channels that will help employees feel their feedback and ideas are valued.
- Monitor the quality of the communication process.

Guiding Principles of Organizational Communications

- Actions speak louder than words; every management decision and action communicates powerfully.
- Brevity is the soul of wit.
- People tend to remember most things only through constant repetition.
- People are most likely to remember the first and last points they hear—and to forget what's in between.
- Positioning the benefit increases acceptance of change.
- Communication is by definition a two-way process.
- Communications should never go over people's heads nor should they underestimate people's intelligence.
- Do not communicate to the point of overkill.

No discussion of alignment is complete without a discussion of rewards and compensation. Traditionally, compensation has been regarded as a major driver of employee behavior. While a considerable body of research suggests that extrinsic rewards may be a less powerful source of motivation than intrinsic rewards—such as the simple pleasure associated with knowing that one has done a good job—tying at least some part of compensation to strategically linked performance measures makes sound business sense. According to William J. Smith, director of the Northwest Compensation Consulting Practice of Watson Wyatt Worldwide, "Effective score-cards provide reasonable, measurable benchmarks with which top management and other employee reward systems can be aligned, with an appropriate balance between short- and long-term perspectives, and different stakeholder influences."

The government's benchmarking study, mentioned earlier, reported that many benchmarking partners stated that measures are not effective without tying incentives to them. It noted that in the best companies, "Performance measurement, tied to incentives and compensation, is employed at all levels of the organization, with clearly assigned and well-understood accountability for results. Most of the (bench-marked) partners linked performance evaluations and rewards to specific measures of success. This, they believed, sent a clear message as to what was important. These measures were almost always different at different levels within the organization, but each was linked to overall organizational strategies."

At Mobil Oil Corporation's Marketing and Refining Division, linking the organization's strategy to compensation through the balanced scorecard was an early step. Edward T. Lewis Jr., as noted earlier in the chapter, relates that the division first needed to understand the direction the scorecard was setting, what the results were, and whether the desired results were being driven. "The existing variable pay compensation program for non-executive employees was a merit-based pay program, similar to what a lot of companies have. The division was granting annual salary increases in the range of 3 to 6 percent, regardless of whether the company was doing well or poorly. Under the new variable pay compensation program, a pot of money is available to employees that, in effect, range up to a maximum 30-percent bonus opportunity. As much as 30 percent of one-time annual salary opportunity bonus is tied to the scorecard measures."[13]

However, tying compensation and incentive to performance measures must be undertaken with care, and especially so at non-executive levels. Changes in the way that people are compensated almost always generate anxiety, and in some cases may run afoul of local constraints or union rules. Moreover, people must feel that the system is fair and the measures are accurate. To this end, managers should avoid penalizing or rewarding people for results they cannot influence, or for observed changes in results that may be due to error or chance variation. We will explore the use of incentives in greater depth in Chapter 11.

Conclusion

MSDR measurement systems allow employees at every level of the organization to contribute to its success. People in the organization "put skin in the game." With a focus on the key strategic drivers, scorecards translate vision into operational measures, which makes the strategy clear and tangible for all parties.

Developing an MSDR measurement system is not easy or without pitfalls. As mentioned, managers often seek the measures at which they are most proficient or that are easily attainable. The key is aligning employees behind a common purpose and goal. MSDR reports offer a common format that accommodate different measures and fall easily from one level to another in a continuous series throughout the organization. Performance measures engage people and bond them to clear and measurable results. With all of the forces of an organization marshaled around its effort, an MSDR measurement system can catapult an organization into a profitable future by providing a significant competitive advantage.

It is important to get both vertical and horizontal alignments in the design of the MSDR scorecard. We spoke extensively in Chapters 8 and 9 about linking the measures to the key success factors. Horizontal alignment is shown in the scorecard examples in Appendix A. The lack of horizontal linkage to the key success factors is, in our opinion, the single largest flaw in scorecard design. It is management's job to ensure the connections are reasonable and proper. You need to ask: "Why these measures?" and "show me how they link."

Much of this chapter is devoted to the vertical alignment or linkages. As depicted in Fig. 9.1 the scorecards need to cascade down the organizational structure. Again, there is no simple way to determine if the scorecards are connected to each layer of the firm. You cannot consolidate results as they do in accounting. Rather, management must check the thematic scorecard links between layers of the organization. Examples V and VI in Appendix A show a good scorecard linkage between corporate and plant operations.

When both the vertical and the horizontal linkages are present, you have the design of a successful scorecard system.

Notes

1. Niven, P. and Mann, S., *Balanced Scorecard Step-by-Step for Government and Nonprofit Agencies,* (Hoboken, NJ: John Wiley & Sons, Inc., 2003).
2. Kaplan, R. and Norton, D. have written extensively about their technique of strategy mapping. Their popular works have created global awareness of the technique. They include the following books: *Execution Premium: Linking Strategy to Operations for Competitive Advantage (2008); Alignment: Using Balanced Scorecards to Create Corporate Synergies (2006); Strategy Maps: Converting Intangible Assets into Tangible Outcomes (2004); Strategy-Focused Organization: How Balanced Scorecard Companies Thrive in the New Business Environment (2001); Balanced Scorecard: Translating Strategy Into Action (1996); All are published by Harvard Business School Press (Boston, MA).*
3. The Balanced Scorecard Institute, Palladium, TOR consulting, Excitant, Performance Measurement Associates, and the Metrus Group concentrate on measurement systems design and alignment.
4. Please see http://www2.dupont.com/Safety_Products/en_US/products/programs_training/index.html for more information about DuPont's STOP Program.
5. Kaplan, R.S., *Mobil USM&R (A), (A1), (A2), (B), (C), (D)*case studies, Harvard Business School case Nos. 197-025, 197-120, 197-121, 197-026, 197-027, 197-028, (Boston MA, 1998).
6. Carr, L., *Ares-Serono* and *Serono,* Babson College cases 131-C97AU and 123-C03 (1997 and 2003).

7. Fonvielle, W. and Carr, L., "Gaining Strategic Alignment: Making Scorecard Work," *Management Accounting Quarterly*, Fall 2001.
8. Brown, M.G., *Keeping Score: Using the Right Metrics to Drive World-class Performance*, AMACOM American Mgmt Assn, (1996).
9. Whiteley, R. and Hessan, D., *Customer Centered Growth*, (Cambridge, MA: Perseus Books Group, 1996).
10. The TransCanada Pipeline case is based on consulting notes of William Fonvielle, principle of Performance Measurement Associates.
11. http://govinfo.library.unt.edu/npr/library/papers/benchmrk/customer.html
12. http://performancemeasures.com, Performance Measurement Associates is an active consultancy in the field and one of the authors is a member of the firm.
13. Kaplan, R.S., op. cit., 1998.

Chapter 10
Gaining Strategic Alignment

Just as in automobiles, your alignment does not last forever; markets change, customer demands fluctuate, new managers bring their ideas, the firm matures, and many other forces can alter the alignment. The MSDR system needs regular checks and tests for alignment. Maintaining alignment is a continual process. Managers must select the proper tools and then apply them correctly to stay on course. This requires constant vigilance and a sound MSDR system. A hard-working system must also indicate your progress toward achieving your strategic goals and signal when you have arrived. All these business-management chores are guided by the MSDR system. In the previous chapter we looked at the vertical linkages, cascading the MSDR system through all the levels of the firm. In this chapter we explore the horizontal alignment of linking the key success factors to the strategy and the MSDR scorecard to the key success factors.

This is asking a lot of the MSDR system and the people who design and manage it. But there are some other tools that can supplement the process. Indeed, the past 15 years have witnessed the introduction of an array of management "power tools" to do just that. These tools have updated and replaced such old-time management "hand tools" as variance analysis of standard cost and budget analysis with month-to-month or year-to-year comparison of expenses. The main flaw of these old tools was that they did not relate results to strategic achievement and could not tell how much progress had been made toward strategic goals. The new tools do. The challenge is to select the right ones, at the right time, and then use them properly. What's in today's modern toolbox? Most managers have ready access to some, if not all, of the following power tools:

- Activity-based management
- Balanced scorecard
- Benchmarking
- Change management
- Core competencies
- Corporate venturing
- Customer relationship management
- Economic value-added analysis
- Knowledge management

L.P. Carr, A.J. Nanni, Jr., *Delivering Results*, DOI 10.1007/978-1-4419-0621-2_10,
© Springer Science+Business Media, LLC 2009

- Lean thinking
- Mission and vision statements
- Outsourcing
- Pay for performance
- Quality of earnings
- Reengineering
- Six-sigma management
- Supply chain management
- Theory of constraints
- Total quality management

Appendix B provides a brief outline of each tool.

While each tool is distinctive, they do share common traits. All were designed to present feedback to management, either by providing data on performance or by offering a unique way of portraying the current competitive situation. The tools provide reliable guidance and mileposts on the strategic journey, enabling management to make better decisions. The tools complement the MSDR system and help provide input for scorecard design. Their proper use hinges on the following: (a) an established, clear sense of direction; (b) an understandable and shared sense of the business model; (c) a focus on results; and (d) the organization's willingness, and ability, to change.

Let's look at how all these variables can work together to build a strong MSDR system with two examples. The first one will be in-depth.

The Nypro Experience

Today, Nypro is a plastics company that operates 52 businesses in 17 countries. It designs plastics products, builds molds, performs plastics injection, supplies other parts needed to assemble plastics parts, assembles the parts, and prepares them for delivery to the firm's customers or its customer's customer.[1]

Nypro's web site flatly states that its customers "use us to make their products because we can do it better, faster and cheaper than anybody else." The company's success is a direct result of alignment on, and superb execution of, its strategy. Not so long ago, however, the company was at a tipping point in its growth. It was operating 38 production facilities throughout the world and had seen its sales double over the proceeding 5 years. How to get bigger?

The company's mission statement back then was quite clear: "To be the best in the world in precision plastics injection molding and related activities ... creating value for our customers, employees and communities." Its strategy was to partner with major precision plastic users in the medical, computer, and communication industries. Further, it offered modern clean-room production facilities and high-quality, globally available plastic parts. The purity of clean room production and high-quality standards appealed to the health-care industry. Nypro customers included Dell, Johnson & Johnson, Verbatim, 3M, H-P, Abbott Labs, and Gillette. It had already come a long way.

History and Strategy

In the early 1970s, Nypro had been just one of more than 2000 injection molders with sales around $4 million per year. Competition, based mainly on price, was fierce. Gordon B. Lankton, driven by an entrepreneurial spirit and a global vision, purchased the company. He quickly changed many of the operating procedures and led the effort to develop a new long-range strategy. He was convinced Nypro could break out of the pack. Key elements of the strategy included the following:

- Develop the capability to make unique plastic pieces of high quality.
- Develop the molding process for large-scale operations.
- Build a worldwide network of custom injection-molding operations.
- Partner and joint venture with employees and other companies.
- Develop clean-room manufacturing capability.

The company started by concentrating on Fortune 50 companies with unique plastic-molding requirements. This focus differentiated Nypro from the competition that was composed mainly of local small molding shops that considered the plastic-molding process as an art form. By contrast, Nypro maintained consistent high-quality standards and production flexibility to meet specific customer requirements. Old-timers liked to recount how Lankton had walked away from a large volume order for a commodity product because it was not unique. Sales grew to $10 million in 1975, $45 million in 1980, $200 million in 1994, more than $500 million in 2001, and to $750 in 2003. Nypro's sales were growing at a pace that doubled in size every 5 years.

Headquarters and several production facilities were housed in a large sprawling former carpet mill in Clinton, Massachusetts. The company renovated the building to provide for manufacturing, engineering, and administrative support facilities. The new main plastic-injection-molding operation consisted of approximately 20 machines in a two-level clean-room environment. As the company expanded it replicated this part of the Clinton operation in 38 locations throughout the world. It built facilities near major customers in order to be a better supply partner. The original operation served as the model and benchmark for these remote facilities.

A clear sense of direction guided Nypro. Its managers knew, indeed lived, the strategy and made sure this destination was communicated throughout the company. Management also understood intimately the business model and the key factors it had to accomplish to be successful. With management and everyone below having a laser focus on achieving the targeted results, the setting was excellent for deploying a MSDR system. And, as it turned out, this mission and vision tool was properly deployed.

Organization

The company had a flat, decentralized organization with a lean headquarters staff. Each molding facility was a profit center with its own general manager and controller. Headquarters coordinated treasury and accounting. The central corporate sales team sold worldwide, using a geographically dispersed sales force.

Management understood the value creation process and how to deploy their supply chain. Meantime, the centralized sale and marketing structure fit the strategy of concentrating on a few large global players. Nypro succeeded in its goal of offering local supply and support, with global reach and standards. In a phrase, they were able to meet their customer's specific needs.

NYPRO was divided into some 35-profit centers. Each profit center and general manager was judged based on his or her stand-alone performance. The operational controllers reported directly to the profit center's general manager and indirectly to the corporate controller, Ted Lapres, for professional and coordination purposes. The general managers received the authority to run their businesses and take the necessary actions to meet their goals. Nypro fostered promotion from within, and placed a high premium on proactive entrepreneurial management. The central sales and marketing group produced about 80% of the sales with the remaining 20% generated by local sales efforts.

Another interesting characteristic of the organization was that each profit center was its own legal entity with an internal Board of Directors. Corporate officers, managers, and other senior profit center managers served on the profit center boards. Lapres, the controller, served on five boards which was about the average number for a senior corporate manager. Some managers, however, served on as many as seven. Each profit center held on-site quarterly board meetings where financial, operational, and other business issues were discussed. As Lapres explains

> This makes for high travel expenses and more time out of the office than I would like. Once I get to the profit center, however, I benefit from the direct talks and the free flow of information. It is difficult when you are traveling to Asia and Europe on a regular basis, but I really get to know what is going on by walking around and talking to the people. If we have a profit center with problems and I am not on the board, I get one of the corporate board members to act as my representative to check into specific problems.[2]

While corporate gave each general manager loads of authority, it still had to approve any major capital expenses. General managers fell into two different groups: those managing plants of 100–200 employees and those managing plants with 500 or more employees. By necessity, the manager of the smaller plant was more of an operations manager, while the manager of the larger plant had to be more of a generalist.

At Nypro's size, the organizational structure appeared to operate well. There were strains, but incremental additions were smoothly assimilated into the company structure. They understood their core competencies and focused on doing these well. Figure 10.1 shows how the choice of strategy requires the organization to operate in a particular manner. We will illustrate later how the MSDR system actually captures the key performance indicators for superior strategic execution.

Strategy	Why?	Consequences
• Unique Product/ Customization	• Product Differentiation • Hi-margins • Entry Barrier	• Specific Market • Less Competition • Higher Profits • Increased Complexity • Marketing Limitations • Increased Utilization
• Few Large Customers	• Higher Volume • Longer Production Runs • Secure Relationships	• Higher Yields • Pricing Pressure • Sales Dependency
• Cookie-cutter, stand alone facilities	• Standard Controls • Lower Costs	• Lower Delivery Costs • Close to Customer • Consistent Control Systems
• Plant Quality	• Differentiation • Justifies High Margins	• Niche Market • High Customer Satisfaction • Demands on Control System

Fig. 10.1 Consequences of NYPRO's strategy

Management clearly focused on the key success factors of unique products, large-volume orders, selected large global customers, a worldwide network, high-quality, and full-facility utilization.

The Process

The injection-molding process involves feeding raw plastic material into the barrel of a molding machine. The small beads of plastic material are melted in the machine and then mixed with various plastic resins and injected into the mold. Once properly cured (hardened and cooled), the new plastic part is ejected from the mold and the process is repeated. This sequence is called a cycle.

The type of plastic, mold cycle, and the tolerances of the part depend on customer specifications. Each part requires a specific set of tools (molds). The molding machines are set up to run a specific job or part. As it grew in scale, Nypro had installed automatic plastic material feed systems on the floor below the machine level. Normally, 20 molding machines were set in a clean-room environment for production. The completed parts were removed from the mold by robot and placed on a conveyer system for assembly and/or packaging and shipment. The process was designed to run 7 days a week, 24 hours a day. Ideally, run time was only interrupted for set-up and scheduled maintenance. The injection-molding machinery was key to maintaining a continuous process and keeping within customer specifications. Nypro partnered with its machine supplier and used state-of-the-art equipment.

Nypro discovered that the complexity of any manufacturing job depended partly on the number of cavities that a specific mold required. The number of cavities could vary from 1 to 400. A complex mold, for instance, might have tight dimensional tolerances and a series of cavities to be filled with each injection. More material was required to fill all the cavities, especially those closer to the machine's injection nozzle, which might cure and receive more material before the cavities at the far end of the mold were filled. Nypro managers learned that a challenging job with a large number of cavities could drive the manufacturing yield numbers down.

They also knew that their "value add" was in the process. They realized that, strictly speaking, they did not make a product. They were actually selling manufacturing services or machine time to companies to make their parts. The more complex parts had given Nypro headaches, but they also allowed the company to charge premium prices for their process know-how and capability.

NYPRO Services

CEO Gordon Lankton liked to point out to employees and customers that NYPRO "doesn't have products . . . just customers and capabilities," an attitude which many credited with creating a sense of mutual trust and long-standing relationships with its customers. NYPRO therefore offered a full menu of services including design, engineering, mold making, production, product assembly, packaging, and distribution. The goal was to provide consistent high-quality production service across all its plants.

Design, Engineering, and Tool Building

Nypro often began working with customers very early in the product-development phase. The designers and engineers would team up with their customer counterparts to insure that the molding and assembly processes met specifications and that a product could be produced most effectively.

The company owned tool-building shops in three locations in the United States and Singapore, where more than 40% of the molds used at Nypro were designed and built. Indeed, mold making (or tool-building as it was called) was the fastest growing part of Nypro's services. According to the company's 1996 annual report, "even more important than the growth of the tool-making capacity is the comprehensive set of global standards to which the tool-making operations and each mold are held. That is why many molding customers who ask Nypro to augment their own molding operations also buy all their molds from Nypro, regardless of whether the molding is done by them or us. The result is uniformity everywhere a customer manufactures and sells product." The molds were almost always owned by the customers and could cost up to $250,000 to produce.

Production

Once the molds were produced and the specifications for the process developed at the headquarters molding facility, they would either be shipped to the plants for production or, if they were more complex, retained for further testing. This allowed production engineers time to refine the production process, eliminate variability, and deal with any unexpected problems. This was especially true of products like contact lenses or certain medical components for which extremely tight tolerances had to be maintained. Eventually, however, even these products might be sent to other plants for production.

Every attempt was made to have identical molding machinery at each plant, in order to maintain global consistency. But since many of the plants had been built to serve the specific needs of individual customers, or had been acquired as turnkey operations, each plant had its own unique set of capabilities. One plant, for example, might have more large tonnage machines appropriate for larger, more complex, or multi-cavity molding, while another might have a clean room for precise and contamination-free operations.

Product Assembly

Customers would often contract with Nypro to produce a number of components for a single product. Nypro, for example, made the components for the Gillette Lady Razor, including a handle, grips for the sides, and a clasp into which the blade assembly was snapped. And, rather than ship the components separately to Gillette for assembly, Nypro developed a robot-assisted technique to assemble the razors itself.

Offering such extra services typified the Nypro attitude toward customer service. Indeed, whenever it appeared that a customer could benefit from additional integrated services, Nypro staff would figure out a way to get it done. Often the solution hinged on robotics, a technology Nypro engineers had become proficient at while designing systems for the injection-molding process.

The Daily P&L Report

To keep tabs on its progress, the company developed a daily P&L tally. This communication served as the primary MSDR data report. By 11:00 a.m., each facility reported the key data for the previous three shifts. Over 30 years, the report has been modified. It had been computerized in the early 1970s and 15 years later was developed into a daily profit and loss statement. This served as the scorecard for corporate management to judge the performance of each production facility and for the general managers to evaluate their operations. The Nypro guideline stated

No company can go forward without profits—profits are needed to buy new equipment, to provide employees with more benefits, and to expand the business. Profits are the scorecard of most businesses—and they are Nypro's scorecard.[3]

At Nypro, the molding machine is the profit center. In the hotel business, it's the hotel room—in the restaurant business, it's the table—in the retail store, it's the shelf space—and in the airline business, it's the seat. Our machines are our hotel rooms. We need to keep them all occupied all of the time. We need to get the best price (value added in terms of dollar per hour) based on providing the best service. We need to improve the standards and improve productivity (yield).

To this day, the bottom of the report summarizes the results of the machines in each of the production facilities. This was the daily report card for each of the facilities. Lankton said:

If you drop in 50 new jobs with new molds, you see an operation's performance deteriorate very quickly. The daily report will show the job value add well below our target of $1,000 per day, and the job yield data should also correlate. This tells me there is a problem at the facility. Something I would see if I could walk around the facility every day the way I did when we were only in Clinton. Hopefully, the daily report helps the local managers gauge the profitability of their jobs. Job complexity and yields are key to making money in this business. We have to bid the job correctly if we want to be profitable.

The daily business report converted operational results into financial terms. Its simplicity and clarity were the backbone of their MSDR report system. It worked well because operational efficiency and machine utilization were not only solid, quantifiable numbers, but key to success. Critical data such as yield and cycle time aligned with the strategy. The wide distribution of the report and its simplicity also made it understandable by everyone. It created a common language to communicate strategic achievement. Among other things, it served as the scorecard for management, helped general managers evaluate operations, served as a gauge to local plant profitability, offered quick response (feedback), and focused on the critical success factor of machine utilization. This deceptively simple device helped all levels of management, and the operators, see the connection between their decisions and actions and financial results. This was critical to managing cash flow in the early stages of the company.

Management understood that this single reporting tool did not capture all of the necessary success factors. Over time, they added further MSDR tools to create a balanced system fine-tuned to achieving their targets.

Other Reports

Soon, other weekly and monthly reports emerged. The weekly ones focused on the key operational data (safety, quality, employees, productivity, and on-time shipments) and listed summary financial information (sales and profits). The monthly reports were primarily financial and contained an analysis of the profit and loss statement, including a detailed assessment of cost and a comparison to budget and forecast. Controller Ted Lapres liked to use it to measure a plant's contribution as a comparative measure of performance.

This puts each plant on equal footing, and I can see how the manager controls the manufac- turing and administrative expenses given the level of sales. The system allows me to look at plants as well as job contribution margins. The percentage contribution is a good common yard stick.

The primary operational measure became the monthly Benchmarking Report. This report, done in chart form, compared all of the facilities. Other benchmarks included accident incidence rate, yield, raw material on hand, on time shipments, gross reject percent, headcount per machine utilized, customer return incidents, value added/employee/week, material percent of sales, pre-tax return on assets, and total payroll percent of sales. Each plant general manager strove to be "Best in Nypro Class." The reports were circulated monthly for each profit center and served as the basis of the monthly performance review.

Nypro management kept on expanding their MSDR tool selection to include Total Quality Management, along with their version of Theory of Constraints, Sup- ply Change Management and Lean Thinking. Management was deploying many of these new power tools in their MSDR system. The culture of openness permitted everyone to keep an eye on the strategic direction. They also avoided the temptation to fill capacity that did not generate profit or cash flow.

Benchmarks

Along with the daily value-added report, Nypro has a scorecard-type system of benchmarking for its profit centers. The company has always kept close track of its ability to deliver on its key success factors. There is a list of ten benchmarks that the company monitors for the molding process, many of which were line items on the daily P&L. Ted Lapres and Gordon Lankton both felt comfortable with these bench- marking measures for the molding activities and understood that the report helped plant managers to evaluate their success against other plants in the Nypro family, as well as competitors. The MSDR Benchmarking tool was deployed to provide more transparent feedback.

In the years since 1995, many Nypro plants, including the original plant in Clin- ton, began to expand their services to include assembly, packaging, design, and after-molding processes. The expansion meant that new measures of productivity and success had to be implemented. As a result, many plants have begun to keep daily assembly reports, similar to their daily P&L reports. But there is no uniformity, as the reports are used only in the individual plants.

The success of Nypro's MSDR systems came about because of a clear under- standing of the core competencies that distinguished the company from its competi- tors. Top management had always tracked profitability and productivity; but as the scope of operations expanded, the same scrutiny needed to be applied to the new activities. They added measures to capture these factors, including an internal web site that offers open access and real-time feedback.

Figure 10.2 shows that the Nypro MSDR system was providing valuable feed- back on the key elements of their strategy. It was not a perfect system. Management was constantly improving the content, format, and timeliness of the MSDR reports.

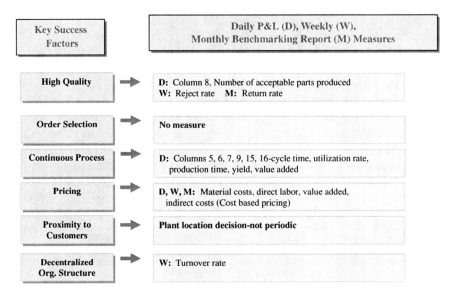

Fig. 10.2 Linking measures to key success factors at NYPRO

There was not a formal MSDR system but all of the parts of their reporting and feedback system linked to the strategy. They were focused and executed well.

The linkages between the strategies, the key success factors, and the measures are displayed in Fig. 10.3. The system also served as a strategic alignment tool for the company. Through the various elements of the MSDR system, Nypro was able to communicate the critical elements of the strategy down to every level in the organization. All the people understood what was important and what role they played in the execution of the strategy. Management made the operating results transparent, and they gained people's attention with a generous variable compensation system based on quarterly results. Nypro serves as a good example of the dynamic and contingent nature of MSDR systems. The company grew quite rapidly. Apace, it refined its strategic direction and modified the reporting system. Historically, the daily business report has served as the operational anchor. But as times changed, it was modified. Management added reports and modified others but aimed the system to keep guiding the organization toward its evolving strategic target.

The company has experienced many changes in recent years. Ted Lapres was named president and CEO in 2006 and they implemented a massive reorganization in 2009. Due to unique market segment demands, they divided the firm into three independent operating business units: Health Care, Consumer Electronics, and Packaging. The lean corporate headquarters now functions as the holding company. With their sound MSDR experiences as discussed above, they chose the balanced scorecard method, outlined in Chapters 8 and 9, as the prime management reporting tool. Ted and the senior management team recognized the power of strategic

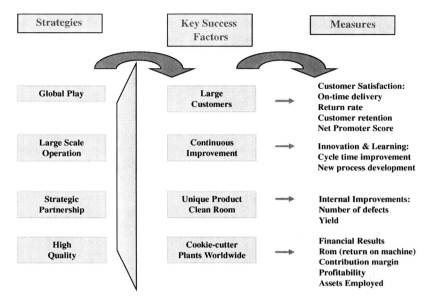

Fig. 10.3 Strategic measurement at NYPRO

alignment, matching accountability with responsibility, to motivate and manage the business units. The scorecard focuses on the key success factors for each business unit and sets mutually agreed strategic targets.

Another Example: Financial Services

Fidelity Investments, a well-known financial services firm, offers a full range of brokerage and investment services to individuals, firms, and non-profit organizations. Facing increasing market competition and intense customer pressure recently altered their strategy to a focus on specific market segments and customer profitability. The proliferation of discount brokers such as Charles Schwab, E*Trade, Scottrade, TD Ameritrade, and others changed the financial service landscape. Customers were demanding and getting more services for less cost. In the past, Fidelity concentrated on building sales volume in the individual and institutional world with a very aggressive sales and marketing plan to attract more customers. They believed that increased sales volume and size were the keys to success in the financial services industry.

Their performance measurements worked with aggregate firm results using primarily revenue growth. They believed that all sales were good, and the largest firm would dominate the market. Profit was managed through tight budget control and close scrutiny of spending. Management believed they were executing the strategy well. They realized rather quickly, however, that changes were needed to attract the more demanding and discriminating customer and to combat the "low price" market entrants. The segmentation and customer profitability emphasis evolved. Size alone was not a good predictor of financial success.[4]

This change in strategy required the firm to adjust its feedback system or their MSDR. In the past, their focus on controlling expenses and very tight budget management produced excellent firm results. The pressure on sales growth fashioned a very aggressive and effective sales force. Over time management began to realize that much of the increased sales volume on the individual and institutional level was not profitable. The larger the firm grew, the less profitable they became. The market was changing, and the size of the "fee" was a real consideration in the customers, purchasing criteria.

Their first response was to look at the various processes used to service the clients. They applied some process analysis streamlining techniques to improve the workflow. They engaged aggressive cost cutting methods to alter their cost model. Over time, Fidelity adopted the six-sigma quality system to eliminate waste and duplication. The popular business press and the financial services industry experts considered this firm as very well managed. They executed their strategy very well and here is one of the prime reasons: they had a responsive and well-developed MSDR system.

As the firm changed their strategy, they also made some major changes in the use of certain management tools. They adopted Activity-Based Costing (ABC) techniques to determine the cause of customer profitability. By looking at firm-wide activities that drove or caused costs, they were able to understand what costs were incurred to service certain accounts. The data were grouped by segment which helped management understand the cost consumption by discrete groups of customers. This 2-year effort, at first, met with strong resistance. The sales, marketing, and operations departments did not trust the data. The transparency of incurred costs by customers was quite revealing and in some cases embarrassing.

Their ABC analysis forced the firm to pay attention to the implementation of their strategy. It helped them focus on their key success factors, customer profitability, and profitable growth. This was a major mind-set shift in the firm. The attention was no longer exclusively on top line sales. Management realized the firm could "grow broke" by just chasing sales volume. Now, they wanted to make sure they received the slice of the pie (market share) with all the fruit (profitable customers). There were a number of financial services segments that offered significant revenue enhancement. Fidelity realized their process and cost structure would not result in a long-term successful venture.

They needed time to trust the data, and gradually, management saw the benefits of making the consumptions of costs transparent. The data from an element of the MSDR system were directly supporting the strategic thrust of understanding customer profitability. Customers were demanding more services for their smaller fees. Fidelity lost track of their value proposition and competed on price alone. The revised MSDR system provided the data to clearly identify what each service cost, and they communicated this to the customer. When services are no longer "free," the consumption changes.

Management was able to change the sales and operational process based on good segmentation data. This allowed them to provide customer value at reduced costs and respond to the market demand. The MSDR system served as a guide to finding the profitable sales growth and changed the mind-set of management to balancing profit with increased sales. Fidelity changed the thrust of their reporting system from a sales focus to a series of measures, financial and non-financial, that captured their process quality levels, operating efficiency, spending by market segment, and customer profitability.

Management did not stop there. In order to drive the proper employee behavior and motivation, they were able to link the key performance indicators for departments in the service delivery process (their balanced scorecard) and the measures of waste and poor quality from the six-sigma program. This created a comprehensive MSDR system that was focused and clearly linked to the firm strategy. Fidelity did what so many firms fail to do. They changed their MSDR scorecard to reflect the new key success factors of their strategy. They realized their revenue growth model was not sustainable in highly competitive financial services market. They had to change their way of doing business and the behavior of the work force. It was a mind-set shift to realize that every customer was not a good customer. Their new scorecard measurement system served as a very strong reinforcement for the behavior change.

Conclusion

The Nypro and Fidelity Investments offer excellent examples of well-deployed MSDR efforts. Each did its job adequately: keeping the focus on key performance indicators linked to strategy, communicating goals broadly and quickly, and reaching out dynamically to add new tools as needed. In Nypro's case, the company even invented a custom power tool of its own, the daily business report, which provided valued performance feedback to everyone in the firm. Fidelity used their MSDR system to help change their alignment to fit the new strategy.

Both companies followed the step-by-step process of horizontal alignment: Strategy → Key Success Factors → Measures (what) → Measurements (how). To emulate these leading firms just follow the process continually checking the linkages between each section. Strategies are forever changing to respond to new market conditions or new opportunities. It is critical that you also change the measures that link to the key success factors of the strategy. The scorecard measures drive behavior and motivate action.

Notes

1. For additional information on Nypro, see the company web site at www.nypro.com.
2. Based on extensive field interviews conducted over the past 8 years.
3. From original internal Nypro documents.
4. Fidelity Investments is a privately held company and specific firm performance data is not publically available.

Chapter 11
Performance and Rewards

Throughout this book, we have been encouraging you to think about a management system that delivers results in a holistic way. The effect of the MSDR is an interaction among the strategy, the culture, and design of the organization, and the specific performance measures in place. Once all those parts are in position, it is time to fuel the system up, time to motivate the strategic behavior. But connecting performance and rewards (even with all the other MSDR parts in place) is far from a simple task. On the surface, the issue is simple—reinforce the good behavior and discourage the bad. Unfortunately, there are plenty of examples all around us of reward systems gone haywire. Before we get into some of those examples and what we can learn from them, let's examine two basic ways in which rewards can be viewed: intrinsic and extrinsic rewards.

Financial and Non-financial Rewards

There is an old saying that a job well done is its own reward. If the strategy is a good one, the culture supports it, the design focuses attention on the target market, and the performance measures highlight key strategic success factors, people can recognize when they've done a good job and reap that intrinsic reward. Typically, however, you will want to match performances to something a bit more explicit.

Looking at the business news, you cannot escape the idea that the vast majority of businesses believe rewards should be financial, especially for executives. You shouldn't overlook the fact, however, that there are plenty of ways to spur motivation without literally dangling a fat annual bonus in front of your employees. In fact, dangling a fat annual bonus can very often backfire. We believe that non-financial incentives are an important part of an MSDR.

Recall our discussion of organizational culture in Chapter 5. Culture can be a powerful determinant in achieving strategic success. One basic task of the reward structure is to reinforce that culture. Good work should be recognized. Teamwork should be celebrated. Non-strategic work should be discouraged. Non-productive work should be eliminated. In short, the reward structure should create a meritocracy.

L.P. Carr, A.J. Nanni, Jr., *Delivering Results*, DOI 10.1007/978-1-4419-0621-2_11,

You can see an example of a meritocracy turned upside down every day in the Dilbert comic strip. Dilbert knows what he should do to improve his company's results, but the strategy and management always seem to discourage his work. The only obvious reward he receives is his extra work when he completes assignments. One of his coworkers is completely unproductive, yet thrives in the organization. Dilbert yearns to be recognized for doing a good job, but his situation is futile.

The Dilbert strip resonates with so many people because they too want to be recognized for doing a good job but very often feel they are not. It is probably our general tendency as human beings to be alarmed about things that are going wrong. Thus, the MSDR has to take a positive action to recognize when things are going well. If you have good performance measures as described in Chapters 8 and 9, it should not be too difficult to recognize when things are going well. Simply pointing that out in a visible way can be a very effective reward. Even a simple occasional handshake can have positive results.

The biggest trap here is to have these recognitions and "attaboys" keep from becoming rote and trite. Putting up a picture of the employee of the month may lose its effectiveness very quickly. However, in the right circumstance giving the employee of the month the best space in the parking lot can be a superb motivator!

Psychologists take as given the idea that random reinforcement assists in the learning process. One manager we know of did a very nice job with random reinforcement in the plant he managed. On an occasional basis, when the performance indicators for his plant have been trending positively, he would close work early on a Friday and have a big barbecue and celebration in the plant parking lot. The experience was like a big tailgate party. It was an effective reward in several ways. First, it was a clear recognition of work well done. Second, there was a strong feeling of camaraderie, which reinforced the plant's key success factors of teamwork and cooperation. Third, it provided a respite from the constant hard work and didn't "reward" good work with more work. Finally, from a financial point of view, the expenses were pretty low. If that manager divided the expenses by headcount and stuffed the money into each worker's paycheck for the month, it would have seemed paltry. However, from the employees' view, it was the recognition not the money.

Another example of an effective use of non-financial rewards appeared at the main plant of Oshkosh Truck from Chapter 2. The plant was organized into work teams. Each team had its own pride board, which prominently displayed its performance measures. As a reward for performance improvement, the work teams were granted more and more autonomy. They were self-managed including the creation of work schedules and the determination of appropriate work procedures. Teams whose performances dipped had some of their privileges revoked. In general, the workforce enjoyed the self-determination. Workers helped their teammates perform better. They self-policed the laggards. The cost of this reward to the plant was not a cost at all! Actually, it was a reduction in costs. The plant was able to operate without nearly the entire prior layer of supervisors.

At this point, we've clearly gotten into the financial side of things. If you are interested in maintaining the positive culture we have just been talking about, it is important to bring some financial recognition into the picture. The first application for this financial reward is simply in the salary and wage structure. If the strategic execution has been good, then the financial performance should follow. If that is the case, then the people responsible for the improved financial situation expect to get a little bit of the incremental income. If the annual raises are consistent with the non-financial recognitions during the year, the overall effect should be positive.

Speaking to the issue of impact on culture, it's important to recognize that there is probably a point at which the size of the financial reward begins to obscure the cultural beliefs. Another cornerstone of psychological research holds that peoples' beliefs are generally formed to be consistent with their behavior. In the workplace context, this means that people doing a good job of executing the strategy will develop the attitude that this is a good thing to do. Two things can upset this psychological connection: substantial threats or rewards. If you get a subordinate to behave in a certain way based on the threat of losing her job, it is unlikely that she'll believe she's doing it because it's the right thing to do. In fact, she may come to believe just the opposite. Likewise, if you pay someone a large reward for achieving a performance target, he may justify the effort by the reward only. That is, his actions did not reflect his beliefs and attitudes. He was only following the money. This is only one of the issues to worry about when devising financial incentive systems that go beyond base pay.

Financial incentives rely more on carrots than sticks in today's management systems. To stimulate results, these carrots take such forms as incentive compensation, bonuses, variable compensation, pay for performance, and "point" systems. Good behavior is rewarded with cash, stock, stock options, trips, gifts, perks, etc. Any financial incentive system is a double-edged sword. Proper use can spur individual and group behavior that's consistent with the goals of the organization. Improper use, however, can create unintended behaviors and results. Unexpected consequences can also stem from the size of rewards, whether too much or too little.

A good example of a well-intentioned bonus system that backfired was one devised for insurance underwriters at a large regional insurance firm. Top management concluded that in order to encourage growth, the company should focus attention on generating new policies. Thus, this well-known insurance company established an incentive system that generously rewarded the underwriters (and their managers) on the number of new policies they generated. The money involved naturally caught the attention of the managers and their underwriting teams. And so, they dutifully concentrated their efforts on writing new policies. The per-policy dollar amounts were not large; but, given the volume they generated, the underwriters could receive close to 100% of their base pay in additional bonus money. The managers could receive a multiple of base salary in these bonuses. The teams began to aggressively pursue new policies.

The result was that the number of new policies grew nicely, as did top line revenues. All had gone according to plan ... up to a point. Unfortunately, company profits started to slip and then fall precipitously. Market share began to erode. What had happened seemed entirely predictable in hindsight. The regional office people focused on building new accounts, but paid scant attention to the renewal of existing ones. The independent agents were happy to make a small commission on renewals when it involved no incremental work on their part. However, when their clients started calling in about delinquent renewals, the agents began to shift policies to the competition (at a higher initial-sale commission rate). Furthermore, the underwriters didn't actually drum up new prospects. The agents did. The only lever the underwriters had at their disposal to encourage new enrollments was their risk assessments. Lower risk assessments resulted in lower prices and more sales. This may have been viewed as inappropriate before the bonus system, but, after all, that's what the company was paying for! The result was more new sales with a higher claims-to-revenues profile. To make matters worse, the company did not understand their process costs. After some analysis, management discovered that it was much more than twice as expensive to process a new account as to renew an existing account. The company had unwittingly spurred people to grow the top line, ignoring the cost structure and the sales mix. Simply put, they motivated completely wrong-headed behavior. Oops!

Another example of a system gone bad was actually told to one of us by the plant management team that built the system. This took place in a manufacturing plant where the plant management team was trying to devise a way to improve operating efficiency. They decided, rightly, that the workforce could make a major contribution by recognizing inefficient processes. They established a reward system that paid people for successful improvement suggestions. The financial incentive was quite strong, 10% of the budgeted annual savings due to implementing the suggestion. The suggestion box system began to generate a growing stream of process improvement suggestions. Eventually, a suggestion with a very large savings effect was submitted. The managers were overjoyed! The annual budgeted savings was in the neighborhood of $400,000. The one unhappy aspect of this was that the process improvement suggestion was for a brand-new process. Why hadn't the process designers seen the flaw to begin with? They had discussed it with the workforce, hadn't they? The flaw in the reward system was exposed during a conversation after the ceremony at which one production worker, we will call him Charlie, was given a check for $40,000. The managers overheard one worker say to another, "That sure was good timing for Charlie. It will pay off that Corvette he bought last month!" Charlie wasn't known to be much of a big spender, so the managers surmised that he knew the payoff was coming. In fact, they later determined, he had detected the flaw when the design team had shown everyone their proposed process plan. Of course, if Charlie had said something then, the plant would have saved even more money by installing the better process the first time. However, Charlie wouldn't have gotten a dime!

Financial Incentive Philosophies

There are two primary financial investment philosophies: profit sharing and rewarding individual or group performance directly. Many firms combine profit sharing and performance-reward methods in their total incentive package.

Profit sharing is based on company, division, or unit performance, or a combination thereof. It normally consists of a formula using some financial ratio as the measurement device, such as ROI, RONA, EBITDA, EP, free cash flow, or other financial metrics. The underpinning is the certainty that the owners (stockholders) wish to share the profits in some form with the people who created the financial gains. The theory maintains that by sharing the profits, the owners encourage those covered by the plan to act in the best interest of both themselves and the owners. This supposedly further reinforces goal congruency between the managers and the stockholders. Recent financial scandals, however, show that true goal congruency is very elusive, especially when stock options are used as the payment currency. Nevertheless, more than 75% of all listed companies use some form of profit-sharing incentives. But the tide may be turning. Recent excessive executive bonuses, outright fraud, the use of a wide array of questionable accounting techniques, and accounting rule changes are causing many firms to abandon stock options for cash bonuses. GE and Microsoft are two leading companies making the change.

The second philosophical approach is to reward individual or group performance based on some set of specific targets, such as budget or spending levels, individual objectives, operational measures, or other specific outputs. The rewards often reinforce formal performance evaluations and are customized to each individual or group. The intent is to reward the achievement of certain agreed-upon goals. Management often unequally divides performance rewards, 75% on objective standards and 25% on discretionary subjective evaluation. They also like to have a mechanism that considers "luck" and "individual attitude."

Let's look at a case history with only slightly happier outcome than the insurance company. A mid-size publicly traded conglomerate also developed a rewards system. This corporation had a small, lean corporate staff that supported six separate business units or divisions operating in different markets with different economic forces.

With the approval of the board of directors, management established a bonus system using the profit-sharing model. It paid cash incentives to corporate staff based on total firm ROI and to division management based on their business unit RONA. Management's argument was that this was needed to remain competitive and attract the very best talent. Payments for managers started at 90% of target and usually paid 25% of base salary at 100% of target, and 50% of base salary at 150% of target. The board set a maximum limit of 25% of the total conglomerate profits to be shared with all management and employees. The limit was never reached but some divisions were occasionally very close to the maximum bonus level.

This typical corporate system worked very well, and the conglomerate prospered. The value of the stock grew greater than the market average and the firm was able to attract excellent management talent. Among factors contributing to the system's success, the bonus system was simple, based on a clear financial formula with very few rules. They were also fortunate in that the divisions were quite independent, with little transfer pricing problems; the headquarters staff was lean, making allocations small; and the division balance sheets were clean and separate with no shared assets. Over time management began to "tweak" its incentive system. They were concerned about the "free rider" problem: Certain individuals contributed more to the results than others and some just chose to go along for the ride. So they modified the systems for all levels below the senior division or corporate management team. Pay-out levels based on financial results were reduced by 50%. But, a 50% subjective bonus was added to compensate for the reduction. The new portion was individual, based on senior management discretion. The company also added a subjective performance component to the reduced profit sharing to correct for bad attitudes, disloyalty, and freeloading.

The company discovered another unexpected problem: The profit-sharing portion of the incentive system (ROI and RONA) had, by its very nature, encouraged managers not to take risks, to focus on the short term, to fully utilize existing assets, and to consider very carefully any additional assets. There was board concern about the lack of corporate risk taking and the stifling of creativity at the business unit level. Some executives felt this caused the overlooking of some very attractive business opportunities. Conglomerate performance began to slip and the senior employee turnover rate increased. Further, some felt that fairness and objectivity were removed with the addition of the subjective component, and the bonus had become more "political".

The system had helped surface these wider problems, but it couldn't make the decisions needed to fix them. Eventually, the financial performance and growth of the firm came to a plateau and a larger public firm eventually acquired it. In this case, a well-intentioned, but flawed, incentive system could not sustain exceptional performance.

There are two lessons to this story. First, if you want financial incentives to work, they have to be clear and simple. Second, financial incentive pay-outs need to be perceived as fair and equitable. This implies that objective measures make better triggers than subjective ones. It also suggests that there ought to be separate methods for dealing with "free riders." Technically, a free rider is someone who doesn't make a contribution to the effort that led to the payoff. A good management system finds and removes free riders; it does not attempt to come up with a complicated formula for incentive payment avoidance. If someone does not make a contribution, why should they be paid at all?

We will explore the various aspects of financial incentive systems by considering the following:

- Are incentives necessary for delivering results?
- Do they aid in achieving goal congruency?
- Do they motivate behavior?
- Is there a link between rewards and results?
- Can incentives be non-monetary, and both financial and non-financial?
- How do you balance subjective-based and objective-based rewards?

Purpose of Financial Incentives

Let's go back to the underlying theory of incentive systems. Their sole intent is to stimulate behavior that aligns the individual actions with the unit goals. They can bestow "positive" rewards or inflict "negative" penalties. In order to be effective, the rewards need to be linked to the measured performance output. More importantly, matching accountability with responsibility for those actually charged with delivering results is critical. An individual or group wants to see the direct connection between actions and decisions and the performance outputs. When this is not clear, the ability to motivate is limited. To summarize, there is a lot of variance between incentive theories and practice. Incentives, in other words, are imperfect at best.

Incentive system rewards tend to be short run in nature, usually covering only a year's performance. Recently, however, there has been a trend to set targets to reward both short-term and long-term objectives. The challenge is to discover the appropriate time horizon for management decisions. When there is a short-term-defined period, there is a great temptation to game or play the incentive system when the end of the period approaches. A common practice at the end of a period is to offer extended dating for customer payment terms. You can borrow from tomorrow for today to increase revenue booked this period.

Other "earnings management" techniques include freezing spending on discretionary items like training, travel, and advertising. Conversely, many firms will perform significant maintenance and repairs, write-off obsolete inventories that they have been carrying for a while or perform capital improvements when a significant external economic event provides some "cover." In accounting circles, this is called "big bath" management—if you are going to take a bath, it may as well be a big one! Decisions are often made in the short run in order to boost incentive trigger measures and improve bonuses. But these actions may actually hurt the firm in the long run. As another example, recall the problem that the conglomerate experienced with a lack of risk talking or building assets for growth. A defined time period for incentive determination definitely increases the temptation for gaming.

Financial incentive systems may not always be rational, but they are always effective at attracting effort. Managers and workers will do all in their power, hopefully within legal guidelines, to maximize their individual reward. Thus, if the bonus targets are not set properly, or not synchronized with the firm's strategy, they can lead to serious dysfunctional behavior. The key is accurately delineating the intended results. The agents (management) can quickly lose sight of the firm's intended strategic targets when large personal gains are at stake.

Adding to the burden of running a good financial incentive system, the extrinsic motivation of money is not lasting and incentive money must be continually applied to be effective. With financial rewards, motivation is there only as long as there is money to pay for it. If reaching the criterion looks hopeless, motivation can completely evaporate. This is a good point to recall our earlier discussion of psychological and social rewards such as recognition, praise, or positive feedback. In contrast to financial incentives, non-financial rewards do not have to be part of a formal system. They can be (apparently) random—a very effective reinforcement pattern. Interestingly, research indicates that these kinds of intrinsic incentive rewards are much more powerful in driving behavior than monetary or extrinsic rewards. Indeed, behavior theorists insist that appealing to intrinsic values, such as being part of a successful team or knowing you are doing a good job, creates a lasting behavioral incentive.

Support for the idea that extrinsic rewards achieve only temporary compliance comes from laboratory, experimental, and field based studies conducted over the past 40 years. W. Edwards Deming made it very clear when he flatly said, "Pay is not a motivator."[1] This begs the question of why so many firms use extrinsic monetary rewards. Much of the answer lies in the simple fact that such programs are easy to do, it is the industry practice, and everyone does it to attract talent. Many firms focus on financial incentives in order to keep pace with the competition for talent. Yet, despite the high level of experience with financial incentives that the business world has accumulated over time, strategic financial incentive programs remain difficult to design and execute.

Why do intrinsic rewards work so well? The book *It's Your Ship*, by Michael Abrashoff, a former commanding officer, provides a wonderful set of examples of how to use intrinsic incentives to positively motivate behavior.[2] As the author notes, "the ship's captain can't hand out pay raises." Rather, Abrashoff had to understand what would motivate the 310-person crew of a modern Navy destroyer, and then create the incentive system using sound intrinsic motivation practices.

He was willing to change the processes to get the desired results and established a management system that made people accountable and responsible for their individual and team outputs. He rewarded achievement with public praise (in person and written), achievement medals, additional liberty in visiting ports, time off, and remembered to thank his crew often for their outstanding work. His sets of intrinsic rewards were very visible and the linkage of individual or group performance to the operations of the ship was very transparent. The ship's crew pulled together to deliver results for themselves and the ship. They flourished in the atmosphere of accountability and trust. This led to pride and a sense of accomplishment and resulted in the ship being recognized as one of the best functioning units in the entire Navy.

Whatever form they take—whether formal or informal, profit sharing, or individual rewards—incentives benefit from the attractiveness provided by achieving external outcomes. This expectancy of reward shapes individual behavior. Well-designed incentives emphatically influence behavior and can drive enhanced results. The challenge is to create a correct design that is properly linked to the intended results. Because good incentive design is tricky, incentive systems often fail. In some cases, they even derail results and de-motivate people. But they are essential tools of leadership.

Organization for Incentive Compensation

To give them shape, financial incentive compensation schemes are generally structured around the firm's organization. They reflect a serious attempt to measure and reward outputs of specific groups (division, subsidiary, department or individual) as part of the total firm. If there is not a clear and specific output measure then the corporate results are generally used. Corporate management and staff are normally incented on the total results.

Yet the organizational structure presents a very serious challenge for incentives. Many companies struggle to clearly define areas of responsibility or specific measurable outputs using their organizational structure. The reason? Cause and effect can become clouded. Management wants the output measures of the parts to link to the total. The tendency is to aggregate the output results to the total, which further separates the relationship between individual action/decisions and firm results. When the link between behavior and outcomes is muddied, this makes incentives much less powerful. The Navy captain's trial-and-error system ultimately worked well not only because he persisted in understanding motivation but also because of a very good match between accountability and responsibility.

Typically, management, with board approval, establishes the size of the incentive compensation pool and the method of determining payment. The tendency today is to make the pool large enough to get the attention of the management and workers. Indeed, there has been an increasing escalation of pool sizes as this form of variable compensation is used to attract and retain good people. Beer and Katz report that executives can expect, on an average, 31% of their compensation in incentives.[3] Many companies use formulas that pay bonuses after certain returns are reached for the stockholders. There is a plethora of financial-based formulas in use, but, generally speaking, the stockholders are willing to pay incentives after they have achieved some minimal target. In 2009, there is an increasing government and public outcry about the size of executive incentives and payment despite poor performance. As we discussed in Chapter 6 on governance, what are the board of directors thinking?

Management then develops financial formulas based on the organization for the distribution of the pool. There are numerous challenges around the pool size formulas and distribution schemes. For example, if management uses return on net assets (RONA) as a standard, it triggers a whole set of questions: Which assets are considered? What about off-balance sheet assets? What about shared assets?

Employing the organizational structure is a sensible way to partition an income statement or budget for incentive calculation purposes. This basically follows the notions of expense centers and profits centers we discussed in Chapter 7. The tricky part is in splitting the balance sheet in order to employ an investment center model for the incentive plan. From a structural point of view, designers want to hold managers accountable for the assets they use to deliver results. Overall financial metrics based on the DuPont formula (ROI, ROA, RONA, ROIC) measure the returns managers generate for the stockholders given the size of the asset pool they use. Mathematically, these types of financial measures produce superior results when the profits are large and the assets low. The challenge is weighting the size and robustness of the assets. Is the firm building for future growth, or are they reducing to maximize returns?

Consider what happens when incentive calculations are based on the DuPont formula. Managers could, in fact, be paid a bonus to maximize short-run returns, while stockholders prefer them to invest for future, long-term growth. Efficient use of assets is good, but a reluctance to invest for the future is short sighted.

Better reward systems do a good job of matching accountability with responsibility. A more difficult feat is structuring incentives around the organization. Some of the major particulars to consider are the following:

- How do you account for shared services (payroll, purchasing, accounting, HR, legal, and others)?
- How is the transfer pricing influencing the internal company results?
- What is the role of corporate services, and what do they cost?
- Are business units performance compared to their competitors in the market, not only to their sister companies?
- How do you balance unit and corporate incentives to get the best decision-making?

Shared services help gain economies of scale in large organizations by harnessing the buying power of the firm. The assets and costs associated with services are managed centrally, with operating units billed separately. The usual design is for the shared service center to break even. The internal fees are benchmarked to external providers for competitiveness. This model is gaining in popularity since it avoids the problems of allocations and the users pay only for what they consume.

More firms, more than 50% today, are moving to a market-based transfer pricing system to value the trades within company units. This prevents the hidden subsidy of a cost-based system and the time-consuming effort of a negotiated system. Market price allows for an eminently fair economic evaluation of unit performance.

The allocation of corporate services to business units has been a perennial bone of contention for managers. They often find allocations arbitrary and excessive. The trend is to keep the central allocated services small by using a shared-services model and having the business units do more for themselves. One of the remarkable achievements of Percy Barnevik, when he formed ABB by combining two large firms, was reducing headquarters headcount from 3000 people to 100, which significantly reduced overall costs and the resulting corporate charge to the 1400 business units.

ABB, often benchmarked for its unique matrix organizational design, properly matched accountability with responsibility to create an incentive plan that worked extremely well. In creating their blueprint, executives considered the many factors that can foul a good incentive system. They started with a central belief in decentralized decision-making, a lean headquarters staff, and minimal allocations. Operating units were left free to create their own service support systems. Transfer pricing was at market, with mechanisms to consider inflation and currency valuation.

They employed an overall measure of ROIC (return on invested capital) that applied a calculated interest charge for the balance sheet assets. The ROIC system was very much like an EVA calculation. Their reporting system was standardized throughout the global organization, using a common language of financial terms. This created an ABB language that senior managers used to evaluate and manage the mammoth organization. The ROIC system placed strong emphasis on managing assets, which was entirely compatible with their key success factors for earning positive returns from an asset-heavy mature business.

A common shortcoming of incentive systems is a tendency to adopt an array of targets that are generically sound but may not be a good fit with the strategic targets. To be effective, the incentive system must reinforce the total organizational targets, with each unit, department and individual working together. It is no easy task to align the staff and support functions with line operations, and only comes from clearly defined roles and responsibilities within the firm. We often observe firms who have been reluctant to take on this work and, instead, take an easier road.

The fallback position to such nitty–gritty definitions is to use financial measures that link to the overall measure of EVA or ROE. This is why ROI and RONA have been popular financial metrics for division and subsidiary incentives. They are understood by senior managers and relate to external stakeholder evaluation. There are, however, some very serious barriers to overcome. Clearly delineating the balance sheet assets employed, and then relating these measures to the parts of the organization is tricky. A clean split of assets employed is often difficult and can lead to arbitrary assignments.

Moreover, many people do not see the connection between their activity and the high-level financial results, and many do not understand the financial metrics. As a consequence, more firms are now employing a set of custom operational and market non-financial measures to calculate incentives. Managers are trying to match rewards with results at all levels of the firm.

Using Non-financial Measures for Financial Incentives

Recognizing the limits of financial measures to capture performance, firms have found creative ways to construct incentives in order to obtain the desired behavior. In the April 1997 issue of *The Accounting Review*, authors Ittner, Larcker, and Rajan examined 317 firms using both financial and non-financial bonus programs.[4] They found that financial measures dominate among companies with stable defender strategies and with powerful CEOs. Non-financial measures were used more often with innovation-oriented prospector strategies, regulated firms, or when there was "noise" in the financial results. In an earlier study Nanni found that incentives based on non-financial measures are preferred at operational levels in the organization, while incentives based on financial results were preferred at the top, strategic level.[5]

It is no surprise that management has devised innovative new measures to deliver results. One study found that the non-financial performance incentives demonstrably link to improved financial results.[6] Both customer satisfaction and profits increased. There was, however, a time lag from 6 to 12 months between improvements in the non-financial performance and the financial performance. This raises the process issue: When do you pay the incentive? Do you trust that the strategic decomposition that identified the non-financial measures? An even more nettlesome issue is: Are you sure the specific individual caused or personally contributed to the results? Are accountability and responsibility properly aligned for that individual?

Normally bonuses are rewarded to groups based on their team output and level in the firm. There is more difficulty in linking action to performance results for staff positions or for those not directly in the line of delivering results. The design challenge when using financial formulas is to trickle down the relevancy of the formula so that those at the lower organizational level see their impact. How, for instance, does the shipping clerk relate to firm ROI?

Because of the difficulty of determining cause and effect when using financial metrics, many firms have added a subjective component to bonus calculations. As noted in the conglomerate example above, management used non-quantifiable tools for bonuses to help with the linkages. Managers indicate that such flexibility gives them the ability to reward attitude and effort. Yet subjectivity is inherently biased and can be misinterpreted as "politics".

One of the prime undertakings of the balanced scorecard and strategy map movement is to actually chart the relationship of overall financial results to each part of the firm. This quest is motivated by a desire to have everyone in the organization understand his or her contributions to the total financial results. The mapping process grew out of the need to link outputs, behavior, and decision-making to the strategy.

A good example of the power of non-financial measures for incentive calculations comes from the Irving Oil example discussed in Chapter 5. To boost market share, the 400 store convenience retail operation launched an incentive system for individual store managers and personnel. The company had always differentiated itself on clean facilities and friendly people. Management wanted to insure that store people would relate to the incentive metrics around customer focus and genuinely see a cause and effect of their behavior. They established five measures. Leading indicators were friendless of staff, pride in property (cleanliness), and overall customer satisfaction. These measures were gathered from regular random customer surveys. The other two results measures were sales compared to budget and payroll expenses as a percentage of total sales. The reports and incentive payments were made quarterly. Managers and store personnel earned bonuses based on their composite score on the three leading indicators.

The incentive system was carefully rolled out. Good internal communications helped ensure significant buy-in by the store managers. The company provided trusted data that was made readily available to all. The result: a steady improvement in the leading indicators and a gradual improvement of the lagging financial indicators. Not surprisingly, management found a strong correlation between the incentive scores and the financial performance of the store. The system highlighted the strong connection between what the store personnel can control (behavior) and their rewards for performance. The incentive program did what it was supposed to do: It rewarded the right employee actions and attitudes which, in turn, produced superior financial results.

Do Rewards Lead to Results?

So why is there a continued heavy emphasis on financial motivation? Good question. The data on the effectiveness of incentives on delivering results performance are actually quite inconclusive. On the face of the rapid growth of variable compensation plans, researchers have questioned their impact on improved results.[7] Several major studies have focused their attention on this issue. Jim Collins, in his very popular book, *Good to Great*, did not find incentives drove firms to greatness. "We found no systematic pattern linking executive compensation to the process of going from good to great. The evidence simply does not support the idea that the specific structure of executive compensation acts as a key lever in taking a company from good to great."[8] On the other hand, the NYSE office of economic research maintains that their survey of members indicates that incentives did improve performance.[9]

Many persistently believe that the increased use of bonuses will enhance performance and that this form of compensation (variable comp) is necessary to attract and retain talent. Yet at the same time, they will also admit that incentives may have little influence on results.[10] Others firmly believe profit sharing will enhance employee satisfaction and sense of ownership. They point to the very successful profit-sharing program at Lincoln Electric. The shared benefits approach leads to cooperation and improved productivity. Success in the process, in turn, leads to trust among members of the firm.[11] The real question is: With all these good feelings for the workers and attractive bonuses for executives, are the firm's results better? The answer is sometimes.

Much field-based and experimental research has probed the effectiveness of incentives. Conclusions come down on both sides of the argument. For ourselves, we believe that incentives can be a powerful motivator and can get the attention of the work force to deliver the desired results or bring about culture change. But, the key is designing the system so that the rewards are truly linked to the desired behavior and performance. This isn't easy. Delivering results is not dependent on incentive systems. Rather, incentives properly designed and executed may allow you to get the desired behavior faster. Financial incentives can turbo-charge effort.

Design Challenges

How do you account for good fortune or bad? It's more than an idle question. Managers need to know whether certain results were actually beyond their control, or are the result, say, of good karma and being in the right place at the right time. They thus want to build into the incentive system a mechanism that will consider good and bad luck. Some argue luck is the result of good planning and insight. The classic question is: What do you do if all the financial targets were hit—ROI, profit, etc.—but the division lost market share? Is this good or poor performance? After all, they achieved the targeted financial results. Yet the market grew faster than anyone predicted and the competition was able to capture more customers. How also do you factor in for natural or unnatural disasters (i.e., 9/11) that devastate an economy or a market? This is when management must perform at their best.

One of us had the dubious pleasure of attending a national meeting of regional sales managers at a telecom equipment manufacturer where this problem came up. The VP of marketing was conducting the meeting. Sales for the prior year were up across the country, but only one sales region, the Northeast, had booked sales at a high enough level to kick in a special bonus. The numbers were indisputably higher than the budgeted target for the region. The regional sales manager was quite pleased. However, the market had expanded very unevenly during the year and market share in the Northeast had actually fallen. This was in contrast to the Midwest, where the sales budget bonus target had not been reached, but market share had increased. Technically, the bonus had to be paid to the Northeast team, but the VP was not going to let the irony of the situation go unremarked. He verbally assaulted the shocked regional manager and, at one point said, "a monkey could have gotten your results last year!"

Rigid financial incentive formulas based on future expectations are certainly sensitive to unanticipated changes in the environment. They're designed to fail. All of which begs the questions: Should good management plan and budget for the unexpected? Or, should unexpected events be removed from the bonus calculations? Most prefer the latter. But that doesn't resolve the basic issue of how should you anticipate the unexpected.

To help manage the murky future, managers often add a subjective management evaluation that allows adjustments to incentives to, well, compensate for unpredicted events. Subjective evaluations for performance are also used as a barometer to adjust for good or bad luck and individual attitudes. When employing this design option, you are also subject to increased gaming and the very real possibility of abusing the incentive system. There needs to be a good balance between the subjective and the objective incentive component. It is impossible to get it to be perfect. Most managers live with the possibilities of some inequity.

Another important consideration is: Who is eligible? Should everyone participate in a bonus system or should there be some cutoff level? How do you scale the incentive plan for different salary levels? Firms employ a variety of mechanisms to create such flexibility. Incentive plan designers must weigh these choices very carefully. We are strong believers in full participation for all employees. People making the difference in delivering results work at all levels. The shipping clerk who catches a wrong address or works late to make an emergency shipment has a big impact on customer satisfaction. Rewarding him also sends a message. Indeed, if workers feel their actions are contributing to the results, and they are recognized, you have established a powerful motivation tool. Cutoffs create separate classes of have and have-nots, as well as strong resentment between groups.

An illustration of the problem of inclusiveness and tiered financial incentives by management level can be found in a global provider of retail payment processing equipment and software. In the late 1990s, the company was highly regarded as an innovative, agile competitor. The company prided itself on being "flat," with few levels of management. Nonetheless, it had a very clear distinction when it came to the incentive plans. Top managers with business segment responsibility were incented with a sharply accelerating bonus plan based on financial targets and EVA for their business units. The bonus range began at 10% of base salary and quickly rose to 100% of base. These targets were isolated to the specific business unit and carried no corporate charges, taxes, or financing. Executives regularly received generous bonus pay-outs. Everyone else participated in a general profit-sharing plan where they could receive approximately 2% of their base pay if the company achieved a target return on sales based on net income after tax. Unfortunately for the rank and file, reported financial results regularly fell just shy of that criterion several years in a row. Shortly thereafter, when a very large technology firm acquired the company in generously proportioned stock-swap, it was shocked to find a decidedly unmotivated work force!

Financial incentives are like candy. A steady diet of them loses its special quality. Experience shows that once incentive systems are in place—and there have been several pay-outs—bonuses are often treated as guaranteed income. It becomes expected. This creates a sense of entitlement and the unwillingness to change goals. Incentives need to be dynamic and endlessly adjustable.

For instance, take the unfortunate case of an electrical component manufacturing division that had established a bonus program based on RONA for all employees in graduated steps for levels in the firm. Happily for them, the company's employees constantly made or exceeded their targets and the workers began to view the early December bonus (about 10% of annual salary) as a given. It became part of their compensation. One year, however, Christmas didn't come. The workers fell behind target and it started to dawn on them that bonuses might not arrive. Many people thought that something dramatic would happen at the last moment to save the year's bonus. It did not. Unfortunately, a number of families spent the "guaranteed" bonus before it was earned. Management had to help several families with debt restructuring and even personal bankruptcy. The CEO pointed out to his management team that there were positive lessons from not achieving the bonus. It removed the guaranteed expectancy and made people realize incentives had to be earned.

The entitlement notion can be made worse by the design of the incentive criteria. Establishment of a fixed level on one or more measures, as opposed to some kind of variable pay-out or measure of incremental improvement provides the foundation of a "good enough" mentality in addition to entitlement. A well-documented example of this phenomenon appeared in a popular business school case on the customer service operation at AT&T Universal Card.[12] Universal Card was introduced in 1990 and pioneered the use of a "no annual fee" card. The services operation was designed to be another differentiating factor for the credit card company, providing high-quality, and efficient operations. It created a bundle of quality metrics and measured them every day. For every day that 95% of the measures in that bundle exceeded a specific target, a bonus payment would be made to every employee in the organization. The results were noteworthy. The company earned a Malcolm Baldrige National Quality Award. The number of bonus-earning days per month approached 100%. Leadership decided that it was time to move to a higher plane of quality outcomes, so they changed both the percentage of measures exceeding criterion needed to earn a bonus and the underlying level of the specific targets. Employees reacted to the double-change in the system as a double-cross and simply a way to pay them less. Quality performance fell. It took concerted effort by management and a softening of the requirements to bring performance back on track.

Bonuses are for delivering results during a specific period of time. As we stated earlier, generally it is a 1-year period, but there is a growing tendency to use longer periods coinciding with the length of the strategic plan. Such lengthening of time periods helps avert the all-too-common phenomenon of making your numbers "creatively". This practice is at the heart of many of the recent ethical transgressions of managers that have become newspaper headlines.

This bonus-maximizing mindset became a very real worry for a publicly traded high-tech firm that we studied. After several initial successful new products rolled out the door, new ideas and longer-term business opportunities were suddenly in short supply. In order to jumpstart entrepreneurial thinking, the firm created an internal venture capital fund. This encouraged people to pursue ideas but structured the accounting so that it would not impact the current bonus calculations. The funding was relatively simple and the pool of funds motivated people to obtain support for their new ideas. The firm had a good cash flow from established products, but until they started the venture fund the number of new growth ideas was embarrassingly meager.

Yet another design snare is the size and nature of the reward. The expectancy theory issue relates to whether the individual efforts exerted toward the reward will be proportional to the size of the reward. Ideally, you want to find the best expected effort for the reward. Related to this is whether it would be more cost effective to use non-monetary rewards, such as trips or dinners. You need to size reward big enough to get individuals' attention and influence their behavior. But not too big. Here's a test: What size and kind of incentive would motivate a salesperson to decide, at 4:55 p.m., to make another sales call rather than head for home?

Linkages

The overriding design consideration is establishing the proper linkages. Whether you take the philosophy of profit sharing or rewarding individual results, an effective incentive system has well-established linkages so that the individual is properly motivated and understands the appropriate action or the correct decision-making rule. Linkages must occur on multiple levels:

- Individual goals linked to the firm goals;
- Accountability linked to responsibility;
- Measures linked to intended actions.

These connections are the same issues we covered in Chapters 4 though 9, but they deserve a quick recap here. The first level strives for companywide goal congruency. This overarching linkage is very difficult to create. It is rare to find the division balanced to the corporation, the department balanced to the division, and the individual balanced to the department. This takes a shared belief system; a clear understanding and acceptance of the strategy; and an awareness of the individual or group role in executing the strategy. The technique of strategy mapping is a popular practice that attempts to create strategic alignment within a firm. Do not assume that once the strategy is articulated then everyone will follow the flag. Business unit strategies do not always fall under the corporate strategy umbrella. Department activities are not always well coordinated. Managers may have different agendas. Individual workers may see no connection or, worse, disagree with the strategic direction. It is imperative that managers spend the time to articulate the strategy and execute an internal marketing plan to get buy-in at all levels.

One of us attended what was supposed to be a major strategy speech from a new company CEO. It was clear that a lot of thought had gone into the CEO's preparation, but he had not prepared the audience! As they were leaving at the end of the talk, one senior executive simply remarked to another, "This, too, shall pass."

Most people have experienced firms with multiple agendas and disagreement between parts of the firm. The causes are many. Disharmony can come from a lack of a clear strategy, a mushy generic strategy (grow and make profit) or no strategy at all. The most challenging circumstance is when there is passive resistance among the managers. No incentive system will function without fundamental agreement on ends and means.

Such a mismatch occurred at a software company that was growing very rapidly. The company had set aggressive growth targets, and sales were doubling every year. But a strategic disconnect between the board of directors and the senior management team led to an incentive program that was at war with itself. During a very challenging year, management made the decision to sacrifice sales and top line growth to preserve profitability. The board, however, had expected growth even at the cost of short-term profitability. They felt the size of the top line drove valuation. There were two strategies but only one incentive program, which meant somebody was wrong. The board substantially reduced the bonuses, creating a rift between the board and the management team that took years to repair.

The message is that managers need to take the time to build consensus around the strategy, clearly define roles, and *continually communicate* internally. No tool or technique can triumph without an open dialogue, one that ensures that the strategy is fully developed and has obtained clear buy-in at all levels. Do not underestimate the internal marketing campaign necessary to get all parts of the organization to understand and accept the strategy.

The second linkage level is ensuring that the unit or individual being incented has the control and freedom to produce the intended outputs. Does the manager have responsibility for all of the factors that will determine the performance results? We very often observe that managers are held accountable for certain result outputs, but they do not control all of the factors needed to produce them. That is the definition of a straw boss: responsibility without authority.

In Chapter 4, we emphasized the importance of matching accountability with responsibility. A mismatch is one of the greatest frustrations managers face. How often we have heard impotent managers say things like: "We do not have the resources to carry out our mission." "With that size of allocation, there is no way we can meet our profit goals." "Given centralized marketing, I have no control over my destiny." It is a rare situation when a manager can control all of the factors necessary for achieving results. But the likelihood of him actually delivering against expectations increases proportionately with his control levels. Effective incentive systems, therefore, make a real effort to match accountability with responsibility.

An excellent example of getting a good match between accountability and responsibility returns us to the Irving Oil chain of convenience stores mentioned earlier. In one specific area, the metric of success was aimed at improving the perceived "friendliness" of store employees. The firm launched an incentive-backed measurement system that systematically surveyed customers about the attitudes and helpfulness of the store personnel. With coaching and training, the store friendliness scores started to dramatically improve. The store associates quickly figured out how their new behavior improved the score and put cash into their pockets. Note that this incentive plan represented a bet on the part of management that service "friendliness" would pay off for the firm, too. Management was delighted with the discovery that the stores with high attitude scores also produced the best financial results.

The final level of linkage is making sure that the measures are properly linked to the desired actions. As we discussed in Chapters 8 and 9, it is critical that managers understand how measures reinforce their actions and decisions. Most incentive measures are dominated by financial results, which link to external market valuation. But it is very difficult to capture a business unit or manager's performance with a few finance-dominated metrics. Such metrics will also skew decision-making. What's needed, however, is balance among conflicting goals. All performance measures are not equal; some measures are used to calculate bonuses and others are used to evaluate performance. When faced with a choice, incentive measures—especially financial ones—will be top of mind and drive individual behavior. This becomes a problem when improved achievement in one area comes at the expense of poor performance in another.

Managers are constantly asked to balance competing forces: short term vs. long term, profit vs. growth, new-equipment vs. renewal of old equipment; develop within vs. bring in from the outside, and so forth. Given the fact that incentives are framed in a time period, managers will make decisions that produce the largest incentive in that slice of time. And this may not be in the best interest of the firm in the long run.

Is exceeding target profit but losing market share good performance? You'd better decide, because most incentive systems use profits over market share to calculate bonuses. You can probably recall a stream of instances in the business press where managers were handsomely rewarded incentive plans despite losing market share, ROI, or market valuation. Such cases are textbook examples of rewarding the wrong results. The use of financial metrics is further compromised with the new trend of restating earnings, often due to a revised accounting rule interpretation. A number of firms are suing their former CEOs to return such engineered bonuses. As a result of the financial crisis of 2009, state and federal governments began to challenge the large bonuses paid to executives in the financial services industry after their firms produced billion dollar losses and needed government assistance to survive.

The incentive design challenge is to link the rewards to the desired output. The difficulty is in identifying the outputs for each group in the organization. As noted above, financial outputs often ignore many actions needed to produce good results. Without the linkages there is little or no behavior change.

If a formal incentive system is used, managers must insure that there is consistency in message between the formal and the informal rewards. Recognition of good work at a meeting, or even in the hallways, needs to be consistent with the formal system. Research indicates that informal rewards have a much greater influence on individual behavior than the formal variety. Positive or negative feedback from a manager demonstrates interest in the individual and has a very strong effect on the behavior.

Implementation

If a firm chooses to use incentives, it then needs to pay very careful attention to how the program is developed and rolled out. Designers must think through the process, rules, linkages, and metrics. A good way to begin is to focus on the execution of the strategy. For example, board members might ask top managers, "What are the top 10 items you must do in order to achieve your strategy and deliver this year's results?" They also want management to link the strategic business plan and the annual operating plan. There is a healthy dialogue with the board to make sure that the 10 items are indeed the ones necessary to deliver the operational plan and are consistent with the long-term strategy.

This process is similar to a brainstorming session where all possibilities are listed and discussed. To build eventual consensus, everyone must be heard in order to balance competing interests, opinions, and objectives. Then, using the final list, the functional and department managers go through the same exercise with their teams. The process is cascaded throughout the organization.

Performance is measured against the targets (objectives) and measurement tools are agreed upon at all organizational levels. The achievement of targets is evaluated on a 5-point scale (5 = far above target, 4 = above target, 3 = target, 2 = below target, and 1 = far below target). At the beginning of the year, a pool of incentive funds is determined with an expected score of 3. There is no hard and fast numeric cutoff. Rather, the score is based on management's overall evaluation. Subjective considerations can be used to balance any good or bad luck or unforeseen market or world events. In the end, it works quite well.

If designed well, the system creates good linkages and then sets the incentive guidelines to accommodate the design challenges. Proper preparation also means that luck and unforeseen events can be accommodated with good judgment. With criteria selection done throughout the firm, system guidelines are not only pressure tested, they cascade downward naturally. Analysis has assured that the size of any reward is sufficient to induce action. The only design challenge that needed close scrutiny was the time parameter and the possibility of gaming. They were able to use the subjective portion of the program to accommodate strange period-end results.

Conclusion

Incentive systems can do many things. They can motivate results. They can create a sense of organizational urgency with a focus on delivering results. They can influence behavior if the incentives are valued, understood, and relate to the individual or group responsibility. And, if well designed, they can create goal congruency between the individuals, the organizational unit, and the firm.

But they are also tricky. Incentives are not neutral. They will motivate behavior. The challenge is to stimulate the desired behavior. The literature is evenly divided between those that maintain that incentives are a critical and useful component of a measurement system and those that argue they are a waste of time. Some believe that the use of incentives is a crutch for poor management and leadership. Incentives are not necessary for delivering results but they can accelerate the process if used properly. We have discussed many of the serious design and implementation traps. Despite these concerns more firms, including not for profit organizations, are implementing incentive programs.

Be careful!

Notes

1. Deming, W.E., PBS video *"The Deming of America"*; (1990)
2. Abrashoff. D. M., *It's Your Ship* (New York: Warner Books, 2002).
3. Beer, M., Harvard Business School and the Center for Organizational Fitness; Nancy Katz, Kennedy School, Harvard University: *"Do Incentives Work? The Perception of a Worldwide Sample of Senior Executives"*. (Boston, MA: Harvard Business School Press, 2003).
4. Ittner, C.D., Larcker, D.F. and Rajan, M.V., *"The Choice of Performance Measures in Annual Bonus Contracts,"* The Accounting Review, (Vol. 72, No. 2, pp. 231–255, April, 1997).
5. Nanni, Alfred J. "Performance Measurement and the Communication of Strategic Priorities: Limits to the Use of Cost Accounting Data," *Economia Aziendale* (Vol. 9, No. 2, pp. 213–231, August, 1990).
6. Banker, R.D., Potter, G., and Srinivasan, D. "An Empirical Investigation of an Incentive Plan that includes Nonfinancial Performance Measures," *The Accounting Review*, (Vol. 75, No. 1, pp. 65–92, January, 2000).
7. Kohn, A., "Why Incentive Plans Cannot Work," *Harvard Business Review*, (September 1993).
8. Collins, J., *Good to Great*, (New York: Harper Collins, 2001), p. 49.
9. New York Stock Exchange, Office of Economic Research, *"People and Productivity : A Challenge to Corporate America,"* (1982).
10. Pepper, S. *Senior Executive Reward*, (Burlington, VT: Gower Publishing, 2006).
11. Dawson, V. P. *Lincoln Electric: A History,* (Cleveland, OH: Lincoln Electric, 1999).
12. Shapiro, R.D., Watkins, M.D., and Rosegrant, S., "A Measure of Delight: The Pursuit of Quality at AT&T Universal Card Services (A) (case 9-964-047)", (Boston, MA: Harvard Business School Publishing, 1993).

Chapter 12
Management as a System: Executing Strategy Through the MSDR

For much of this book, we have been peeling back layers of the MSDR and examining its components. We started by giving you a sort of "parts inventory," enumerating different kinds of mechanisms for directing attention and providing feedback. From there, we proceeded to a discussion of strategy. We cited some well-known management models and placed them within three broad tactics for MSDR design. Since then, we have examined a series of MSDR parts related to those design principles—organizational culture, organizational design, balanced and aligned performance measures, and rewards and incentives. Now we need to put all those parts together and show you how a complete MSDR supports the execution of the company strategy.

The time has come to return to the initial premise of this book. Management Systems that Deliver Results need to be viewed from a holistic, systems perspective. The parts of the MSDR must fit the strategy and must work together harmoniously to support the execution of the strategy. The management system is more than the sum of its parts. There should be a positive, goal-oriented synergy. In order for the management system to deliver results reliably, the parts need to reinforce each other in guiding organizational members toward strategic behavior, motivating and reinforcing that behavior.

Assembling an MSDR

As we peeled back the layers of an MSDR throughout this book, we did so generally in the order of responsiveness to change. We started with the organizational culture not only because shared attitudes, beliefs, and behavioral habits are powerful motivators and have a profound effect on strategy execution but also because, by its nature, organizational culture is slow to change. It takes a long while for people to establish a common social platform, even if they are selected for membership in the firm based heavily on their attitudes and traits. You can certainly influence your organization's culture, but you cannot change it on command. The next layer we examined, organizational design and structure, is much more directly under your direction as a manager. But changes in these characteristics are complicated and

L.P. Carr, A.J. Nanni, Jr., *Delivering Results*, DOI 10.1007/978-1-4419-0621-2_12, © Springer Science+Business Media, LLC 2009 time consuming. Such changes require deliberate planning, not only in design but also in implementation. We discussed performance measures at the next level. You can adjust performance measures much more quickly than either organizational culture or organizational design. Performance measures, too, need to be planned and implemented carefully, but such changes are possible over shorter periods. Finally, we introduced rewards and incentives. These system features can be attached to new or existing performance criteria very quickly and, at least for new reward plans, they can be implemented very quickly, too. The germination period for each part of the MSDR system is different. We need to plan our MSDR garden so that all of the flowers bloom at the right time to complement each other. This is accomplished by taking a holistic approach. We must consider the total garden not just the individual flower beds.

This gardening analogy may sound a bit flowery (excuse the pun), but we think it is an appropriate one. You can't have a decent garden if you plant and manage one section independently from the others. While you are working on one section, another may become full of weeds, overgrow its boundaries, or die from lack of water. We can apply the "peel back the layers" logic to management system components in isolation, but once we start thinking about putting them all together, that logic breaks down. Now the central objective is to make the parts fit together and work in unison to support execution of the strategy. Every aspect of an MSDR affects every other aspect. For example, changing the performance measures will have an effect on the attitudes and beliefs of the people whose work activity is captured in the measurement. In fact, that's the whole idea! You can put together an MSDR by starting with "off the shelf" seeds, but they have to be precisely planted and then carefully tended in order to assure that the system will actually deliver strategic results. The best way to describe that gardening process is through an example.

Looking Inside Management Systems

We have tried to provide frequent examples to illustrate effective and ineffective management systems. Those examples have fallen into three broad categories. Probably the most recognizable examples are the ones we might call management system horror stories. These have been the examples of management systems gone wrong, examples of management systems that delivered bad results. The great majority of such stories came to us via third parties. These are the kinds of stories that you are apt to run into in the business press. This is natural. After all, disasters make more interesting news than pleasant cruises. When management systems go wrong, they attract attention!

A second broad category of examples has been illustrations of companies who experienced a strategy execution glitch, but not a management system failure. These firms were able to recover by having a system that was able to be adjusted to "go right." A critical task of an MSDR is to right the organizational ship when an unanticipated disturbance knocks it off course. These stories are far less frequent in the business press. When they appear, it is typically because the event that threw the company off course was noteworthy. If no one outside the company noticed the problem, the correction would be invisible, too. Examples of organizations where something had gone wrong but had been repaired usually came to us after the fact. Members of these organizations were happy to tell their stories, but only after they had found a way out of the adversity.

Finally, we have presented a handful of examples where companies truly had an MSDR. These systems not only delivered results, but they were the focus of intense management attention and, as a result, continuously improved. In most cases, examples of the best management systems came to us while they were in progress. These examples were revealed directly to us by the organizations. We (nor you) would have been able to detect them by external observation. This fact reveals an important truth about MSDRs. While it is relatively easy to see when the parts of a management system don't fit, an effective MSDR is nearly invisible! From an external perspective, it just appears that management is doing a good job of strategy execution. Management systems reveal themselves to the outside world when they blow up. A seamless MSDR makes managers look good and makes management look easy. However, it should be clear to you by now that creating an MSDR takes serious, thoughtful planning, and continuous attention. Their managers are always weeding, pruning, and watering their MSDR gardens, but they are also always thinking about how to do even better next season.

In retrospect, how these examples were revealed to us all makes sense. Organizations that have not managed their whole management systems "garden" don't need consultation, they need to plow it under and begin a complete redesign. Organizations that are experiencing major challenges to their management system need immediate remedies, not development. But organizations that are doing a good job with their management systems are the ones that are constantly examining, tweaking, and improving those systems. In other words, they are vigilant gardeners. With that kind of focus, they are the most likely to be looking for opinions, consultation, and advice.

In order to illustrate how those management system parts fit and work together, we will focus on a single pair of related examples—two businesses owned by a single entrepreneur who, coincidentally, is a graduate of our college. In keeping with the discussion above, it should not be so surprising to learn that these examples came to us rather than us going out searching for them. It was a pleasant surprise to find an example of a very compelling MSDR in what is arguably our own backyard!

Jefferson Vander Wolk brought the story of his MSDR to us through an indirect route. Jeff is a Babson graduate from well before either of us joined the faculty. One of us was introduced to him over lunch during a visit he made to our campus for other purposes. The antennae went up when he asked, within 15 minutes of our introduction, "Why don't more companies use the Lincoln Electric model?" You may recall from our discussions in Chapters 5 and 11 that Lincoln Electric has long had a very effective profit-sharing program. True, the Lincoln Electric story is well known in our academic circles, but it's not something we expect to come up in a casual conversation! Obviously, this was a business manager who was intensely interested in management systems, enough to have done his own reading and research.

Interestingly, Jeff Vander Wolk's pursuit of a highly effective management system began at roughly the same time as each of us began our own examinations of the characteristics of MSDR's. While we were running, studying, and consulting on management systems, Jeff Vander Wolk was running experiments on his own businesses. Those experiments eventually resulted in a pair of MSDR's which we believe illustrate many of the basic principles we have put forward in this book. For the rest of this chapter, we will use those systems and the businesses in which they reside to illustrate how the parts of an MSDR fit together and reinforce each other.

An MSDR at Work: The Waterway Café and The Inn of the Governors

Jeff Vander Wolk had been a successful real estate developer. Over the years, he had progressed from developing properties to operating some of them, too. Currently, his business interests include a popular restaurant in South Florida and a busy hotel and restaurant in New Mexico. He has installed his management systems in both of these businesses. The two businesses share some common features, but there are some notable differences, too. We believe it will be helpful to look at each of them.

The Waterway Café is a restaurant located on the Intracoastal Waterway several miles north of West Palm Beach, Florida. The Intracoastal Waterway is an engineering-enhanced natural break between the Florida mainland and the Atlantic beaches of southern Florida. In front of the Waterway Café, it carries a fairly steady traffic of pleasure boats and small commercial craft moving between the open Atlantic, major bays, and inland mooring locations. The restaurant is, as you might expect, nautically themed. In fact, two of its special physical characteristics are related to the waterway. There is a "floating bar" comprised of a gangway running to gazebo-topped barge on the waterway. The layout of the floating bar is similar to a bull's-eye. The center is the bar with stools around it. Then next ring is an access aisle. The outer ring is comprised of dining tables. Furthermore, about 300 hundred feet of mooring space is available for watercraft visitors. Boaters can radio ahead for take-out or to reserve a table.

The great majority of the restaurant's traffic, however, comes by automobile. Here, the proximity to the water is a bit of an inconvenience. The Café is immediately adjacent to a bridge that runs from the beach to the mainland on a major thoroughfare. Because it is a divided road, you can only enter the parking lot from the eastbound direction. Because the bridge must clear the water high enough to let water craft pass underneath, the causeway ramps extend well inland from the waterway. The result is that the entrance to the Café's parking lot is well away from the restaurant itself. If you aren't paying close attention, you can easily miss it, despite the signage. If you do miss the entrance, then your recovery is complicated. You must go over the bridge to an intersection on the beach side, make a u-turn, go back over the bridge to an inland intersection, make another u-turn, and try again. You certainly have to want to go there more than you are worried about driving convenience!

The Inn of the Governors is a hotel and restaurant situated at the edge of the downtown section of Santa Fe, New Mexico. It is laid out like a large stucco-walled hacienda, with three interconnected buildings in the compound and parking in what might have been large courtyards a century ago. One of the main physical advantages of the Inn is that it lies within easy walking distance of Santa Fe's main plaza, major art galleries, and upscale shops. Hence, it is a destination for tourists. Nonetheless, many locals patronize the Del Charro Saloon, the Inn's restaurant and bar. Like the Waterway Café, the Inn's location also has a downside. Santa Fe's downtown area derives part of its charm from its narrow roads and alleys, but narrow roads and alleys are not conducive to free movement for modern American vehicles (and modern American travelers). The route to the Inn's entrance is not nearly as simple as pulling off the highway into a typical motel. Beyond that, the act of parking in the Inn's courtyard spaces represent a level of effort two or three times more difficult than the angle parking typical of those locations. Again, convenience of access isn't why you go to the Inn of the Governors.

The Strategies

If an MSDR is a tightly woven, synergistic whole, then where do we begin to examine one? The answer is simple, and it reprises one of the major themes of this book—start with the strategy. The two businesses share several common traits. Both businesses serve similar target markets. They are both "mid-price casual" establishments, not too different in price or clientele from many of the national restaurant or hotel chains. They compete head to head with those familiar institutions and do not have the national name recognition or advertising to rely upon.

These businesses do not try to differentiate themselves on novelty. There are no particular gimmicks—no animatronic talking moose in the lobby, no soaring foyers or open glass elevators. (The irony of novelty in the hospitality business is that it gets old quickly.) Instead, the Café serves eclectic American food with a South Florida accent. The Del Charro serves southwest-inspired American food. The Inn has the kinds of room you would expect from a mid-price hotel, ranging from roughly 250 to 450 square feet in size and priced on a basis relative to size. Both businesses have tasteful, thematic décor. Neither business relies on uniqueness of the physical offering as its customer value proposition. Instead, these businesses pursue a more enduring form of competitive advantage. They both have a strategy predicated on excellent customer service.

Your initial reaction may be that "customer service" as a strategic emphasis is not particularly creative or different. You'd be right! But is that so surprising? If you and your competitors are aiming for the same customers, and those customers have an identifiable need to be met, wouldn't you expect that you would all come up with roughly the same value proposition to address those needs? So how would you differentiate your business and gain a competitive advantage? In short, you would need to execute that strategy better than your competitors. That's why you need an MSDR. Let's now look at how the Waterway Café and the Inn of the Governors do that.

For both businesses, the strategic proposition is that pleased customers become loyal customers. Loyal customers not only return, but they tell their friends. This brings in new customers, who then become loyal customers, who tell *their* friends. The result is a growing and reliable string of customers and a growing and reliable revenue stream.

So what is required to please customers enough for them to become loyal customers and sources of referrals? Certainly, there is some base set of requirements that are necessary, but not sufficient. For example, the bathrooms need to be stocked with soaps and towels. The premises must be clean. The food must be fresh, well prepared, and delivered when ready. You may be able to recall stays at hotels or meals at restaurants where these minimal criteria were not met. Odds are, you didn't return if you were able to avoid it. But would simply meeting these criteria make you a *loyal* customer?

Think about some of the less obvious things that diminished your experience at a restaurant or hotel. Usually, it isn't the core things. The food may have been fine, but maybe the service was inattentive or slow. The place was busy and the wait was long, but, even so, you felt like you were forgotten. Worse yet, when you noticed that there were empty tables and asked what the holdup was, you were told that the delay was due to the fact that the restaurant was out of clean napkins and flatware. The room was decent, but you couldn't get the cleaning service to refresh the room on a schedule convenient to you. You got someone else's wake-up call. You probably remember thinking, "How hard is it to do this stuff?"

The problem is the people—not any single one of them, but the result of all of them. Each person in the organization may be focused on his or her task, but things slip between the cracks. The hand-offs fail. Thus, at the Waterway Café and the Inn of the Governors, the objective is to create a system where nothing falls between the cracks. The goal is to have seamless service and that requires high-performance teams.

It may help to think about a high-performance team as a professional basketball team. You may not be a big basketball fan, but you don't need to be an expert to see the fluidity and responsiveness of the five members of a basketball squad. When play starts, each member of the team has as assigned primary role. However, as the game proceeds, the roles adjust spontaneously in response to the challenges and opportunities that arise. There are several important implications we can extract from this analogy. First, to have a high-performance team, every member must have the capability to be able to do the other's job, even if not quite as skillfully. That calls for training and development. Second, each player on the team as a whole has to be able to anticipate the other players' moves. That requires coaching, familiarity with each other, and practice. Third, each player has to be able to anticipate the challenges and opportunities that are about to arise, or, at least, recognize them immediately when they do. That is a consequence of intensity and focus on the goal and an ability to read the situation. Finally, the whole team needs to have the same strong drive to win. That implies that everyone on the team has an "all for one and one for all" mentality which, in turn, implies that a win for one *is* actually a win for all.

That last statement may sound a bit strange. Of course, when a basketball team wins a game, everyone on the team wins. But in a hotel or restaurant, that shared outcome isn't always (or even often) the case. "Winning" customers does not have the same outcome for the waiter, the hostess, and the dishwasher, even though all three have to contribute to secure the win.

So here is the causal chain:

1. Pleasing the customer requires high-performance teams;
2. High-performance teams need cross-functional capabilities;
3. High-performance teams need coaching, practice, and experience with each other;
4. High-performance teams need to focus on the goal;
5. Every member of a high-performance team needs to share in the outcome.

The management systems at the Waterway Café and the Inn of the Governors needed to have all five of those characteristics in order to execute a strategy that would differentiate them from their competition based on excellent customer service.

Let's now look at those management systems in detail to see how their parts fit with each other to support and encourage customer service excellence. Over the next few sections of this chapter, we will introduce each MDSR component in the same order as we looked at them in the book. However, keep in mind that we are now focused on the system as a whole. Therefore, the discussion of the MSDR at the Waterway Café and the Inn of the Governors will not be so linear. We will regularly make some references to all of the components as we describe each one!

We began our "peel back" examination of management system components with the organizational culture back in Chapter 5, so we will start there.

Culture and Values in the Hospitality Industry

In Chapter 5, we talked about how an organization's culture can provide a powerful set of limits and strong focus for the behavior of the members of the organization. The catch, of course, is that the limits should be on non-strategic behaviors and the focus should be on strategic behavior. We also talked about how it takes a long time to foster a culture that supports the firm's strategy.

Nurturing a culture that aligns with strategy in the hospitality industry is problematical. If organizational culture is about shared beliefs and attitudes and about behavioral habits, how do you foster a service-centric team culture in the industry where employee turnover is traditionally the highest?[1] How do you shape a customer service culture in organizations where the employees don't even all speak the same language, share a common cultural background, or even have much personal experience from their customers' perspective? That's certainly the case for both of the businesses we are looking at. A substantial percentage of the employees at the Café are natives of the Caribbean and Latin America and speak a variety of dialects of English, French, Spanish, and Portuguese. At the Inn, the variety is somewhat less, but there are many employees whose native language is Spanish, some of whom speak only minimal English. This is not a unique feature of these businesses. In the highly labor intensive hospitality industry, this is close to the norm.

With high turnover, many restaurants and hotels are forced to focus simply on training such employees in the specifics of their jobs (this is the protocol for cleaning a room—these are the rules for cleaning a table). The Inn and the Café focus on something altogether different. They aim to educate their employees on how to work together as a team to make customers happy and loyal and to work more efficiently. We will get to how they motivate their employees and develop these capabilities later. First, we will spend some time talking about the contrast between training a service staff and creating a service culture.

Actually, it is quite difficult to provide customer service through a formula. Training employees to do their jobs in operational terms does not create flexibility of responses. Furthermore, it allows many simple service activities to fall through the cracks. The dishwasher is told to fill up the rack with flatware before putting it into the washer. This keeps the cost of washing low, but what about when table turnover is slow at peak times? Will there be sufficient clean flatware when a table turns over? The housekeeper is told to clean all of the rooms in the hallway in a particular order. That may be efficient, but is it customer focused? These employees are trained, in a sense, to be invisible to—and independent of—the customers. So what if, instead, they were encouraged to be part of the customer experience? That is the cultural norm at both the Waterway Café and the Inn of the Governors.

Here is an example of what that culture looks like in action. One of us was at the Inn a few years ago and witnessed a rather tense couple pulling their rollaway bags across the courtyard. They were asking each other where, again, their room was. It was clear from the exchange that there was some lingering friction that had probably begun during their drive. The wife suggested, "Well, why don't you just go ask someone?" A moment later, a member of the housekeeping staff emerged from one of the buildings with some towels draped over one arm. The husband called to her. "Can you tell me where this room is?" He held out the key card. It was fairly clear that the housekeeper didn't speak English very well, but she got the picture, smiled at him, and responded, "Come, I take you." She then took the handle of the woman's rollaway bag, turned, and headed off in a new direction, signaling for the two to follow her. At first, the couple looked a bit stunned. This response from the housekeeper did not "compute." It was totally unexpected. Then their faces smoothed over. The husband gestured for his wife to proceed and then fell quietly into line behind her.

It is difficult to convey the whole effect of this event. It is not simply that the housekeeper provided assistance. Of course, this, in itself, is noteworthy. It would have been easy for the housekeeper to feign a complete lack of understanding. It would have been easy for her to simply point to one of the buildings and continue on her assigned task. But she went out of her way to assure that the customers got what they needed. Beyond providing a "full service" experience for the customers and clearly taking a significant detour from her task in process, she connected with those customers at a personal level. Her behavior was not mechanical. The connection was unforced. This kind of interaction with customers is the norm at the Inn.

In a series of interviews, many of the employees at the Inn reinforced this perspective. One characterized the attitude as "You've got to wow them when they come in the door." However, the level of difficulty for instilling both a passion for the customer experience and an appreciation for what it takes to please the customer cannot be overstated. For many new employees, one manager told us, "There was a need to teach them what hospitality was all about. I'm not sure if they had ever been a customer in a similar setting—they didn't make the connections."

At a meeting with the wait staff at the Waterway Café, another aspect of the culture was discussed. The group described themselves as a family. Their basic approach was to help each other, rather than react in ways they had experienced elsewhere, like "you're bothering me," or "it's not my problem." One server said that, if something goes wrong, "we figure that the system is the problem, not the people." By this he meant that a problem is something they can work together to fix, and beyond that, to prevent in the future. But this point of view was also a result of another aspect of the culture. To an extent, this really was a family. Of the eight wait staff and hostesses in the room at the time, five were friends and relatives who had recruited each other. The three others had been customers who were impressed by what they saw and later returned seeking jobs. All of these people had made the cut as members of the family, but not everybody did. One server told us, "You can tell in the first week if someone is going to make it." If the new person did not make the cut, the peer group made it clear—and encouraged the person to leave, directly and indirectly. "We do management's job," one said. Employment was "a few days and out or stay a long time" according to another. The "free-rider" problem isn't an issue at either business! The culture demands that each employee contribute value to the team effort. It reinforces the requirements for high-performance teams that the entire team be capable and be focused on the goal.

The cultures at both businesses are strikingly similar. In both locations it is the norm to work together, to connect with the customers, and to "wow" them. These are all critical elements in implementing a strategy of customer service excellence through high-performance teams. Currently, the two cultures are strong enough to maintain themselves to some extent. They have powerful informal means of policing new organizational members. Clearly, however, these cultures did not emerge spontaneously. They had to be managed into place. This did not happen by writing some rules of behavior. Instead, it was the result of the joint effect of the other components of the MSDR.

Here is an example of one of those interactive effects. Another interesting positive contribution of the culture is that, for those who are accepted as part of the "family," there is a tendency to stay a long time. The average employee tenure at the Inn of the Governors is several times as long as for the hotel industry in general. Similar employee longevity is a trait of the Waterway Café. This means that the teams get more practice and experience working together and, given the nature of the structure and the coaching role played by management, their team performance can become fully developed. This is another required trait of high-performance teams. The organizational culture clearly works hand in hand with the team-style structure to support the strategy of customer service excellence. We will now look more closely at the organizational structure in each of the two businesses.

Organizational Structure and High-Performance Teams

In Chapter 7, we discussed two basic alternatives to structuring an organization: functional orientation and market orientation. We then described a hybrid of those two approaches, the matrix organizational model. In general, hotels and restaurants tend to be functionally organized. It's hard to get around this. You probably don't want the chefs registering new guests. You probably don't want the housekeepers preparing the meals. Nonetheless, the hotel and restaurant guests are the market and you want the market to be served well. At the very least, the coordination among the parts of the service delivery chain must be very tight. Each member of the overall service team must have some understanding of what needs to be done throughout the chain to make the customer happy.

While many hotels and restaurants are divided into functional departments, the structure at the Inn and at the Café is much more matrix-like. If you've tried to put together an organizational chart for the Inn of the Governors, for example, the result would be a fairly typical looking functional chart. At the top is the manager. At the next level would be assistant managers for the restaurant, the business administration, and the hotel. Then, within the hotel the workforce would be organized around the front desk, housekeeping, and maintenance. Each one of those departments would have someone in an apparent supervisor role. However, such an organization chart implies a serial chain of command. The reality in these two businesses is far from that! These groups and subgroups are more like a team of teams. The managers play the role of coaches. They motivate the staff and facilitate team-managed performance improvement. Similarly, the supervisors are more like team captains. Their job is not to tell their team members what to do, but to help the team, as a group, to *discover* what to do. Since the objective is to develop high-performance teams, the emphasis is on teamwork. While everyone has a primary task responsibility, his or her ultimate job is improving the customer experience.

In a visit to the Inn several years ago, one of us attended a meeting of the entire housekeeping team conducted by the manager of the Inn. He didn't spend his time telling the housekeeping staff what to do. He didn't give a lecture on task objectives. Instead, he facilitated a discussion about potential process improvements. The staff provided suggestions, followed by a general discussion of the idea. One suggestion related to a maintenance issue. The manager duly noted this suggestion and said he would bring it before the maintenance team.

The process is similar at the Café. The focus is on learning and improvement. This approach was captured neatly by one of the wait staff at the Café. He told us that the Café's manager "allows us to fail" and, therefore, encourages experimentation and risk taking. The wait staff group described a collaborative effort to respond to mistakes and, beyond that, to identify unproductive responses. Their consensus was that productivity was a group result, but a personal responsibility. A quite intentional result of this team structure has been a continual reduction in the need for supervisors.

You may have had an experience at a restaurant where a minute or so after the server has asked, "Can I get you anything else" and left, you decided that you would, after all, like to have another glass of wine. The problem, of course, is that your server has moved on to another part of his or her standard cycle. It may take quite a while before that cycle returns to you. (Sometimes, it's hard not to think that your server is out in the back chatting on a cell phone!) Meanwhile, it's difficult to get anyone else on the staff to even look at you. Many restaurants profess to have their wait staff work as a team, but this often turns out to mean simply that the person who delivers your meal is not the one who took your order. One critical difference between that kind of team and a high-performance team is that members of a high-performance team are focused on the customer, while members of the typical work group are focused on the task.

If you visit the Inn of the Governors or the Waterway Café, you can see this kind of high-performance teamwork in action. You will have to watch closely, though, because the mechanism of a high-performance team system is nearly invisible. On a visit to the bar and grill section of Del Charro Saloon on a busy night, we took a seat at a small table. A minute or two later, a waitress came out of the kitchen and delivered appetizers to a table some distance away. After a short, amiable chat with the customers, she turned to face the bartender. It appeared that he was waiting for her to look his way. When they made eye contact he signaled with his chin toward the table where we sat (without interrupting his pour). A moment later she was at the table to welcome us and take our order. Through a silent and nearly imperceptible connection, the two of them had worked together to assure that we would be promptly served.

A similar example of fluid teamwork was observed on another night—a year earlier and several thousand miles away—at the Waterway Café. This time, the team members were a waiter and a runner. A runner at the Waterway Café is a sort of assistant waiter. We were in the midst of a discussion when a runner came by. It was clear he didn't want to interrupt us, so he simply made eye contact, raised the water pitcher he was carrying and pointed to it with his empty hand. We nodded and carried on our conversation without interruption while he refilled our water glasses. Perhaps 10 minutes later, he was passing by as we pushed back our salad plates. He stopped in his tracks and asked, "Can I take those for you?" Not 30 seconds later, our waiter came by to tell us that our entrées should be ready shortly and that he was on his way to the kitchen to check on their status. It was clear that a customer care "hand-off" had taken place outside our view.

On their own, neither of these experiences was a big deal. However, in each case we felt that the staff was going out of its way to look after us. In neither case, however, did it feel like they were hovering over us. Rather, they seemed to be anticipating our needs. Instead of being focused on their tasks of the moment, they seemed to be focused on the customer! What's more, it clearly wasn't an individual effort, but a team effort. Experiences like this add up.

So you can see that the team-based organizational structure at each of these two businesses is designed to enhance customer service excellence by encouraging cross-functional activity, coordination, and a focus on the goal of serving the customer. But the structure does not create those skills, develop that coordination, or inculcate that focus. In fact, you may feel that what we have just described isn't even organizational structure at all. It sounds more like the organizational culture—shared goals, beliefs, and behavioral norms. To some extent, you would be correct. The seamless integration of parts in a MSDR should result in a system where the parts seem to blend together. A cooperative culture at both organizations reinforces and is reinforced by this blurring of functional distinctions. Even at the Inn, where the hotel and restaurant responsibilities are fairly distinct, it would not be particularly unusual to see a waiter stopping to tidy-up a table while passing through the hotel lobby. One hotel employee described it as a "system to support a personal responsibility to be productive." This is an example of how the culture and structure work together and reinforce each other in the effort to execute a strategy of customer service excellence. The culture grows out of the use of problem-solving teams. The teams' performance is enhanced by the cultural norms of connecting with the customer and working together. Neither MSDR component is quite as effective in creating the positive customer experience without the other.

But this culture and the team-oriented structure would not be very effective without a way to provide feedback on the effect of the team members' actions. Beyond feedback, there also needed to be a mechanism for helping everyone connect what they do and how they do it to customer service outcomes and final business results. Training had to be designed to focus on the critical skills that the organizational members had to have in order to provide excellent customer service. Performance measures had to be assembled that would encourage problem solving and learning.

Balancing and Aligning Performance Measures

The set of performance measures at the Inn was not established through a formal balanced scorecard methodology of the sort we described in Chapter 8. However, it reflects a similar management system, structure, and thought process to the "classic" Kaplan and Norton balanced scorecard model we described there. Recall the basic design of a balanced scorecard from Chapter 8. It provides feedback from four different perspectives—the financial perspective, the customer perspective, the business operations perspective, and the innovation and learning perspective. These views are causally related. Positive results from the customer perspectives should lead to revenues and top line growth from the financial perspective. In turn, effectiveness of business operations is defined by what makes things look good from the customer perspective. Efficiency of business operations contributes to financial results by managing the cost side of the profit equation. Innovation and learning reflects improvements in the efficacy and efficiency of business operation, leading to improved customer satisfaction, more revenue, less cost per dollar of revenue, and, in the end, superior financial performance.

You won't be surprised to learn that management of both the Waterway Café and the Inn of the Governors pay close attention to financial results. You might, however, be surprised to learn how far into the organizations this information is communicated. Virtually everyone is aware of the business financial performance. For instance, in the housekeeper's control center at the Inn (affectionately known as "the dungeon" since it is located in the basement below the hotel lobby), there is a "pride board" on which an array of performance measures is posted. Perhaps the most striking feature of this pride board is the variety of financial measures. These include rather specific figures—both year to date and trailing 12 month—on cost, revenue, profit, and "gainshare" numbers. (We will explain more about what a "gainshare" is later in the chapter.) These data are provided in raw numerical form and in the form of graphs. A parallel set of data related to the Del Charro is posted for the restaurant staff. Similar numbers are posted at the Waterway Café.

The Inn and the Café utilize relatively standard formal measures of customer satisfaction. Each business collects customer survey data which get reported throughout the businesses. But another major source of customer satisfaction information is an informal, relatively free-form kind of feedback. Both businesses pay close attention to online information sources like TripAdvisor. Since both the Inn and the Café rely heavily on word of mouth for promotion, this source of customer satisfaction data closely aligns with the strategy, consistent with our discussion in Chapter 9. Also, the way in which this information is used closely aligns with strategy execution through high-performance teams.

Online customer reviews are not read by everyone in the organization. There is no expectation for them to do so. Instead, it is management's job to attend to these reviews, interpret them, and pass the feedback on to the relevant teams. It seems to be a truism that online reviewers don't hold back. Thus, negative reviews provide explicit feedback for performance improvement. Negative statements from a review are not treated as individual failures. Rather, they are viewed as a problem to be solved in the team's operation. Similarly, everyone on the hotel and restaurant staffs can see the relationship between positive reviews (customer perspective) and improving financial results (financial perspective).

Another dimension of the use of online feedback is that it provides a very stringent hurdle for assessing innovation and learning. Online reviewers tend to refer to other reviewers' comments when they write their own reviews. Thus, rave reviews increase expectations for the next reviewer and, consequently, raise the bar for judging execution. Negative comments in a review increase the likelihood of scrutiny for the same issue by the next reviewer. Finally, and perhaps most importantly, this feedback is completely unscripted by the businesses. There is no need to anticipate what is important to customers in order to create a survey. Online reviewers tell you what is important to them without being asked! This avoids problems created by asking the wrong question. In Chapter 3, we talked about the need to monitor the external environment and not simply rely on an internal view of the ways to meet customer needs. The use of online reviews makes great use of this principle.

The various service teams in both businesses are essentially self-managed. Thus, operating performance data are collected by the teams on an informal basis. Again, as in a balanced scorecard framework, the operations performance data are related to both customer experience and cost efficiency. The focus is on what to do in order to improve operations on both dimensions. Thus, the innovation and learning aspect of the balanced scorecard framework is assured through these continuous improvement efforts. Note that the strong culture at work in each of these businesses contributes an important dose of informal performance measurement. Team members know whether they are contributing to the common goal or their peers will find a way of letting them know they are not!

At the Inn of the Governors, the lead housekeeper regularly has discussions with the housekeeping team about structural or policy changes that will help make work easier and more effective. One example mentioned to us was a change in how some of the windows at the Inn open. Originally, all of the windows slid wide open. However, the housekeepers noticed that sometimes children staying in the rooms would open them all the way in order to climb in and out! This was dangerous, a source of unnecessary wear and tear, and, simply, an avenue for soiling the rooms. The windows were modified to make it difficult for anyone but an adult to open the window all the way.

The combination of formal and informal performance measures is designed to support effective teamwork in pursuit of a positive customer experience and improved profitability. However, even the triangulation among the customer-centric culture, the team structure, and the focused strategic feedback does not account fully for the final business performance in either business. In order for performance measurement to be an effective source of performance improvement, the members of the organization must possess the requisite skills and knowledge. Ongoing training captures this aspect of learning perspective. Training is a critical ingredient in making the rest of the MSDR work. It has been a major focus of management system development effort. It deserves to be described in a little detail.

All of the parts of the MSDR we have described so far may already have a lot of traction for an experienced business manager or for a typical MBA student. Perhaps the whole system we have laid out here would have made sense to you when you were a teenager. However, what if you didn't even know how to balance a checkbook? What if you had never even had a checkbook? For some of the employees in these businesses, that may have been the case. Management of personal finances may have been a matter of cashing a paycheck and hoping the cash lasted until the next check. To be sure, this was not the case for every new employee. We even found an MBA working as a server at the Waterway Café as a way to learn how to run a successful restaurant business. However, Jeff Vander Wolk clearly understood the challenge of making his MSDR work. The employees had to be educated, not simply trained, before all of the MSDR gears would mesh. Thus, the development program had to do many things. It had to help employees learn how to set long-term goals and come up with a plan to pursue them or the idea of performance improvement would be meaningless. It had to educate employees on basic concepts of financial measurement or the logic of pursuing cost reduction and revenue increases would be a mystery. If customer service excellence and the customer experience were the goals, then everyone would have to know how to engage the customer, not simply perform tasks. If performance improvement was critical, then everyone would need to have skills in problem identification and root cause analysis.

Employee development is provided through a series of workshops that employees attend on company time. These workshops proceed from basic to advanced levels. Since an important part of the measurement system is understanding the organization's financial results, there is even some training in basic financial acumen.

Later workshops are focused on tools for both self-improvement and performance improvement. These include team building and "customer relationship" skills. Groups are not naturally effective teams. Many organizations have found it valuable to provide team-building and team-management training for employees ranging from production teams to service teams and all the way up the organization to top management teams. Here, such team-building skills are critical if the benefits of longer job tenure and performance improvement are going to be reaped. Similarly, if the objective is for every team member to positively engage the customer, then every team member has to understand how to do that. This development is necessary in order to allow the employees to actually become able to work together to discover, anticipate, and satisfy customer needs.

The program includes quality improvement techniques and methodologies for analyzing the root cause of problems, including such practices as Toyota's "five whys."[2] Development of such skills is necessary to close the loop between motivating employees to improve financial performance of their businesses and giving them the skills and knowledge to provide the ever-improving level of customer experience that will drive improved profits.

A high-performance team needs training, development, and feedback. The performance measures and performance improvements at The Inn of the Governors and The Waterway Café are focused on these distinctions.

The MSDR we have shown you so far includes a culture based on the shared belief that everyone needs to work together to provide the customer a positive experience. This supports the core of the strategy. Competitive advantage comes from customers actually enjoying their experience, not just having a non-negative one. The businesses are organized into task-oriented teams to reinforce the notion of teamwork. The teams are organized into a coalition of teams so that all aspects of the customer experience can be addressed. The performance measures connect the customer experience to financial outcomes that everyone sees. The performance measures also include informal sources that guarantee that the feedback is truly from the external customer perspective, not simply a set of internal specifications about what the customer should get. The training and education program provides both the knowledge and the skills to allow the teams to continually improve their ability to be effective and efficient.

All of the parts of the MSDR fit together and reinforce each other. They support the development of high-performance teams. Those teams are focused on the goal and that focus is reinforced by every component of the MSDR. The teams are trained to develop cross-functional capabilities and have coaching, practice, and experience with each other in using those capabilities. But there is still one missing ingredient.

The desire to be part of a high-performance team had to start somewhere. What first motivated members of these organizations to be focused so intently on the customer experience? What drew them toward working as a coherent whole? What invested them with a feeling that they all had a share in the outcome? The answer is that another part of the MSDR provided that drive. Each of these businesses utilizes a financial incentive system that literally gives every employee a share in the outcome.

Profit Sharing as the Motivator

Both the Inn of the Governors and the Waterway Café employ a very simple but powerful profit-sharing program modeled after the one at Lincoln Electric. Recall that Jeff Vander Wolk asked us why more companies did not use that approach at our first introduction. He wasn't asking out of idle philosophical curiosity. He wasn't asking to see if we felt there were any drawbacks. He was asking because it seemed so illogical to him! That model has worked very well in both of these businesses.

Both in concept and in practice, the system is quite straightforward. It has to be. The employees earning profit shares are not financial analysts and MBAs! After a required level of profit is reached, all incremental profits go into the profit-sharing pool. The total pool is divided by the number of employee shares. Each employee then receives his or her share.

The mechanics work like this. The profit-sharing pool is essentially determined by a version of residual income as described in Chapter 7. Management sets a hurdle rate, a required return on investment level that must be met. All profits that exceed the investment base multiplied by the hurdle rate comprise the profit-sharing pool. So, for example, if the investment base was $5 million and the hurdle rate was 15%, then any profit in excess of $750,000 would go into the profit-sharing pool.

Every employee of the company who has met a minimum employment term qualifies for what these organizations term a "gainshare." The distributable pool is calculated periodically and divided by the number of outstanding gainshares. Everyone then gets a check. For some employees, the gainshare check can be close to 100% of their base pay for that period!

This sounds pretty simple and, in concept, it is. However, the balance and the details are quite deliberate. Remember that the central purpose for this model is to motivate employees to do a better job of executing the strategy. The design of the gainshare system reflects Jeff Vander Wolk's beliefs. As a successful entrepreneur, Jeff believes that working hard and working smart should have an economic benefit. Thus, if he expects that kind of behavior from his employees, he has to be ready to let them share the benefits.

One of the critical aspects of the plan is that *everyone* has a share in the outcome. This is one of the requirements for a high-performance team. A few managers qualify for an extra gainshare or two, but basically everyone has an equal share of the pool. There is more of an incentive to work hard when you don't have the feeling that your hard work is paying off for someone else more than it is for you. We talked about the desirability of such shared outcomes in Chapter 11. That notion extends to ownership, too. In Chapter 11, we mentioned a company whose general rank and file seldom got to participate in profit sharing because the required return on sales level was set just beyond reach. Meanwhile, the managers of that firm earned very high incentive payments. The return on investment target at the Café and at the Inn is both a reasonable level for the ownership return and an achievable level for the workforce. The difference in incentive pay between the dishwasher and the business manager is relatively small.

Another critical feature of the gainshare system design is that there are two segments of the gainshare pool. Seventy percent of the pool is the distributable portion, which goes directly to pay-outs. The other 30% is reinvested in the business according to the priorities determined by the employees. This has two interesting results. First, the employees are encouraged to think about how the business could run better from the owner's point of view. That is, if having another flatware rack for the dishwasher would allow the kitchen to better pursue its goal of pleasing the customer, then that is an adjustment that can be made. If the consensus is that better signage would improve business, then that investment is made. Second, this reinvestment increases the investment base. Thus, as the business improves, so does the dollar yield, both for the owner and for the employees. The incentive system is the fertilizer for the MSDR garden.

There are several important effects resulting from the gainshare system. First, the financial rewards extend employee tenure. The prospect of higher income means that the job is not interchangeable with similar jobs at other companies. Second, longer employee tenure allows time for the development of high-performance teams. Team members get to know each other well and learn how to work together effectively. The benefits of training and learning can be reaped. Third, the profit-sharing program guarantees that everybody has a common goal. Everybody has a stake in winning.

There is one more important link that we have not yet mentioned. Although everyone may be motivated by the prospect of more money, how can this motivation be converted into a long-term commitment? An effective MSDR won't leave this to chance. The incentive system has to be integrated with all of the other components in the MSDR.

The connection to the organizational culture may be obvious. At the very least, you can now understand why these two businesses tend to have low employee turnover. The employees can make more money than they would for similar work at other establishments.

However, it goes beyond the money. The culture becomes a meritocracy. Everyone can feel proud of their contribution and the fact that it is recognized. As part of an active decision-making team, each employee can derive a higher sense of fulfillment working at the Café or the Inn than they might in an organization where they would essentially be regarded as commodities. Furthermore, they have firm evidence that management appreciates the job they do.

You can probably also understand why the employees fiercely protect the integrity of their teams. The financial incentive is designed in such a way to encourage employees to keep their numbers low and improve their efficiency. In general, the fewer people there are in the pool, the higher the individual gainshare. An extra person is justified only if his or her presence can deliver more than another share of additional profit. Thus, team members value each other because each contributing team member actually increases the wealth of his or her peers. As a result, they are apt to police their own ranks and weed out poor performers early. This is a neat solution to the free-rider problem!

The gainshare system is integrated into the training program, too. In order to ensure that the gainshare program will be truly effective, the early training workshops at the Inn and at the Café focus on helping employees to understand the mechanics of the gainshare program as well as to understand how their efforts can increase their gainshare earnings. A critical feature of the workshops is also some basic training on creating, prioritizing, and achieving personal goals. The immediate goals of this early part of the development program are (1) to get the employees to understand how the gainshare program works, so that it can be effective in motivating behavior and (2) to help employees develop a long-term view on financial goals, emphasizing the creation of cause and effect pathways. The net effect is to provide a social benefit to staff members, cement their relationship to the organization, and make the gainshare program more meaningful and effective at motivating performance improvement. That interlocking reinforcement makes the entire system more effective. Motivated by the gainshare program, employees want to be part of the high-performance teams. They want to learn how to engage the customer. They are ready to find ways of producing positive customer experiences without more labor. They are cautious of spending that doesn't produce more benefit than cost.

The performance measurement system incorporates the gainshare system, too. It's hard to be motivated if you cannot see the payoff from the effort. Certainly, the gainshare payments are a direct form of feedback. However, the performance measurement system puts those checks into perspective. It shows the long-term effect of the overall team effort. Figure 12.1 shows one of the items that we found posted in the housekeeping "control center" at the Inn several years ago. This is a graph of the trailing 12-month average annual gainshare value. The different lines each depict a different year. The bottom line is the base year of 2002/2003. The next higher line is 2003/2004. The third line from the bottom is 2004/2005. The top line is for 2005/2006, the year this chart was posted. The year-over-year and month-over-month trends are quite compelling. The annual profit-share bonus each

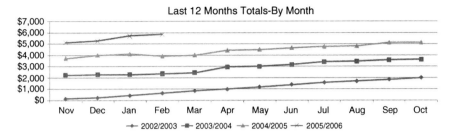

Fig . 12.1 Inn of the Governors Gainshares

employee was taking home during this period kept growing at a fairly constant pace. As of February 2006, the annualized bonus for every employee of the Inn was nearly $6000. This may not sound like much from an executive pay perspective, but imagine the percent of total income this represents for someone of the housekeeping staff!

In Chapter 11, we made it a point to acknowledge the dangerous downside of incentive systems. Incentives that are localized to individual managers or to a single part of the business carry significant risk of unanticipated consequences and increase the motivation to game the system. That risk is minimized at the Inn and the Café, since the incentives are tied to company performance. However, it is important to recognize that the gainshare systems at those two businesses are also carefully integrated with the other MSDR components. It is not enough simply to establish a potential to motivate every employee in a goal congruent direction. The incentive system reinforces the team structure. The training system provides important connections between the incentives and the individuals. The performance measures track both the relationship between strategy implementation (positive customer experience) and the financial performance, but also provide clear data about the relationship between business financial performance and personal financial performance. All of the parts, working together, reinforce the culture's focus on teamwork and customer experience.

The Holistic Effect—An MSDR

So now you should have a feel for what makes these two businesses so special. The answer is the synergy across the parts of the MSDR! As a last illustration of the cumulative effect of the MSDR at the Inn of the Governors, here is an exchange between a server and a couple having breakfast in the dining room of the Del Charro.

Customer: This is our last breakfast here. We're leaving today.
Server: That's too bad. Where are you going?
Customer: Home—back to work.
Server: Everybody's got to work.
Customer: Yes, well, then we can save up. Then we will come back.
Server: Good! I'll be here. . . .I love this place!

It's clear from this exchange that both the customer and the employee enjoy their experience at the Inn of the Governors. This is the ultimate effect of the MSDR. Good experiences are addictive—you want to repeat them. The system is designed to get the customers to have those good experiences so they will come back, so they will tell their friends and, in this internet age, so they will tell the world! The system is also designed to focus the work force on providing that good experience for the customer and doing it in a way that makes them feel good, too—appreciated, recognized, valuable, proud of their work and, of course, wealthier.

All the parts fit and work together. Each feature of the system is designed to reinforce the effects of the other features, aim the work force in the right direction, and give them the power to make progress toward their goals. The incentive system motivates the employees to *work together* to improve profits. The organization structure reinforces this concept of teamwork and establishes a framework for self-management by the teams. The shared outcomes and team structures reinforce a culture predicated on contribution, cooperation, and merit. This engenders a level of loyalty among the employees that allows them to view mishaps as "engineering" problems, not personality issues. The connection between customer experience and profitability is made explicit. The performance measures focus efforts on the long-term results, but encourage immediate problem solving as the means to achieve those long-term results. The employee development program is designed to fill-in the connective tissue between desire and ability. The final effect is continually improving customer service and resulting improvement in profitability.

The relationships among the parts of the MSDR are complex. That makes them hard to create and manage, but, ultimately, also makes them hard for your competitors to copy. It took years of cultivation before these two businesses could count on a consistent bloom from their gardens. As we were completing this book, we asked Jeff Vander Wolk[3] to review this chapter and provide us with some comments. He had some important updates.

He told us that the details of the MSDR mechanics in the two businesses have changed since we observed them. The changes in the MSDRs were not parallel in the two businesses, either. Neither of these revelations was a surprise! The MSDR garden needs constant tending. The vigilant gardener is never satisfied with the outcome. What is the effect of the weather? Are there new pests to deal with? Would a rearrangement of the garden result in a more pleasing outcome? There is always something to respond to, something to learn, something new to try.

The economic weather tested both businesses, and, indeed, the hotel and restaurant industry in general, in 2008 and 2009. Yet, while hotel bookings in the Santa Fe area fell, the Inn held its own. In fact, revenue per available room (REVPAR, a traditional hotel industry barometer) was higher at the Inn in February of 2009 than it had been in February of 2008 and 152% of the downtown Santa Fe average.

The Waterway Café faced even more tests over recent months. First, there was a highway reconstruction project that exacerbated the already difficult access to the restaurant. This was followed in quick succession by the openings of some 50 new restaurants within a 5 mile radius of the Café. Then came the economic slump. The Café's business suffered and the MSDR, especially the gainshare system, was modified in response. Notably, however, the business, itself, was never in question. Meanwhile, many of the new restaurants in the area have foundered. As this book was going to press, the Café opened an additional 80-seat section.

Conclusion

The MSDRs at The Waterway Cafe and The Inn of the Governors illustrate both the dramatic impact of an effective system and the level of care it takes to design and implement one. Everything we have talked about in this book is evident in the MSDR designs and the processes with which they are executed.

Jeff Vander Wolk has been nurturing a cohesive, customer-focused culture in each business for many years. Both businesses are organized in a matrix design that emphasizes customer-focused service teams, an important focus of the strategy. The performance measures focus on key strategic success factors and, despite the absence of a formal balanced scorecard mechanism, address those success factors in financial, customer, operational, and developmental terms. The incentive systems ensure goal congruence. Critically, all of the parts are designed to work together and reinforce each other. As events in the environment change the business context, details of the MSDR are tweaked in response. The result has been an increasingly resilient competitive advantage for each business in its local market.

Epilog

Our objective in writing this book has been to provide you with a practical guide to help you think about how to create a strategic management delivery system for your organization. The result is not a "how to" book, nor it is it an argument for a particular management tool. Instead, we hope the result is a source of insight and inspiration for you as you craft your system for strategy delivery.

An MSDR must be custom-built for your business and its strategy. Like any system, an MSDR has many parts. Those parts must all fit together and mesh to achieve a particular objective – executing the strategy. That fit and goal orientation is what makes an MSDR work.

The design of the book took you through a list of those parts and described their functions. That list began with the strategy. We also continually returned to the strategy in our discussions of each part on the MSDR list. Every part of your MSDR needs to be directed toward creating the desired strategic effect on your target customers. Strategies do not have to be tricky or unique to be effective. In fact, the more complicated the strategy, the more difficult it will be design an MSDR. The most difficult part of designing the strategy may be analyzing the environment (industry trends, economic trends, market trends) and trying to find a strategic position that you can both achieve and "bet" on. This may result in the formulation of a strategy that looks very much like some of your competitors'. In that case, your strategic advantage will rest entirely upon your ability to create a supporting MSDR.

We started with the external environment because it is the context of your management system. Generally speaking, you cannot do much about the economy, what customers want, or what your competitors are doing. We then proceeded through the things you can do something about. We started with those things that can only be moved slowly – like the organizational culture – and progressed to MSDR parts that could be changed and adjusted more directly and more quickly – organizational design, performance measures, and incentives.

It is critical to recognize that, although each part of an MSDR can be discussed separately, all parts of an MSDR are interdependent. In this final chapter, we illustrated both the holistic nature of the parts of an MSDR working together and the way harmony among those parts reinforces the overall effect. Management Systems that Deliver Results are not the simple additive effect of a handful of independently conjured control mechanisms.

Contrary to the implied promises of so many management fads of the day, there is no universal, one size fits all approach to management systems. Yet many managers continue to search for some miracle ingredient that will make their garden grow, regardless of the conditions and pests that challenge it. As we said at the beginning of this book, MSDRs require hard work and constant attention. They need to be cultivated over time. The focus must be on how the parts fit and work together – the synergistic effect – rather than on technical adherence to the precision of individual components. You cannot build an MSDR one piece at a time. You have to build it all at once – and then keep improving it. That is the hallmark of a Management System that Delivers Results.

Notes

1. *www.hr.com/hr/communities/turnover_rates_cause_concern_for_organizations_eng.html*
2. The "five whys" is a simple root cause analysis technique. It begins by asking "why" a certain problem arose. The answer to that question is then probed for its cause with another "why," and so on. The method was popularized by Toyota in the 1970s and after.
3. Jeff also informed us that he is currently working with a co-author, Lou Savary, on a short book on his management philosophies and techniques. It is tentatively entitled *A Kinder Capitalism Where Everybody Wins*. Further details about his MSDR design and program can be found at the website www.teamplusalliance.org.

Appendix A: MSDR Scorecard Examples

Balanced Measurement Systems

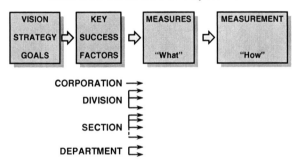

We outline six scorecards from different types of firms and from different levels in the organization. We start from the Key Success Factors and link to "*what*" they measure and "how" they measure. Chapter 9 addresses the critical linkage between Strategy and Key Success Factors.

L.P. Carr, A.J. Nanni, Jr., *Delivering Results*, DOI 10.1007/978-1-4419-0621-2_BM2,
© Springer Science+Business Media, LLC 2009

I: Insurance Company Call Center. A new call center for an insurance company was established to help combat the increasing policy lapse rate. Customers complained about the service and let their policies lapse and moved to another insurance carrier. The management concerns were the productivity of the new center, customer service perception, acceptance by the insurance agents, response time to calls, and reduction in the laps rate.

Insurance Company Call Center

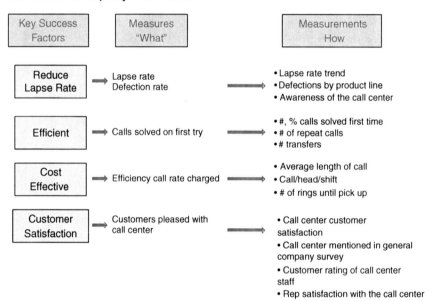

Key Success Factors	Measures "What"	Measurements How
Reduce Lapse Rate	Lapse rate Defection rate	• Lapse rate trend • Defections by product line • Awareness of the call center
Efficient	Calls solved on first try	• #, % calls solved first time • # of repeat calls • # transfers
Cost Effective	Efficiency call rate charged	• Average length of call • Call/head/shift • # of rings until pick up
Customer Satisfaction	Customers pleased with call center	• Call center customer satisfaction • Call center mentioned in general company survey • Customer rating of call center staff • Rep satisfaction with the call center

II: Bio Tech Firm. This is the US division of a biotech firm. They are expanding the served therapeutic areas and are interested in growing the business.

Bio Tech Firm

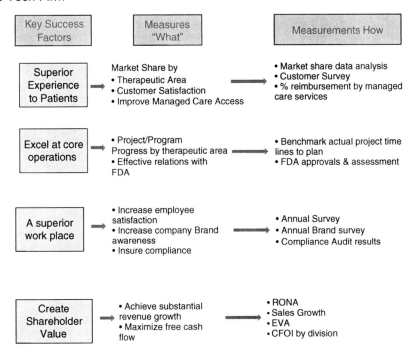

III: Retail Clothing Chain. A major retail clothing chain competes in a very competitive market and they are concerned with brand image.

Retail Clothing Chain

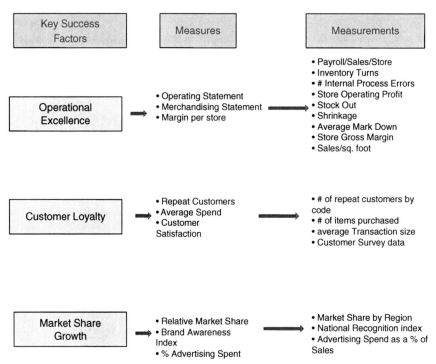

IV: Convenience Retail Chain. A regional convenience retail chain has taken a differentiation strategy competing on the enhanced customer experience rather than price.

Convenience Retail Chain

Key Success Factors	Measures	Measurements
	Customer Satisfaction Data	• Survey every 20th customer • Rating on attitude • Store/restroom cleanliness
Superior Customer Service	Increased # of Store Visits	• Number of transactions per store
	Increased Size of Spend	• Average size of transaction
	Brand Awareness	• Brand survey data
Efficient Operations	Operational Standards	• Performance store audit
	Optimize People Utilization	• Revenue per employee
	Employee Retention	• Employee turnover rate
Store Profitability	Store Profitability	• Actual expenses to budget • Coverage ratio (store/fuel) sales ratio • Net operating costs • Actual revenue performance

V: Contract Manufacturer (Corporate). This contract manufacturer has over 50 global locations offering superior quality and services to large global firms. Each of their production facilities are the same design. This is the corporate scorecard.

Contract Manufacturer (Corporate)

Key Success Factors	Measures	Measurements
Large Scale Customers	Size of Customer	• # of $1m customers • Customer retention • Net promoter score
Continuous Support	New Process Development	• Cycle time improvement • # of new process defects • # of implemented employee suggestions
Unique Process Clean Room	Internal Improvements	• # of defects • Yield rates • # of safety incidents
Cookie-cutter Plants world wide	Financial Results	• ROM (Return on Machine) • Contribution margin • Profitability • Assets employed
	Employee Satisfaction	• Survey results • Employee turnover rate

VI: Contract Manufacturer (Plant). This is the same contract manufacturer as above (V) but looking at the plant scorecard.

Contract Manufacturer (Plant)

Key Success Factors	Measures	Measurements
Quality	Reject Rate Employee Satisfaction	• Material quality score • Yield rate per machine and per job Employee survey data
Order Selection	Complexity/Order Volume/Order	• # cavities/product • # of setups per job • Production run time
Continuous Process	Utilization Rate	• # machine hours • Cycle time
Pricing	Material Costs/Unit	• Contribution margin
Customer Satisfaction	Net Promoter Score	• On time delivery • # of customers • Customer survey

Appendix B: Glossary of Modern Management Tools

Activity-Based Management (ABM): An approach to the management of activities within business processes as a way to continuously improve both the value received by customers and the profit earned by providing this value. Causes of activities are identified, measured, and used along with other activity information for performance evaluation; emphasis is on the reduction or elimination of non-value-adding activities. ABM focuses on managing activities to reduce costs and improve customer value and draws on Activity-Based Costing (ABC) data as a major source for information.

Balanced Scorecard: A framework that attempts to incorporate all quantitative and abstract measures of true importance to a company so that managers have the instrumentation necessary to promote future competitive success and shareholder value. A balanced scorecard is a set of performance measures constructed for four dimensions of performance. The dimensions are financial, customer, internal processes, and learning and growth. By not limiting focus on financial outcomes, the Balanced Scorecard helps provide a more comprehensive view of a business, which in turn helps organizations act in their best long-term interests.

Benchmarking: A process of comparing a company's performance to that of another using objective and subjective criteria. The process compares programs and strategic positions of competitors or exemplary organizations to those in the company. This then allows the company to better understand their market position and to develop plans on how to make improvements, usually with the aim of increasing some aspect of performance and reviewing its status for use as reference points in the formation of organization decisions and objectives.

Change Management: The process of developing a planned approach to change in an organization with the objective to maximize the collective benefits for all people involved in the change and minimize the risk of failure of implementing the change.

Core Competencies: The things a company does well that provides consumer benefits are difficult for competitors to imitate and can be leveraged widely across many products and markets. Core competencies can take many forms including technical expertise, operational efficiency, R&D know-how, and company culture.

Corporate Venturing: An alternative to traditional methods of company growth. A company invests in new products or technologies by funding businesses that have a reasonably autonomous management team and separate human resource policies. The goals can be to develop products to expand the core business, to enter new industries or markets, or to develop "breakthrough technologies" that could substantially change the industry. Corporate Venturing can be done in one of four ways: by taking a passive, minority position in outside businesses (corporate venture capital), by taking an active interest in an outside company, by building a new business as a stand-alone unit, or by building a new business inside the existing firm with a structure allowing for management independence.

Customer Relationship Management (CRM): An integrated information system that is used to plan, schedule, and control the presales and post-sales activities in an organization. CRM embraces all aspects of dealing with prospects and customers, including the call center, sales force, marketing, technical support, and field service. The primary goal of CRM is to improve long-term growth and profitability through a better understanding of customer behavior.

Economic Valued Added (EVA): A measure of a company's financial performance based on residual wealth calculated by deducting cost of capital from operating profit. The formula for calculating EVA is as follows: EVA = Net Operating Profit After Taxes (NOPAT)–(Capital × Cost of Capital)

Knowledge Management (KM): The process of connecting people to people and people to information to create a competitive advantage. KM is comprised of a range of practices used in an organization to identify, create, represent, distribute, and enable adoption of employee insights and experiences. Such insights and experiences can help individuals and groups to share valuable customer and competitive learnings, to reduce redundant work, to reduce training time for new employees, to help retain intellectual capital within the company despite employee turnover, and to allow the company to adapt to changing market conditions and competitive threats with more ease.

Lean Thinking: The continual effort to increase productivity and eliminate waste without decreasing value to the customer. Put simply, companies practicing lean thinking want more value with less work and cost.

Mission and Vision Statements: The Vision Statement describes the future identity of the organization. Since the vision statement describes what the company wants to be, it is a source of inspiration for employees and shareholders. The Mission Statement describes how the Vision Statement will be achieved by staying routed in the present: current purpose, customers, and processes of the organization.

Outsourcing: The delegation of non-core operations or jobs from internal production within a business to an external entity that specializes in that operation. Outsourcing is a business decision that is often made to lower costs or focus on core competencies.

Pay for Performance: A motivational concept in human resources in which pay decisions are based on defined performance levels, rather than entitlement, tenure, or other non-performance-related factors.

Quality of Earnings: The amount of earnings attributable to higher sales or lower costs rather than artificial profits created by accounting anomalies such as inflation of inventory. The purpose of quality of earnings is to reflect the cash that the company's businesses are generating and how well their balance sheets reflect their true economic position. Companies with good earnings quality will generate sustainable cash from operations, whereas companies with poor earnings quality will have boosted their reported earnings with such tricks as un-expensed stock options, low tax rates, asset sales, off-balance-sheet financing, and deferred maintenance of the pension fund. Overall, earnings that are calculated conservatively are considered to have higher quality than those calculated by aggressive accounting policies.

Reengineering: A management approach that examines all aspects of a business and its interactions and attempts to improve the efficiency of the underlying processes. The business reasons for making such changes could include poor financial performance, external competition, erosion of market share, or emerging market opportunities. Reengineering will examine and change any one of five components of the business: strategy, processes, technology, organization, and culture, or a combination.

Sarbanes-Oxley Act (SOX): A US federal law passed in 2002 in response to corporate scandals including Enron, Tyco, Adelphia, Word Com, and others. It established required internal controls, corporate governance structures, stricter audit independence, and individual management responsibility for compliance. Major elements include: a) Senior executives are held individually responsible for compliance; b) Audit firms cannot provide consulting services; c) The audit process is regulated; d) Specific individual criminal penalties were established for fraud by manipulation or destruction of financial records.

Six-Sigma Management: A process to identify and remove the causes of defects and errors in manufacturing and business processes. Six-sigma is an organizational initiative designed to reduce defects ten-fold while simultaneously reducing processing time by 50% every 2 years. The objective of Six-sigma Management is to create processes that are twice as good as the customer demands so that if the process mean shifts down, the process will not generate more than 3.4 defects per million opportunities.

Supply Chain Management: An inventory process involving planning and processing orders; handling; transporting and storing all materials purchased, processed, or distributed; and managing inventories in a coordinated manner among all suppliers, manufacturers, distributors, and retailers on the chain to fulfill customer orders as they arise, rather than to build up stock level to fulfill anticipated future demand.

Theory of Constraints: An approach to continuous improvement (reducing operating expenses and inventory and increasing throughput) based on a five-step procedure: (1) identifying constraints, (2) exploiting the binding constraints, (3) subordinating everything else to the decisions made in the second step, (4) increasing capacity of the binding constraints, and (5) repeating the process when new binding constraints are identified. It seeks to identify a company's constraints or bottlenecks and exploit them so that throughput is maximized and inventories and operating costs are minimized.

Total Quality Management: Approach to quality that emphasizes continuous improvement, striving for zero defects, and elimination of all waste. It is a concept of using quality methods and techniques to strategic advantage across all departments and employees as well as extending backward and forward to include both suppliers and clients, customers, and shareholders.

Suggested Reading and Interesting Web Sites

Suggested Readings

Anthony, R., *The Management Control Function* (Boston, MA: Harvard Business School Press, 1988).

Beer, M., Harvard Business School, and the Center for Organizational Fitness; Nancy Katz, Kennedy School, Harvard University: *"Do Incentives Work? The Perception of a Worldwide Sample of Senior Executives"*. (Boston, MA: Harvard Business School Press, 2003).

Collins, J., *Good to Great.* (New York: Harper Collins, 2001).

Dixon, R., Nanni, A., and Vollmann, T., *The New Performance Challenges: Measuring Operations for World Class Competition* (Homewood, IL: Dow-Jones Irwin, 1980).

Epstein, M.J. and Hanson, K.O. (eds.), *The Accountable Corporation* (4 volumes) (Westport, CT: Greenwood Publishing Group, 2005).

Ittner, C. and Larcker, D., "Innovations in Performance Measurement: Trends and Research Implications." *Journal of Management Accounting Research* 10: 34 (1998).

Ittner, C. and Larker, D., "Coming up Short." *Harvard Business Review*, November 2003.

Johnson, H.T. and Kaplan, R.S., *Relevance Lost: The Rise and Fall of Management Accounting* (Boston, MA: Harvard Business School Press, 1987).

Kaplan, R. and Norton, D., have written extensively about their technique of strategy mapping. Their popular works have created global awareness of the technique. They include the following books: *Execution Premium: Linking Strategy to Operations for Competitive Advantage (2008); Alignment: Using Balanced Scorecards to Create Corporate Synergies (2006); Strategy Maps: Converting Intangible Assets into Tangible Outcomes (2004); Strategy-Focused Organization: How Balanced Scorecard Companies Thrive in the New Business Environment (2001); Balanced Scorecard: Translating Strategy Into Action (1996), All are published by Harvard Business School Press* (Boston, MA).

Kohn, A., "Why Incentive Plans Cannot Work." *Harvard Business Review*, September 1993.

Livingstone, J.L. and Theodore G., *The Portable MBA in Finance and Accounting* (3rd edition) (New York: John Wiley and Sons, 2001).

Lynch, R.L. and Cross, K.F., *Measure Up: Yardsticks for Continuous Improvement* (Cambridge, MA: Blackwell Publishers, 1991).

Merchant, K., *Control in Business Organizations* (Boston, MA: Pitman Pub, 1995).

Niven, P., *Balanced Scorecard Step-by-Step for Government and Nonprofit Agencies* (New York: John Wiley & Sons, Inc., 2003).

Otley, D., "Management Control in Contemporary Organizations: Towards a Wider Framework." *Management Accounting Research* 5(4): 289–299 (1994).

Ouchi, William G., "The Transmission of Control Through Organizational Hierarchy." *Academy of Management Journal*, 1978 and "Types of Organizational Control and Their Relationship to Emotional Well-Being", *Administrative Science Quarterly*, 1978.

Porter, M., "What is Strategy." *Harvard Business Review* 76(6): 61 (1996).

Salmon, W.J., Lorsch, J.W., and Donaldson, G., *Harvard Business Review on Corporate Governance*, (Boston, MA: Harvard Business School Press, 2000).

Simons, R., Levers of Control. *Harvard Business Review* 73 (1995).

Simons, R., *Performance Measurement and Control Systems for Implementing Strategy* (Upper Saddle River, NJ: Prentice Hall, 1995).

Web Sites for Performance Measurement

Entering "scorecards" in you search engine such as Google will produce hundreds of hits. Here are a few we find very informative.

www.balancedscorecard.org
The Balanced Scorecard Institute

www.performanceportal.org
Performance Measurement Association

www.Performancemeasures.com
Performance Measurement Associates, Inc.

www.fpm.com
The Foundation for Performance Measurement

www.2gc.co.uk/resources
2GC Active Management

About the Authors

Lawrence P. Carr, Ph.D., is a Professor of Management Accounting at Babson College, Wellesley, MA. He teaches in the Graduate School of Business and the School of Executive Education. His courses, Managing and Achieving Strategic Results and Managing and Measuring Performance, stimulated the need for this book. He is a recipient of several teaching awards and has published over 30 articles and 25 teaching cases. He is a co-author of *Total Quality Management: A Cross-Functional Perspective.* Prior to his academic career, he spent 18 years in industry, serving as a Division Controller and Vice President for Kollmorgen Corporation and President and CEO of OSRAM, Corp., the United States and Canadian subsidiary of OSRAM GmbH, part of Siemens. He is an active consultant working for firms such as H.J. Heinz, Accenture, Irving Oil, Siemens, Intel, Novartis, and others.

Alfred J. Nanni, Jr., Ph.D., is Chairman of the Division of Accounting & Law and a Professor of Management Accounting at Babson College in Wellesley, MA. He holds the Vander Wolk Chair in Management Accounting and Operational Performance. He currently teaches in a variety of MBA programs at the Olin Graduate School at Babson as well as in the Executive Programs.

He has published and spoken extensively on the topic of strategic performance and execution for academic and practitioner audiences in both the United States and Europe. He is a co-author of *The New Performance Challenge: Measuring Performance for World-Class Competition.*

Many of his publications and presentations have drawn on his consulting experience with clients, including Cabot Corporation, IBM, Johnson & Johnson's Advanced Materials Group, McNeil Pharmaceuticals, Nortel Networks, Polaroid, R.R. Donnelly, the Strategic Pricing Group, Texas Instruments, 3M Europe, and the US Department of Defense.

Index